Destroyer
Weapons
of World War 2

The standard US World War 2 destroyer main armament, the 5in/38cal DP gun, here aboard USS *Laub*.
USN

Destroyer
Weapons
of World War 2

by Peter Hodges and Norman Friedman

NAVAL INSTITUTE PRESS

Published and distributed in the United States of America by
the Naval Institute Press, Annapolis, Maryland 21402

ISBN 0 87021 929 4
Library of Congress Catalog No 79-84585
Printed and bound in the United Kingdom

Authors' Notes

Some years ago, I wrote a monograph on 'Battle' class destroyers, whose moderate success encouraged me to treat 'Tribal' class destroyers in the same way. My original intention was to produce a third work along the same lines that would bridge the gap between these two outstanding British destroyer designs. As the draft of this third book developed, it became clear that it was fundamentally about the development of destroyer weapon systems; eventually it became equally clear that for the sake of completeness it should include the 'Tribals' and 'Battles' too. The expansion in fact embraces the prototype *Amazon* and *Ambuscade* of 1926 and the 'Battle' class of the mid-1940s and thus covers the 'between wars' vessels and the last class whose early units were actually in commission at the end of World War II.

Arguably, the post-war 'Weapon' and *Daring* class might also have been included, but neither saw any war service, nor could they claim to be 'classic' British destroyers. The 'Weapons' were effectively AA/AS Escort ships, while the *Darings* were hopefully described as 'light cruisers' at one stage of their careers, and at another were simply known as '*Daring* class ships', being considered too powerfully armed to be classified as mere *destroyers*. How this could be justified when they, with six 4.5in and six 40mm Bofors, were compared with, say, an American *Gearing* class vessel with six 5in, six 3in AA, four 40mm Bofors and eleven 20mm Oerlikon is hard to understand.

Writing a book and then expanding it by a 'top-and-tail' method is an odd procedure and not one to be recommended. Consequently, while I have endeavoured to treat the preliminary and final sections in the same manner as the original, the chronological presentation of certain weapon equipments is regrettably not so tidy as might have been the case.

During the lifetime of the ships, there were several changes in terminology – generally made as a means of more accurately describing a particular function or employment of equipment.

Because the bulk of pre-war naval gunnery was concerned with engagements against surface targets; and because, by its very position high up in the superstructure, the Director was more often than not actually in *depression* when it was 'on' an enemy ship, this movement was known as 'Director Setting'. Its counterpart in the horizontal plane was called 'Line of Sight Training'.

With the introduction of the High Angle control systems, the expression 'Director Elevation' became more meaningful; and in 1943, this term superseded 'Director Setting' while 'Director Training' defined the other motion. At about the same time, the old terms 'Roll' and 'Cross-roll' became 'Level' and 'Cross-level' (since, strictly speaking,

'Roll' was related only to ship movement, while 'Level' was related more accurately to 'Ship movement along the line of sight to the target').

In 1947, the expressions 'High Angle' and 'Low Angle', abbreviated to HA and LA, were replaced by AA and Su ('Anti-Aircraft' and 'Surface' respectively); and in 1950, the use of roman numerals was abandoned in favour of arabic. Thus what had been known as the 'HA/LA Director, Mk VI' became the 'AA/Su Director, Mk 6.'

Throughout the text, the contemporary expressions have been used as nearly as possible, so that the chronological development of the single 4.5in mounting, for example, becomes 4.5in Mk V, Mk V*, Mk 5* Mod 1, and Mk 5* Mod 2.

My thanks are due to Chris Ellis for sowing the original seeds; to Antony Preston for enthusiastic endeavours on my behalf; to my wife Diana for a great deal of earnest typing; and to the following for permission to reproduce photographs: The Ministry of Defence (Navy); The Imperial War Museum; The Public Archives of Canada; PA Vicary, of Cromer, Norfolk; Anthony Pavia of Birkirka, Malta GC; Wright and Logan, Southsea; Messrs Vickers, (Shipbuilders) Ltd) Messrs Vosper-Thornycroft Ltd; and Mrs Beryl Fraser of Toronto, Canada.

Peter Hodges

Most of the material for the US section was taken from various files held by the US Navy Operational Archives at the Washington Navy Yard. For assistance in its use I am grateful to Dr Dean Allard and to his able as le assistants, most notably Gerri Judkins, Kathleen Lloyd (now retired), and Nina Statem. A D Baker III assisted me with photographs as well as advice based on his long experience in researching the appearance of US warships. I am also very grateful to Norman Polmar and to Charles Haberlein for their assistance. However, this work would have been impossible but for the patience and forebearance of my wife, Rhea.

Basic material on US destroyer development through 1950 was taken from the files of the former General Board, held, like the other material cited, by the US Navy Operational Archives at the Washington Navy Yard. Notes on wartime modifications were taken from the CNO/ Cominch correspondence file and from 1945 SCB weekly memoranda; I also used the Bureau of Ordnance Armament Summaries as well as the file of bi-weekly changes to them, 1942-1944. The accounts of weapon development are based partly on the multivolume BuOrd History held in manuscript form by the Navy Library; on data in the BuOrd *Gun Mount and Turret Catalog;* and (for ASW) on the monthly formerly classified *Fleet Antisubmarine Bulletin*. Radar material has been taken from my book, *US Naval Radar* (Annapolis: Leeward Publications, 1979). Finally, I have benefited greatly from A D Baker III's article on the 1945 Emergency AA conversions in *Warship International* 1978 No 1.

Norman Friedman

Contents

Part 1.
Royal Navy Destroyers

The quad Vickers 0.5in machine gun.
MoD

1. A to I Classes

AMAZON AND AMBUSCADE

The springboard from which subsequent 'between-wars' British Fleet Destroyers developed was the joint creation of Thornycroft and Yarrow whose independent designs for an improvement to the Modified 'W' class were accepted by the Admiralty. Each company built a 'private-venture' destroyer – *Amazon* from Thornycroft's Woolston yard, and *Ambuscade* from Yarrow's at Scotstoun – and both survived from 1926 until well after World War II. Apart from the two special J Samuel White Type 4 'Hunt' class, no further commercial designs were called for by the Admiralty, until, in the present decade, Thornycroft – by now Vosper-Thornycroft – and Yarrow produced their Type 21 Frigates for the Ministry of Defence (Navy). That *Amazon* and *Ambuscade* should again be the chosen names for the two lead ships of the class was almost an inevitable decision.

The two earlier ships were very similar in performance and were identically armed with four 4.7in BL Mk I guns in single CP Mk VI** mountings; two Vickers 2pdr QF Mk II guns in single Mk II HA mountings; and two sets of triple torpedo tubes. Indeed, there was nothing novel in the weapon fit, which largely followed that of the previous 'Shakespeare's and 'Scott's, except for the omission of their 3in HA in favour of the two pompoms.

Amazon and *Ambuscade* were the last destroyers to be built with the old 'Breech-loading' 4.7s (as distinct from the later QF guns) and also the last to be armed with triple torpedo tubes (apart from the Type 4 'Hunts'). The 4.7in CP Mk VI** mounting was strictly a 'surface' weapon, with a maximum elevation of 30°, and was weakly protected by only a shallow sprayshield.

The 4.7in Mk IX gun on the simple 30° CP Mk XIV mounting, as fitted to the pre-war 'A' to 'D' class destroyers. This was the first destroyer 4.7 with a QF Breech and succeeded the 4.7in BL Mk 1 on the CP Mk VI mounting introduced on the modified 'W' class. This is the 'B' gun of *Kempenfelt*, June 1936.
P A Vicary

The 2pdr was the original 'pompom' and had a rate of fire of 200rpm. It was belt-fed, but the belts themselves were made of canvas and the displacement of rounds within them led to numerous jams. The muzzle velocity was only 2000fs and thus the weapon became progressively less effective in the ensuing years as aircraft speeds steadily increased.

The Fire Control for the 4.7in guns was rudimentary. Range was measured by an open 9ft rangefinder MQ 1 on a pedestal in the rear of the bridge and the guns were directed by a Destroyer Director Sight. This, on a short pedestal, was protected by a small curved windshield (rather like a gun-less gunshield) and sent elevation and training gun orders by electrical transmitters to the four mountings and to the searchlight.

Like the majority of the 'between-wars' destroyers up to the 'I' class, both ships were eventually converted to Escorts during the war.

THE 'A' TO 'I' CLASSES

The prototype designs were developed in the succeeding classes with detail changes in outline and improvements to the weapon equipment. Each class had its own 'Leader', generally distinguished by a fifth 4.7in mounting on a 'bandstand' between the funnels. Oddly, in the first three classes the 'Leader's' name did not alphabetically match her flotilla. Thus, *Codrington* led the 'A's, *Keith*, the 'B's, and *Kempenfelt* the half-flotilla of 'C's. (The latter group, together with their 'Leader', were all later transferred to the Royal Canadian Navy, adopting Canadian names and joining *Saguenay* and *Skeena*, both built to a commercial Thornycroft design.) Thereafter, the 'Leader's' name matched the respective flotilla - *Duncan* with the 'D's, *Exmouth* with the 'E's, *Faulknor* with the 'F's, *Grenville* with the 'G's, *Hardy* with the 'H's and *Inglefield* with the 'I's.

Left: After an interim Mk XVII mounting for the 'E', 'F' and 'G' classes, the 40° Mk XVIII was designed for the 'H's and 'I's. It was this mark that was fitted to the earlier War Emergency classes. Note that the gunshield bears a marked similarity to that of the Mk XIV, but that breech trunnioning has created the need for a heavier balance weight, over which the spent cartridge catch net has been laid. Although the breech worker (on the right) has an on-mounting platform, the tray worker stands on the deck, and follows the mounting around as it trains. Hand ramming was effected by hauling on the hand grip, and the tray worker reset the rammer head by pulling it back to the rear of the loading tray. *IWM*

Centre: The 4.7in CP Mk XVIII mounting fitted in the 'H', 'I', 'O', 'Q' and 'R' classes. Layer, trainer, sight setter and breech worker were carried on the rotating structure, but loading and rammer numbers followed the mounting around as it trained. The dark 'V'-shaped tubular structure over the cradle is the sight counterbalance, and the vertical shaft on the gunshield secured the canvas gun-curtain. *MoD*

Right: A front view of the CP Mk XVIII. Note the pattern of rivets showing the stiffening girders and the characteristic box-shape of the gun-shield. The shaft and cranks beneath the barrel operated the 'safety-firing' cut-off gear to prevent the gun from firing into its own ship's structure. *MoD*

FAULKNOR, JUNE 1937

1 DCT
2 Type MS 20 9ft Rangefinder, on 'Three-Man' Rangefinder Mounting
3 Pole foremast
4 Signal yard
5 Combined signal/main roof radio aerial yard
6 'Q' 4.7in CP Mk XVII mounting
7 Quadruple 21in torpedo tube mounting QR Mk VI*
8 24in searchlight
9 Main roof aerial yard
10 Depth charge thrower

FAULKNOR, JANUARY 1945

1 MF/DF aerial
2 Radar Type 285 on Rangefinder Director Mk II (W)
3 Radar Type 291 General Warning
4 'TBS' radio aerial
5 Quadruple 2pdr Mk VII mounting
6 'Cut-down' after funnel
7 Main mast for main roof radio aerial
8 After 21in torpedo tube mounting QR Mk VI* (re-installed in 1942)
9 HF/DF aerial
10 Repositioned HA, originally on site of after torpedo tubes
11 Single 20mm Oerlikon mounting
12 Twin Mk V 20mm Oerlikon mounting

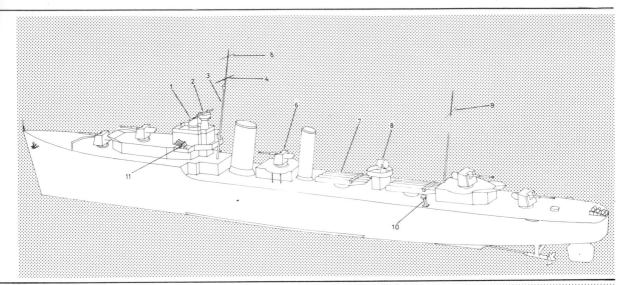

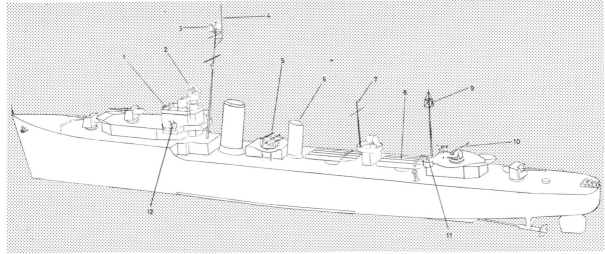

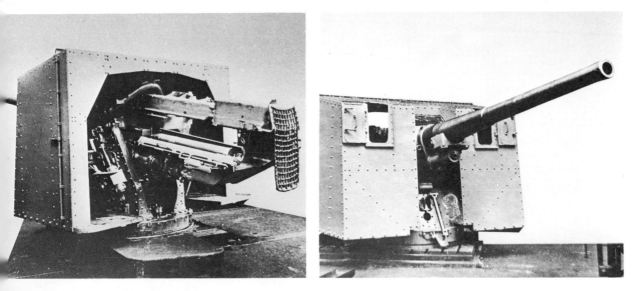

ARMAMENT AND FIRE CONTROL

The 'A' class introduced a Quick-Fire version of the 4.7in gun (ie with a sliding, instead of a screwed, breech block). The gun, the Mk IX or IX*, was mounted in the CP Mk XIV mounting, was again only capable of 30° elevation, but was protected by a more substantial box-shaped shield. The newly developed quadruple torpedo tube mounting was installed but the close-range AA armament and Fire Control remained as before. This class were given the 'Two-Speed Destroyer Sweep' (TSDS) to meet a Fleet requirement for minesweeping at high speed ahead of the Fleet (to the detriment of the A/S armament). Only three ships of the class survived the war, by then having been converted for escort duties.

The 'B's were virtually identical with regard to their armament except that, as a flotilla, they were equipped for the AS rôle (having Asdic, DC mortars and one DC oversern rack) instead of the TSDS. Four ships, including the 'Leader' *Keith* survived the war, by which time they too had been converted for escort duties.

The important change implemented in the original 'C' class, was the appearance of the Destroyer DCT on the bridge in association with the Admir-

alty Fire Control Clock Mk I for the control of the 4.7in guns, which were again in CP Mk XIV mountings. A 3in HA was mounted between the funnels but was later removed, and the 2pdrs, previously on the fo'c's'le deck, were remounted in the vacant 3in position. Both TSDS and Asdic were fitted, but only stern racks were provided for depth charge discharge.

SINGLE 2-PDR POMPOM

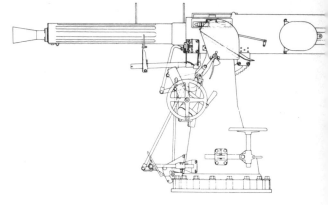

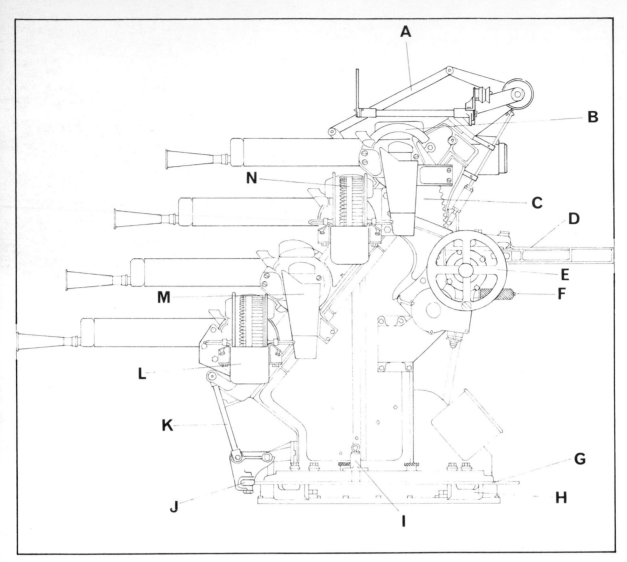

VICKERS QUADRUPLE .5IN 'M' MK II MOUNTING

A Sight linkage
B Elevation scale
C Elevation arc connected to No 2 gun (all guns connected to No 2 by linkage)
D Layer's body-rest
E Elevating handwheel
F Training clutch lever, disconnecting geared drive
G Safety firing cam rail
H Mounting jumping clip
I Housing locking bolt
J Safety firing cam roller follower
K Safety firing linkage
L Guard tray beneath ammunition drum
M Spent cartridge tray
N Ammunition drum

The quadruple Vickers .5in machine gun mounting – a pre-war standard close range AA weapon which was replaced by the 20mm Oerlikon.
IWM

The 'D' class repeated the 'C's, but were given the more comprehensive A/S arrangements of the 'B's. The 2pdr single mountings were replaced (in four ships) by the newly-developed quadruple .5 inch Vickers machine gun mountings, and the 'as-built' 3in HA was suppressed. With the 'E's a policy change occurred in that minelaying was added to the already overburdened 'maids-of-all-work'. When the ships were operating in this rôle, 'A' and 'Y' mountings, together with the torpedo tube mountings, were landed, while the seaboat stowages were shifted forward to the fo'c's'le deck, to leave the Iron Deck clear for the mine rails. Details of this equipment appear later in the book. The Fire Control remained as before, but a new model of 4.7in mounting was installed. This, the CP Mk XVII, had portable deck plates around the training base, which when removed allowed the gun to elevate to 40° for marginally better AA defence. Since, however, no anti-aircraft fire control was included in the ships' equipment, only barrage fire was possible, and the 'removable-deck-plate' scheme was patently so impractical that it is astonishing that it was ever even conceived, let alone adopted.

No major changes occurred with the 'F' class, and the usual wartime modifications – a 12pdr AA in place of the after set of torpedo tubes, a shortened after funnel and the mainmast removed to improve 'sky-arcs', installation of warning radar and a sprinkling of 20mm Oerlikons – were made as the war progressed, and finally the four survivors were modified for A/S escort duties. *Faulknor*, the 'Leader', had the old rangefinder removed from the bridge, shipping in its place a Rangefinder Director in association with a Fuze Keeping Clock for AA gunfire control, as did *Foxhound*. The 'Leader' and four ships survived the war, *Fame*, sold to the Dominican Government in 1948, lasting into the 1960s.

Top left:
Thornycroft's prototype *Amazon*, virtually unchanged in September 1937. Her distinctive flat-sided funnels, typical of her builder's design, made her easily recognisable from *Ambuscade*, which had the 'V' and 'W' style 'Woodbine' after funnel. Note the small spray shields on the 4.7in guns, the 2pdr pompoms between the funnels, and the torpedo tubes with its third tube above and between the outers.
Wright & Logan

Top right:
Codrington, the 'Leader' of the 'A' class with a brave display of signals, approaching Portsmouth in the summer of 1935. Like most of the succeeding Flotilla 'Leaders', she has a fifth 4.7in gun between the funnels. Note the tall mainmast, supported by heavily insulated wire shrouds.
Wright & Logan

Right:
The mine-layer's 'fantail' can be seen in this October 1942 shot of *Icarus*. She is painted to the Admiralty 'Western Approaches' scheme and still has her TSDS davits on the quarters. Her after tubes have been replaced by a 12pdr HA.
MoD by courtesy of John Roberts.

The established weapon layout now became virtually a standard fit in the 'G's, 'H's and 'I's with, of course, some exceptions. The prototype 'Pentad', or five-fold torpedo tube mounting, was installed in *Glowworm*, and the 'H' class introduced the 4.7in CP Mk XVIII mounting designed for 40° maximum elevation. The 'I's – the last of the long run built for the Royal Navy – introduced the later 'standard' angled bridge front and 'Pentad' torpedo tube mountings. *Icarus*, *Impulsive*, *Intrepid* and *Ivanhoe* served as minelayers in the early part of the war (together with two 'E's), but later reverted to their original rôle. All had Asdic, two DC mortars, overstern DC discharge rails and TSDS.

Of this group of 27 ships, only two 'G's, two 'H's and three 'I's survived the war, when both 'G's and one 'H' were serving in Allied or Commonwealth Navies.

The Royal Navy gained a further flotilla of similar destroyers when six vessels ordered by Brazil and two of an order of four ships for Turkey were requisitioned on the stocks. The Brazilian ships were given 'H' names, and the Turkish pair became extra 'I's. They closely resembled their true RN counterparts, but had the wartime shortened funnels and benefited by being given a combined DCT and rangefinder – an advantage not enjoyed by the British ships. Three of the eight remained afloat in

H.M.S. "ESCAPADE." 1934.

1945, when the one 'Turkish' survivor was delivered to its rightful owners (a somewhat delayed event). The Brazilians, however, had by this time built their own replacements and their remaining two 'H' class vessels, *Havelock* and *Highlander*, were scrapped in the UK.

Apart from one or two wartime re-equipments, none of this large pre-war group had an anti-aircraft fire control calculator, while the earlier vessels had but rudimentary surface fire control capabilities. All were armed with 4.7s designed for ship-to-ship actions and as a whole their anti-aircraft defence was lamentably weak. Hence they were modified for escort rôles, retaining a proportion of their main armament. Generally they lost 'Y' gun to make space for increased DC stowages and dischargers in the form of DC mortars and overstern rails. Additionally, either 'A' or 'B' gun might be removed for the 'Hedgehog' spigot mortar, and AA defence was marginally improved by installing four single 20mm Oerlikons. Another common modification was the complete removal of the obsolete DCT and range-finder from the bridge and its replacement by the surface warning radar Type 271 'lantern'. The remaining 4.7s were then controlled locally, their principal function being to engage U-boats on the surface.

Above: A typical 12pdr AA of early vintage which was fitted in the 'A' to 'I' classes during the early part of the WWII in place of the after set of torpedo tubes. Against the aircraft of the day, and locally aimed and fired, it was almost totally ineffectual.
MoD

Left: *Escapade*, which survived the war, secured to a buoy in 1934. The height of the heavily-stayed pole mainmast was made necessary by International Maritime regulations, which demanded that any powered vessel should exhibit two white masthead lights, the after higher than the other.
MoD by courtesy of John Roberts

Top: Appropriately named, the long-lived *Fame* in February 1947 shows the typical wartime Escort conversion of those pre-war Fleet destroyers fortunate enough to survive. While still retaining 'A', 'B' and 'X' 4.7in guns, she has a split 'Hedgehog' abreast 'A' mounting; triple 2in rocket flare launchers on 'B' gunshield; MFDF projecting from the bridge-front; surface warning Radar Type 271 on the bridge roof; Air Warning Radar Type 291 on the foremast; single 20mm Oerlikons between the funnels and abreast the old searchlight platform; cut-down after funnel; HF/DF pylon mast rising from the after superstructure; 'Y'

mounting and the after set of torpedo tubes removed; and increased depth charge discharge arrangements on the quarterdeck. She was sold to Dominica and was still serving in the 1960s. *Wright & Logan*

Bottom: *Icarus* survived the war, although by its end had been relegated to the Escort rôle. Earlier, she had been fitted both for and with minelaying gear, but here, in April 1946, she has only the vestigial remains of her original armament while yet retaining the 'fantail' mine conveyers. *Wright & Logan*

The wartime modifications were of course progressive, and *Faulknor's* armament appeared thus[1]:

January 1941 3in HA in place of after tubes; mainmast removed; stump mast (for 'main roof') fitted to forward edge of searchlight platform.

January 1942 RF director with radar Type 285 in place of rangefinder; after funnel cut down; multiple machine guns shifted to sponsons abreast searchlight platform with radar Type 286 at foremast head; funnel-height mainmast replaced 'stump'; HF/DF pylon on forward edge of 'X' gundeck; MF/DF aerial on front face of bridge.

January 1943 'X' 4.7in removed and replaced by 3in HA; after set of tubes replaced; multiple machine guns removed and single 20mm Oerlikons on bridge wings and on sponsons on forward corners of 'X' gundeck added; radar Type 286 replaced by Type 291.

January 1945 Bridge wing single 20mm Oerlikons replaced by twin Mk V 20mm Oerlikon mountings; 'Q' 4.7in mounting removed and replaced by 2pdr quad Mk VII mounting.

[1] Details from *Destroyer Leader*, Peter C Smith, William Kimber, 1968.

2. Tribal Class

THE 'TRIBAL' CLASS

The rearmament scramble of the second half of the 1930s saw major foreign powers building large destroyers of around 2000 tons displacement with main armaments of up to eight 5in DP in four twin mountings. The British reply was the 'Tribal' class, for which at one time ten 4.7in in five twin mountings had been proposed. Eventually, the design settled on eight 4.7in in four, and such was the urgency of the hour that all sixteen ships were launched in 1937. Ten were completed in the following year and the remaining six well before the outbreak of war in September 1939.

The impact of these ships on the Fleet must have been akin to that which *Dreadnought* had made some thirty years earlier. Not only was the order for sixteen units, but their main armament was double that of the previous types (with the exception, of course, of the five-gun 'Leaders'). Much has been written about their often legendary exploits in the Second World War, and this is not relevant here. The weapons however are of considerable interest.

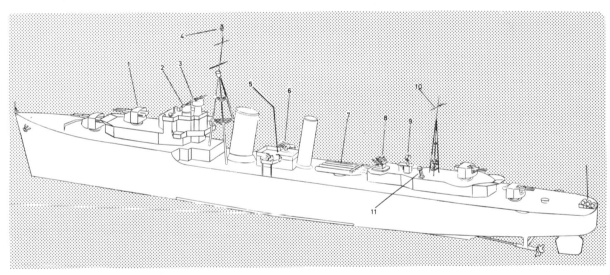

COSSACK, JUNE 1938

1   Twin 4.7in CP Mk XIX mounting
2   DCT
3   Rangefinder Director Mk II
4   D/F Aerial
5   Site for proposed 'Q' 4.7in or pompom mounting
6   Vickers .5in MG mounting Mk III
7   Quadruple torpedo tube mounting, QR Mk IX
8   Quadruple 2pdr Mk VII mounting
9   24in searchlight
10 Main roof radio aerial yard
11 DC thrower

THE TWIN 4.7IN CP MK XIX MOUNTING

The 4.7in Twin Mk XIX first underwent trials on board HMS *Hereward*. The mounting housed two QF Mk XII guns in a common elevation cradle, and it was the first twin and the first power mounting specially designed for destroyers.

The Mk XIX was hydraulic-powered and ran on a pressure of 1000psi delivered from two turbo-hydraulic units. Its all-up weight was 25.5 tons and the maximum training speed (in power) was 10° per second. With a fully trained crew, and power ramming, a rate of fire of 12 rounds per minute for each gun could be achieved. The design included alternative hand-drives, local gunsights and on-mounting AA fuze-setting positions on both sides of the mounting platform. Although open to the rear, it was well protected by a distinctive gunshield, and its greatest drawback lay in the fact that its maximum elevation was still only 40°.

'Quarters Clean Guns' was a regular occurrence and one of *Ashanti's* gun's crews are seen engaged in cleaning and maintenance on a 4.7in Mk XIX. *IWM by courtesy of Dave Sambrook*

THE QUADRUPLE 2PDR MK VII (SERIES) MOUNTING

The earliest model of this anti-aircraft weapon was the '(M)', which had been developed from the much larger 8-barrelled Mk VI (M) installed on capital ships. In fact in the early design stages the latter weapon was proposed for the 'Tribals' but it was eventually ruled out for reasons of topweight.

As the drawing shows, the barrels were staggered in pairs to give access to the loading trays. Ammunition was made up in sections of 14-round articulated steel link belts. These lengths could themselves be connected, concertina fashion, to a total of 112 rounds for each of the four loading trays, and thus a considerable stock of ammunition was immediately available. The internal gun mechanism was complex in the extreme and 'pompoms' needed considerable skilled maintenance. Each gun fired at approximately 100 rounds per minute, and they were triggered to operate in pairs, but despite some improvement over the older ammunition-belt system, jams were still frequent.

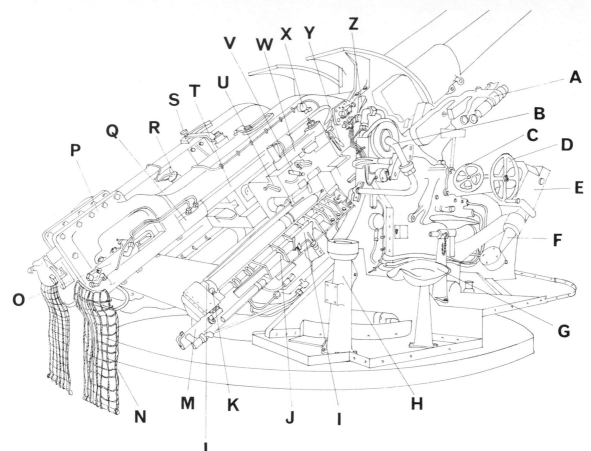

4.7IN CP TWIN MK XIX MOUNTING

A Trainer's monocular sight
B Hydraulic exhaust take-off from elevating structure
C Trainer's power handwheel
D Trainer's hand drive
E Training receiver
F Drive to training receiver 'mechanical' pointer
G Fuze-setter's seat
H Fuze-setting pedestal
I Loading tray unlocking palm lever
J Loading tray
K Hand rammer head
L Power rammer head
M Rammer cylinder
N Spent cartridge catch net
O Intensifier connected to recuperator cylinder gland
P Balance weights
Q Recuperator cylinder
R Loading light
S Semi-automatic/quickfire changeover lever
T Recuperator ram
U Breech mechanism lever locking lever
V Safe-fire lever
W Breech mechanism lever
X 'Rounds fired' counter
Y Breech worker's percussion firing hand-grip
Z Firing circuit 'interceptor' (circuit breaker)

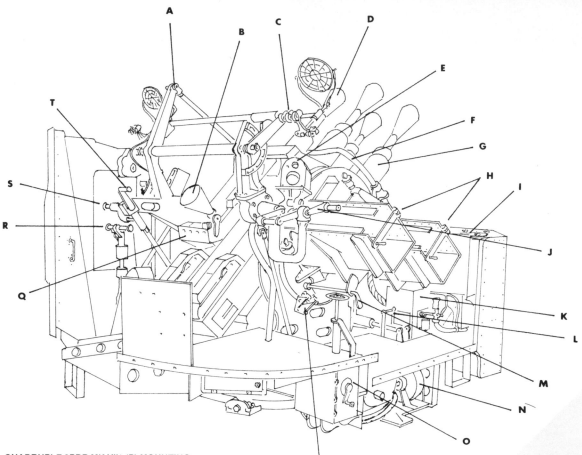

QUADRUPLE 2PDR MK VII* (P) MOUNTING

A Sight linkage
B Water-cooling filling position
C Back-sight, with blank outer eye piece
D Flame guard
E Training receiver
F Water-cooling pipe
G Water-jacket
H Ammunition trays, each holding 112 rounds
I Circulating water tank
J Training hand-cranks
K Oil tank
L Safety firing gear
M Firing interruptor lever
N Hydraulic training motor
O Pump motor starter
P Elevation and depression buffer
Q Loading indication lamp box
R Power joystick
S Elevation hand-cranks
T Firing hand-cranks

The famous 'Quad' pompom, mounted in the common position immediately abaft the funnel in a destroyer (note the port siren and the ladder to the siren platform). The ammunition was made up in belts of 14 rounds, which could be clipped to existing rounds in the ammunition feed-trays. The difficulty of aiming at high elevations is made very clear by the attitude of the layer and trainer. Between them – in a more comfortable position – is a rating manning the firing hand-cranks. These were later replaced by an electric firing motor drive. The manual firing arrangements and the absence of a splinter shield around the mounting date this as an early-war photograph.
IWM

Early mountings had hand-crank operated firing gear, but this was later duplicated by a powered drive, as indeed, was the mounting itself. An electric pump motor, hydraulic pump and hydraulic training and elevating motors were added, giving a maximum speed of 25° per second. Power control was effected from the hand-crank (which could be clutched to 'hand' in an emergency) in what was called 'power-assisted hand control'. In this mode, moving the hand crank opened a control valve, the mounting following, but a differential drive closed the valve. Thus, the Layer and Trainer still turned their hand-cranks to keep the mounting in motion, but of course, the effort so to do was minimal. A 'scooter' (or 'joystick') controller was also added for the Captain of the mounting by which he could slew it rapidly on to the firing bearing and, indeed, fully control the weapon in action if required. Further modifications included the fitting of conical flame guards to the muzzles and the addition of splinter shields for crew protection. As a result the all-up weight reached 11 tons – approaching that of the twin 4in HA.

With director control and RPC – refinements only possible in larger ships – the multiple 2pdr weapons were reasonably effective but suffered from their inadequate muzzle velocity and consequent poor maximum range. Nevertheless, the 'quad' gave the 'Tribals' a considerable edge over the weakly-armed earlier Flotillas, whose gunnery officers must have envied their more fortunate colleagues in the larger ships.

THE QUADRUPLE .5INCH 'M' MK III MOUNTING

This mounting completed the AA armament of the 'Tribals', if one discounts the occasional single and twin Lewis .303 machine guns (which must have been manned more in the hope than the expectation of hitting anything, and least of all of doing any real damage). The .5in weapons were also virtually useless, and although retained in many ships in the early war years they were replaced by the more efficient 20mm Oerlikon when production allowed.

In the Mk III quad the four barrels were staggered back from bottom to top and the circular ammunition belt drums alternated with the spent cartridge trays. The rate of fire was 700 rounds per minute per barrel, but the range was lamentably short and the hitting power weak. The Layer had a geared elevation drive and the Trainer a geared drive which could be de-clutched to allow the mounting to be pushed around. Few modifications were made to the mounting in its wartime service other than the addition of a splinter shield.

Its barrels were deliberately misaligned from each other to give a 'scatter' effect, and later mathematical calculations showed that when firing an approximate ten-second burst at 1000yds range, and assuming the *total* target area was within the pattern of spread for the duration of the burst, 40 rounds of the 500 fired might hit the target. This sounded hopeful, but took no account of the fact that keeping the target within the pattern depended on both Layer and Trainer, independently yet concurrently, exactly judging the speed of the aircraft as well as constantly tracking it by hand-follow on a rolling and pitching deck for ten seconds.

Two of these mountings were carried on a gundeck between the funnels, with the bridge wing sponsons once again glaringly vacant. One wonders why single 2pdrs (which at least fired a 40mm calibre exploding shell) had not been fitted in the first instance, if only for the sake of a common ammunition supply.

FIRE CONTROL

Having already claimed 'destroyer-firsts' with their twin 4.7s and their quad pompom, the 'Tribals' added another scalp in being provided with an AA predictor. Surface fire control was directed from the established Destroyer DCT on the bridge in association with the usual Admiralty Fire Control Clock; but the earlier rangefinder was replaced by the Rangefinder Director Mk II. This functioned purely as a rangefinder in surface firing, following DCT training by a follow-the-pointer bearing receiver, but in AA fire it became a director in its own right. Details of both pieces of equipment appear later in the book.

TORPEDO AND ANTI-SUBMARINE WEAPONS

With space and topweight bought up by the surface weapon layout, the torpedo armament was halved by the general standard of the day and only one torpedo tube mounting was fitted in what was geographically the site of the forward set in earlier classes. However, to compensate to some degree, the QR Mk IX was designed for power operation (yet another 'first'). The side elevation shows the general arrangement, and the background to torpedo tube mountings as a whole, again, appears later.

A short overstern rack for three depth charges was set on the centreline, and a DC thrower was sited (rather unusually) on each side of the forward edges of 'X' gundeck, to what advantage at that height has not been discovered.

Bottom left: The legendary *Cossack* on Contractors Sea Trials in the Tyne area in 1938 in the 'as first fitted' state. She commissioned at Portsmouth in June of that year and was 'half-Leader' of the 1st (Tribal) Destroyer Flotilla in the Mediterranean. *IWM*

Bottom right: Earlier, in 1941, further general wartime changes had already been implemented in *Zulu*. Radar Type 285 has been added to the RF Director, single 2pdrs are fitted on the bridge sponsons, the tripod mainmast has been replaced by a stump mast carrying the HF/DF aerial and the after funnel has been cut down. *IWM*

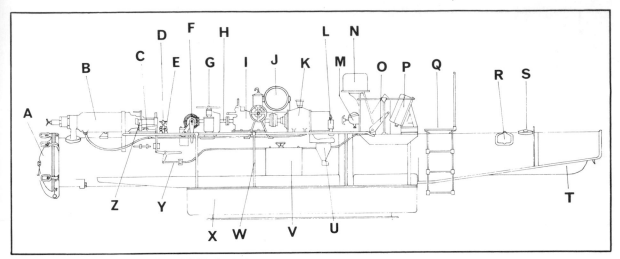

QUADRUPLE 21IN TORPEDO TUBE MOUNTING QR MK IX

A   Rear door
B   Explosion chamber
C   Set gyro angle
D   Set torpedo speed
E   Set 'pattern-run' (30°zig-zag course)
F   Hand-training drive
G   Set torpedo running depth
H   Training shaft drive output from torque converter
I   Torque converter (combined hydraulic pump and motor)
J   Training receiver
K   Electric drive motor for torque converter
L   Cordite gas-operated 'Top stop'
M   'Tube ready' switch (one for each tube)
N   Local torpedo sight
O   Local firing lever (one for each tube)
P   Tube order receiver
Q   Access platform across tubes
R   Access flap to torpedo 'pistol'
S   Access plug to depth and roll recorder (practice torpedo only)
T   21in Mk IX torpedo, 11 000 yards range at 40kts
U   Tube operator's seat
V   Electric motor starter
W   Guard rails
X   Cover over training rollers
Y   Flexible cable from firing lever
Z   Explosion chamber breech

WARTIME CHANGES

The lessons of Narvik and Dunkirk saw the 'X' 4.7in mounting replaced by a twin 4in HA Mk XIX, and since, concurrently, most destroyers had their after set of tubes replaced by a single 12pdr HA to give them some measure of anti-aircraft defence, the 'Tribals' with *power-operated* torpedo tubes ended up better off insofar as torpedo armament was concerned.

Other improvements followed the pattern of the day. Early radars appeared, the after funnel was cut down and the mainmast dispensed with. Oerlikons (and in some cases single 2pdrs on the bridge sponsons!) replaced the Vickers machine guns, and splinter shields were added to the 'quad' and on the gundecks.

Two of the class were lost in 1940, three in 1941, and seven in 1942; and only the four survivors – *Ashanti*, *Eskimo*, *Nubian* and *Tartar* – enjoyed the

full benefit of wartime refits. By 1945, *Nubian's* armament and radars comprised:-

3 x twin 4.7in
1 x twin 4in HA
1 x quad pompom
2 x single Bofors
4 x twin Oerlikon
1 x quad torpedo tubes
2 x DC throwers
Radar Types 285, 291 and 293
IFF, MF/DF and HF/DF

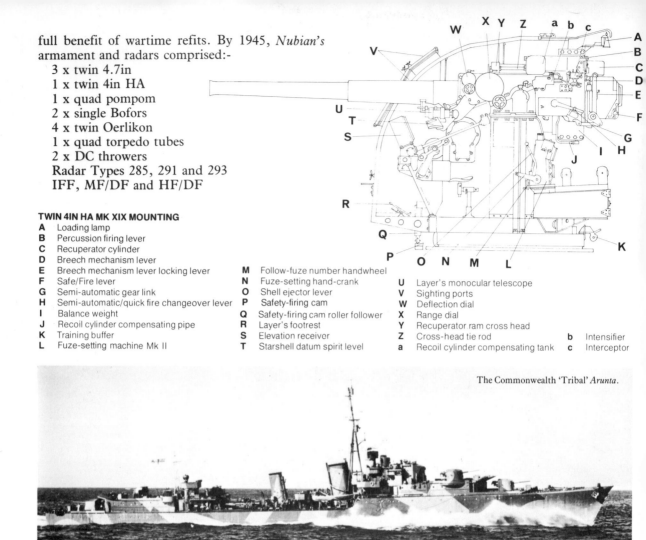

TWIN 4IN HA MK XIX MOUNTING

A	Loading lamp					
B	Percussion firing lever					
C	Recuperator cylinder					
D	Breech mechanism lever					
E	Breech mechanism lever locking lever	**M**	Follow-fuze number handwheel			
F	Safe/Fire lever	**N**	Fuze-setting hand-crank	**U**	Layer's monocular telescope	
G	Semi-automatic gear link	**O**	Shell ejector lever	**V**	Sighting ports	
H	Semi-automatic/quick fire changeover lever	**P**	Safety-firing cam	**W**	Deflection dial	
I	Balance weight	**Q**	Safety-firing cam roller follower	**X**	Range dial	
J	Recoil cylinder compensating pipe	**R**	Layer's footrest	**Y**	Recuperator ram cross head	
K	Training buffer	**S**	Elevation receiver	**Z**	Cross-head tie rod	**b** Intensifier
L	Fuze-setting machine Mk II	**T**	Starshell datum spirit level	**a**	Recoil cylinder compensating tank	**c** Interceptor

The Commonwealth 'Tribal' *Arunta.*

THE COMMONWEALTH 'TRIBALS'

Three ships – basically to the early-war improvement standard of the RN vessels – were built in Australia, four were built for the RCN by Vickers on Tyneside and a further four were constructed by the Canadians at Halifax, although none of the last group saw any service in World War II.

The comparatively late building programme of the British-built Canadian quartet allowed even further improvements to be implemented, most notably the re-siting of the quad pompom. This was transposed in the fore-and-aft line with the searchlight, and at the same time raised on a platform to improve the sky arcs. The (by now) established Oerlikon positions – bridge sponsons, between the funnels, and in the original DC thrower sites on 'X' gundeck – were first occupied by singles but later by power-operated twin Mk Vs, whilst the DC throwers themselves were dropped one deck to what was in any case the more usual Iron Deck level.

The first two Canadian-built ships carried the final fit of twin 4.7in Mk XIXs in 'A' 'B' and 'Y' positions, while the second pair – *Nootka* and *Athabaskan (II)* (named after the only Commonwealth 'Tribal' lost in World War II) – were completed with twin 4in HA Mk XIXs throughout. In due course, all were brought to a common standard: 'X' mounting became a USN 3in/50 cal twin AA, and 'Squid' mortars were mounted on the quarterdeck. The Commonwealth ships survived into the 1960s, and *Haida* has been preserved on Lake Ontario as a reminder of an outstanding warship class.

Not only were the 'Tribals' the first British destroyers capable of delivering an 8-gun broadside – they were also the last. They enjoyed and thoroughly deserved the considerable respect of all who knew them.

3. J, K and N Classes

THE 'J' CLASS

There were several instances between the two world wars when an established type of British warship was followed into service by a 'cut down' version. It happened with the building of the cruisers *Exeter* and *York* – reduced by one turret from the previous 'County' class; it happened again when the *Arethusas* followed the four-turret *Leanders* and *Amphions*. Much the same occurred with the destroyer flotilla that came immediately after the 'Tribals'. Although the latter class were revolutionary in the Royal Navy, they had been produced in reply to the similarly large destroyers being introduced by foreign naval powers. But if the 'Tribals' were revolutionary, so too, in many ways, were their successors.

As the erstwhile peaceful nations of the world drew breath for the forthcoming conflict, so the need for a more balanced destroyer design arose. For the feature of the 'Tribals' that raised perhaps more controversy than any other was their much reduced torpedo armament – then reckoned as the raison d'etre of the Fleet Destroyer. Their newly introduced power-operated twin gun mountings were complex, costly and took many months to construct. Similarly, their fire control was novel, expensive and largely untried. All this, coupled with the addition of a quadruple 2pdr pompom, pushed their size and maintenance loading to limits which would become intolerable in repeated classes.

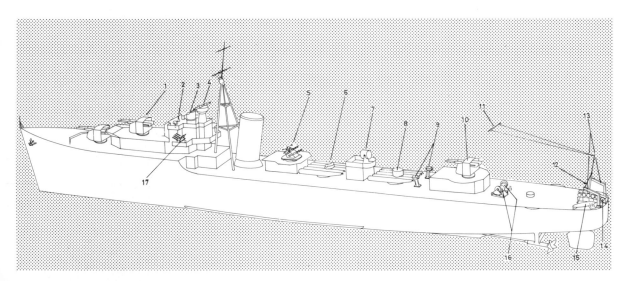

J & K CLASS AS DESIGNED

1	4.7in Twin Mk XIX mounting	10	'X' 4.7in mounting, stowed forward
2	Captain's sight	11	Spreader for main roof radio aerials
3	Destroyer DCT	12	Port support strut for ensign staff
4	'Three-man Rangefinder'	13	Port and starboard minesweeping davits
5	Unshielded 2pdr 'M' Mk VII pompom mounting	14	Single 6-charge overstern rails and trap
6	Windshield on PR Mk II torpedo tubes	15	Port minesweeping paravane
7	44in searchlight	16	Port and starboard steam minesweeping winches
8	Enclosed splinter shield on PR Mk II torpedo tubes	17	Quadruple Vickers 'M' Mk II 5in machine gun mounting
9	Mk II depth charge throwers		

The complexity of the 'Tribals' was soon appreciated at high level, and for the next generation of destroyers the Naval Staff made sweeping changes. To ease future production, the construction of the hull itself was radically altered by the adoption of longitudinal framing rather than the long-established transverse variety. In the face of declared misgivings only two boilers were to be fitted, trunked into a single funnel: and by the reduction of the main armament to three twin mountings, extra deck space was provided for a return to two sets of torpedo tubes. A bow less raked than that of the 'Tribals' helped towards a reduction in overall length of nearly 20ft; displacement was reduced by 200 tons; and with engines developing 40 000 shp, the nominal maximum speed was still 36 knots. Altogether, the design was a very accomplished juggling act.

MAIN MACHINERY AND LAYOUT

The two Admiralty three-drum boilers were housed in separate boiler rooms and provided steam at 300 pounds per sq in (psi) to two Parsons geared turbines in the engine room. 'Revolutions for knots' proportioned out at approximately 10:1, so that at 350rpm, the engines developed full power for the top speed. The ships could cruise quite happily up to about 23 knots on one boiler and at the economical speed of 20 knots had oil fuel for over 3500 miles. In the 'cruising' state, it was usual to run on one boiler, thereby conserving oil and easing the boiler room watchkeeping rota. Abaft the engine room, the drive was geared down in a Gearing Compartment, from which the propeller shafts proper were driven. This main machinery remained standard for all the succeeding classes except for the 'L's and 'M's where the horsepower was upgraded.

The ventilation trunking for the forward boiler room emerged in the rear of the bridge superstructure and that of the after boiler room formed an apparent 'deckhouse' abaft the funnel. In the same way, the engine room trunks formed a smaller 'deckhouse' abaft midships, above which was the accepted searchlight position. Boiler room trunking was always larger than engine room trunking because the boiler rooms were under forced draught conditions and needed a large and continuous air supply. In the case of the engine room – which was open to the atmosphere – the ventilation was straightforward. The after superstructure was set above the accommodation spaces where the wardroom and officers' cabins were sited. The officers' galley was also aft (with its own 'Charlie Noble' funnel) so that in a destroyer, particularly, they lived in actual isolation.

No special ninth 'Leader' was built for the 'J' class (although one was intended in the first instance) but *Jervis* was fitted out to act as such and her after superstructure was extended forward close up to the second set of tubes. The extra space provided the accommodation for Captain (D)'s staff.

GUN ARMAMENT

Twin 4·7in Mk XIX mountings were carried in 'A' and 'B' positions with the third at 'X'; and it was the after mounting which raised early arguments. In the 'Tribals' – which had introduced the weapon – the 'X' mounting was unable to fire on arcs close to the bow because it was 'wooded' by the mainmast, searchlight platform and pompom. A Mk XIX mounting had a total training movement of about 320° between its limit stops, and in these ships midtraining was dead ahead for the forward pair and dead astern for the after mountings. In the 'J' class, 'X' mounting had arcs specially extended out to 340° but, oddly, the Naval Staff elected to centre the after

Jervis, the 'Leader' of the 'J's, off Portland July, 1939. Note the 'pill-box' on the after tubes, the extended after superstructure, 'X' gun stowed muzzles forward, and the absence of the TSDS davits on the quarters. *P A Vicary*

mounting's training on zero, too, so it stowed muzzles forward. The effect was that it could not bear dead astern and to train from the port quarter to the starboard (and vice versa) necessitated a slew the 'long way round'. 'As Built' photographs always show 'X' mounting housed with muzzles forward, but early in the war the stops were altered to allow the guns to stow at 180°.

The absence of a second funnel and the large after boiler room vent trunking structure made this a suitable site for the pompom where it enjoyed wide sky arcs, particularly in the absence of any form of mainmast (the 'main roof' radio aerials were slung between a foreyard and a spreader secured by wire pendants from the ensign staff). The pompom was supplemented by quadruple ·5in Vickers Mk III machine gun mountings on the bridge wings.

FIRE CONTROL

With the benefit of hindsight, one can now see that the Admiralty took a retrograde step with the fire control installation of the 'J' class. Like their immediate predecessors, they had an Admiralty Fire Control Clock Mk I as the Surface calculator, a Fuze Keeping Clock Mk II for AA prediction, and a 'Destroyer DCT' on the bridge; but instead of having the newly designed Rangefinder Director Mk II as the controlling unit in AA fire, the DCT was modified to accept AA fire control instruments and worked in association with a simple 'Three-man Rangefinder'.

The latter, manned by Rangetaker, Layer and Trainer, was set on a tall pedestal abaft the DCT and provided only target range in either a surface or an anti-aircraft engagement. It was given an elevation and training receiver so that its crew could follow the point of aim of the DCT. If one accepts the Naval Staff policy of a separate rangefinder (itself in many ways an odd arrangement) the theoretical advantage of the 'J' class system lay in the fact that one director – the DCT – was used in all forms of fire control. But in the event, the DCT was found to be unsuitable in the AA mode and, in mid-1941, the arrangements were completely revised.

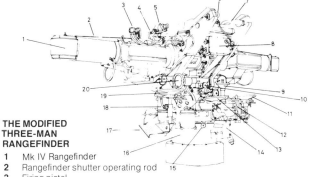

THE MODIFIED THREE-MAN RANGEFINDER

1. Mk IV Rangefinder
2. Rangefinder shutter operating rod
3. Firing pistol
4. Director Setting repeat receiver
5. Layer's monocular sight telescope
6. Control Officer's binoculars
7. Binocular elevating arm
8. Angle of Presentation setting unit
9. Two-speed training handwheel
10. Range-taker's range setting handwheel
11. Trainer's seat
12. Range-taker's vertical seat adjustment handwheel
13. Range-taker's seat
14. Telephone stowage box
15. Training locking bolt hand-grip
16. Fixed pedestal base
17. Layer's footrest
18. Layer's vertical seat adjustment lock
19. Layer's seat
20. Two-speed elevation handwheel

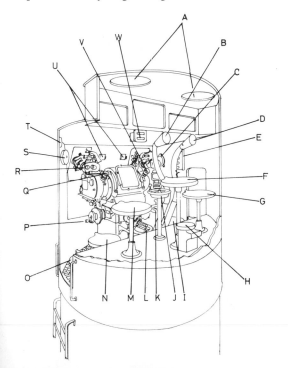

THE DESTROYER DIRECTOR CONTROL TOWER

A. Look out hatches
B. Voice pipe to Transmitting Station
C. Fire gong
D. Voice pipe to Captain and Rangetaker
E. Gun ready lamp box
F. Control Officer's seat
G. Spotting Officer's seat
H. Gyro compass bearing receiver
I. Trainer's seat
J. Control Officer's training handwheel
K. Trainer's handwheel
L. Firing circuit changeover switch and firing pistol
M. Rate Officer's seat
N. Layer's seat
O. Cross-level operator's seat
P. Director elevation handwheel
Q. Eyepiece of layer's stabilised sight
R. Layer's stabilised sight binoculars
S. Check fire bell
T. 'Fall of shot' warning rattler
U. Stabilised sighting port 'Clear view' screen switches
V. Eyepiece of trainer's stabilised sight
W. Combined range and deflection receiver

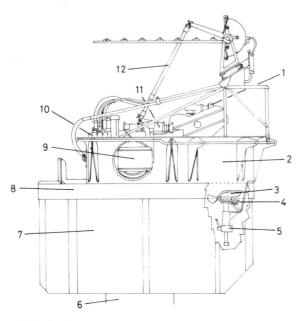

MODIFIED THREE-MAN RANGEFINDER WINDSHIELD AND
RADAR TYPE 285M AERIAL
1   Control Officer's binoculars
2   Windscreen
3   Control Officer's seat, attached to windscreen
4   Seat lateral adjustment
5   Seat vertical adjustment
6   Fixed pedestal base
7   Fixed windscreen
8   Rotating windscreen base
9   Rangefinder
10 Radar Beam Switch Unit
11 Layer's monocular telescope
12 Aerial array elevating link arm

The DCT was 'de-modified' to solely low angle fire control duties and the rangefinder was itself rebuilt to become a 'Modified Three-man Rangefinder'. In its original state, it had been surrounded by a fixed drum-shaped windshield over which the rangefinder 'arms' projected; when modified, an extension shield was added. It was ring-shaped, attached to the rotating structure, and it thus revolved over the fixed shield as the rangefinder trained. A centrally placed seat for the Control Officer was attached to the moving part of the shield, and a light tubular framework was added above it to carry the radar Type 285 'fishbone' aerial array. 'Angle of Presentation' binoculars for the control officer were fitted above the rangefinder, together with electrical elevation and training transmitters, linked to the Fuze Keeping Clock,

and a director firing pistol for the layer transformed the unit into an independent Rangefinder Director. Indeed, the two were almost indistinguishable, and both functioned as directors in their own right in AA fire but were manned simply as rangefinders in surface control.

TORPEDO ARMAMENT

As though to compensate the torpedo specialists for the neglect they felt had been shown them in the 'Tribals', the 'J' class were provided with two five-fold torpedo tube mountings. They were known as 'Pentads' and not 'quintuple' as some writers frequently refer to them. In both sets, the local control position housing the alternative torpedo sights and tube firing levers was positioned above the tubes, rather than to one side, but only the after set had a 'pill-box' cupola, perhaps for evaluation. The forward set had an open-topped spray shield and both had an adjacent deck-edge mounted torpedo davit.

Nerissa, shown here at Malta in April 1944, ran under the Polish flag as *Piorun* between 1940 and 1946. She was then returned to the Royal Navy, and renamed *Noble*, and she survived until 1955. The original *Noble* had already been transferred to the Royal Netherlands Navy as *Van Galen* in 1942.
P A Vicary

MINESWEEPING GEAR AND ANTI-SUBMARINE WEAPONS

It was common practice between the wars to equip some destroyer flotillas with minesweeping gear, often instead of depth charge arrangements. The idea was to provide a high-speed sweeping capability ahead of the main fleet and the legendary 'maids of all work' were the only suitable craft. A special set of gear called the 'Two-Speed Destroyer Sweep' (TSDS) was designed, consisting of two minesweeping paravanes handled by a pair of heavy davits on the quarters and streamed from individual steam-driven winches near the after superstructure.

The general clutter precluded anything other than a single overstern depth charge rail used in conjunction with a pair of DC throwers set abaft the after torpedo tube mounting. These were the proposed arrangements for the 'J's but some omitted the TSDS. When fitted, its presence was always revealed by the davits on the quarters.

WARTIME CHANGES

A significant change came in mid–1941, when the removal of the after set of torpedo tubes was officially authorised. Their place was taken by a single 4in HA gun, fitted to give some measure of AA defence not otherwise provided by the low-angle main armament. The long term intention was to provide a special additional fire control calculator that would allow the 4in to be controlled with the main armament despite the difference in its ballistic characteristics compared with the 4.7in

guns, but initially, pending the production of the control equipment, the HA gun was capable of only independent barrage fire between 4000 and 500 yards. In fact, the benefit gained from the 4in at the expense of half the torpedo armament was minimal in all the British destroyer classes; however, the 'Tribals', could afford the comparative luxury of a twin 4in in 'X' position and eventually had the 'dual ballistics' arrangements fitted.

In the 'J's, anti-aircraft defence was later improved when the 20mm Oerlikon became available. These were added on platforms amidships abreast the searchlight and replaced the inadequate machine guns on the bridge wings. Some ships suffered from coincidentally clashing requirements at this time, for *Jervis*, *Jupiter* (and *Kashmir*) had been given a single 20mm Oerlikon on the searchlight platform and another on the after end of 'X' gundeck, in what were originally 'X' gun's 'blind arcs'. When the stop gear of the after 4.7in was altered the Oerlikon had to be shifted and was then paired-up with the other single on the searchlight platform.

Nizam was one of four 'N's which served in the RAN. Here, in December 1945, she is seen in Grand Harbour, Valletta, Malta, on her way back to the UK. She had single 20mm Oerlikons on the bridge wings, twins amidships and a single 40mm Mk III* mounting on the rebuilt searchlight platform.
A & J Pavia by courtesy of John Roberts

By May 1942 five of the eight ships had been lost and at the end of the same year it was concluded that the inaccuracies inherent in the fire control system rendered the 4in almost valueless outside the ranges already bracketed by the newly installed close range weapons, resulting in its removal and the re-installation of the after tubes.

Later in the war, twin power-operated Oerlikons replaced the singles on the bridge wings, and finally, the only two survivors of the class – *Jervis* and *Javelin* – were refitted with lattice masts to carry the improved and more extensive radar aerials.

THE 'K' CLASS

This class was laid down and completed more or less concurrently with the 'J' class (*Javelin* and *Kashmir*, in fact, changed names with each other while building) and both were virtually identical and were similarly modified. The name-ship *Kelly* took the name of Admiral Sir John Kelly, who had died in 1936, and *Kelvin* was so called as a tribute to Lord Kelvin, the nineteenth century inventor of a number of important shipborne devices, but the others – including, in some ways, *Kipling* – had names strongly associated with the British Empire. Only *Kelvin* and *Kimberley* survived the war, each having lattice masts by the time hostilities ceased, and both were scrapped in 1949.

Of the combined group of 16 destroyers, Lord Louis Mountbatten's command *Kelly* is probably the best remembered, for like Vian's *Cossack* she became almost a legend in her own short lifetime and it was upon her exploits in the Home and Mediterranean theatres that Noël Coward based his epic film 'In Which We Serve'.

THE 'N' CLASS

Although alphabetically out of order, these eight ships were repeats of the 'J's and 'K's and are conveniently dealt with at this point. The two earlier groups were all in commission by December 1939, when it had become obvious that the completion of the bigger 'L' and 'M' classes would be delayed. Thus, the 'N' class, laid down in the late autumn of 1939, began to enter service in the winter of 1940-41 while many of the 'M' class were still on the stocks. The pattern is seen in this example of the launch dates from Fairfield's yard:

Juno	December 1938
Kelvin	January 1939
Napier	May 1940
Nestor	July 1940
Musketeer	December 1941
Myrmidon	March 1942

Their fitting-out coincided with the general removal of torpedo tubes and the introduction of Oerlikons; and they were completed with a 4in HA and single 20mm gun on the bridge wings. A pair of twin .5in machine gun mountings were installed on the quarterdeck as a stop-gap measure to improve AA defence, but like the quad Vickers, they had neither the range nor the hitting power to be effective. After all, there was little to be said for firing upwards at an aircraft with a gun of much the same calibre as he could fire downwards at the ship. The class as a whole later followed the pattern of up-gunning with Oerlikons, the removal of the 4in HA and the addition of improved radars.

Seven of the class were transferred to other Allied navies – one going to the Poles, two to the Dutch and four to the Royal Australian Navy – and only *Nepal* stayed with the Royal Navy. It was cynically observed at the time that 'They' might just as well have kept her original name (*Norseman*) and given her to the Norwegians. As it was, the name *Nepal* was chosen in recognition of the Gurkha Regiments after the two ships bearing their country's name (an original 'Tribal' and *Larne* of the 'L' class, renamed to perpetuate the theme) had both been lost.

4. L and M Classes

THE 'L' AND 'M' CLASSES

These really represented the last fling of the Naval Staff in terms of pre-war destroyer design. The initial intention was to produce a vessel with a better margin of speed above that of the new capital ships, but preliminary studies showed that this could only be achieved by an unacceptably large and costly ship. Even so, as basically only extensions of the 'J' and 'K' classes, the 'L's came out bigger all round. Full load displacement rose by over 300 tons and engine power was upgraded to 48 000 shp to give

the same nominal speed as the others.

Their most distinctive feature was undoubtedly the very large twin 4.7in Mk XX mountings, sited in the 'J' class positions, coupled to a heavy dual purpose director. Apart from the post-war *Daring* class they were the only other British destroyers to have three totally enclosed gunhouses but although they have been credited as being the first to have 'turrets', this is not strictly true. However, the big twins certainly did *look* like turrets and are explained in more detail later in this section.

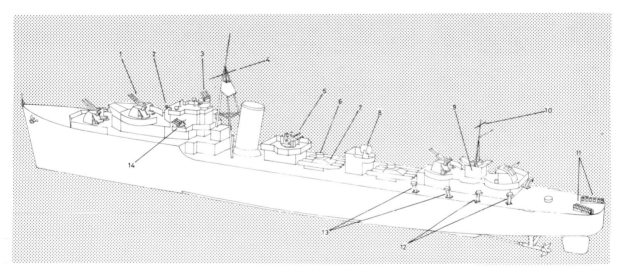

GURKHA (EX-LARNE) JULY 1941

1 4in Twin HA Mk XIX mounting
2 MF/DF aerial
3 Radar Type 285 aerial on Rangefinder Director Mk V**
4 Combined signal and main roof radio aerial yard
5 2pdr Mk VII pompom mounting
6 Tube operator's splinter shield
7 Enclosed central tube trainer's position on QR Mk X torpedo tube mounting
8 44in searchlight
9 4in gun crew's shelter on extended after superstructure
10 Main roof aerial yard on stump mainmast
11 6-charge DC rails and traps
12 'Quarter' Mk II Throwers
13 'Beam' Mk II Throwers
14 Quadruple Vickers 'M' Mk III .5in machine gun mounting

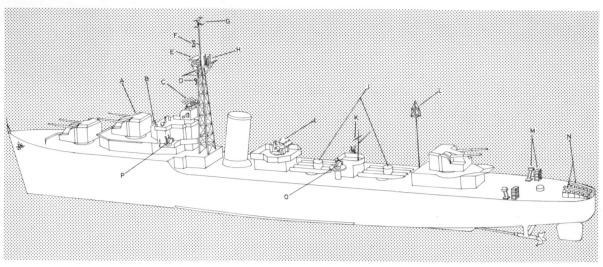

ARMAMENT

A good deal of adverse comment has been levelled at the armament of British destroyers – particularly in their inability to cope with high level and dive bomber attacks – and it therefore seems appropriate at this point to examine the problem that beset the weapon designers.

The 4.7in calibre was adopted by the Royal Navy for destroyer fitting in the middle years of World War I as a means of up-gunning the Modified 'W' class. The calibre itself was not a novelty, for it had formed the secondary armament of the Victorian battleships *Nile* and *Trafalgar* when they first entered service in the late 1880s; but the only up-to-date 4.7in suitable for fitting in a central pivot mounting was a military weapon. The alternative proposal was to develop a 5in gun, but in order to save time, the Naval Staff decided upon the 4.7in and in opting for the fractional calibre, they cast a die whose face was not to be changed for some 25 years.

When the First World War ended, Britain cancelled more than forty of the destroyers that she had on order, but the United States completed the tremendous building programme that she had initiated and went on launching her famous 'four-stackers' well into 1920.

MATCHLESS APRIL 1946

A 4.7in Twin Mk XX mounting
B MF/DF aerial
C Radar Type 285 aerial on Mk IV TP HA/LA director
D Combined wind speed and direction unit
E Radar Type 293 aerial
F IFF aerial
G Radar Type 291 aerial
H IFF 243 aerial
I 2pdr Mk VII* P pompom mounting
J QR Mk VIII*** torpedo tube mountings
K Mainyard for main roof radio aerials
L HF/DF aerial
M 'Parbuckle' stowage and Mk IV DC thrower
N 6-charge oversStern rails and traps
O & P 20mm Oerlikon twin Mk V mountings

A fine view of the imposing twin 4.7in Mk XX mountings on the Polish-manned *Orkan*. Launched as *Myrmidon* in March 1942, she was lost in October 1943. She has the 'Western Approaches' camouflage pattern, single 20mm Oerlikons on the bridge wings and amidships, and a 4in HA in place of the after 'tubes'.
MoD by courtesy of John Roberts

It was not until the mid-1930s that the United States embarked on a New Construction programme, but although this started later than the Royal Navy's, the Americans were quick to appreciate the need for some sort of 'standard' dual purpose gun, linked to a dual purpose fire control system. Their standard gun was a 5in/38 calibre piece, which they eventually fitted into enclosed single and twin mounts in association with an integral director and computer. It formed the main armament of their destroyers and the secondary armament of larger ships, with great benefits in logistic support and in personnel familiarisation. British new construction, on the other hand, saw the continuation of the 4.7in calibre in destroyers, 4.5in in aircraft carriers, 4in in cruisers, and 5.25in in battleships.

In the Royal Navy, destroyer gun mountings were Low Angle weapons and although quite adequate in the anti-ship rôle, were not designed for AA fire. None of the pre-'Tribal' class ships – in other words, a very large proportion of British destroyer strength – had any High Angle fire control arrangements, and even when this control was provided in later classes, it was still linked to Low Angle gun mountings.

A point that immediately arises is that the absolute maximum theoretical range of any gun of given muzzle velocity is produced when the barrel is elevated to an angle of 45° to the horizontal. This is a fact governed by inescapable physical laws; and further investigation shows that the increase in range achieved between 40° and 45° elevation is so small that it is hardly worth considering. For

purely surface fire, therefore, a maximum elevation of 40° is a quite practical limit, but the latter is in any case dictated by the maximum effective range of whatever fire control system happens to be associated with the gun. In the 'A' to 'D' class destroyers, which had only rudimentary arrangements, the maximum gun elevation was 30°; and at this low limit, the barrel can be trunnioned at more or less its natural point of balance. It is when more elevation is demanded that the problems begin to arise.

The 4.7in shell weighed 50lb and its brass cartridge case 30lb, which, in combination, was too heavy for a man to handle at speed in a small, lively ship. Thus the ammunition was split into two components. This in turn led to the need for a loading tray in the rear of the breech mechanism, but on a 'naturally' balanced gun, its presence further restricted the elevation.

To relieve this problem, the principle of 'breech-trunnioning' was adopted, which simply means that the breech was moved towards the trunnion axis to create more space although, of course, making the gun severely muzzle-heavy. To bring it back into equilibrium, a balance weight was required which was set conveniently above the supporting structure of the loading tray, but the complete arrangement increased the all-up weight of the mounting. The old 4in gun in the First World War destroyers weighed 5¼ tons; with the 4.7in Mk XVIII of the 'H' and 'I' classes it had risen to 10¾ tons. As well as supporting this weight,

the ship's structure had to withstand the considerable shock of gunfire – in the case of a 4.7in being of the order of a 20 ton blow.

The designers had four main options open to them if they wished to produce a destroyer with a High Angle armament. The first, and fairly obvious one, was to reduce the calibre of the guns, because this significantly reduced the weight of the shell and cordite to a level that would allow it to be 'fixed' and yet light enough to be manhandled. A combined shell and cartridge – in other words 'fixed' ammunition – could, if it were light enough, be loaded directly by hand, thus obviating the need for a loading tray with its inherent restriction to elevation.

The second option was to reduce substantially the recoil length of the gun because this, too, affected the maximum elevation at which it could be fired. Obviously, the breech could not be allowed to come into contact with the mounting base. The chief objection to a short recoil length is that less shock is absorbed in the buffer and more is transmitted to the ship's structure, so the destroyer 4.7in was designed with a long recoil of 26½in to keep the ship's framing as light as possible.

Recoil shock is also diminished, of course, if the calibre is reduced, so that on a hull of given structural strength one can have either a long recoil 4.7in or a short recoil 4in. It was precisely along these lines that the well known twin 4in HA Mk XIX mounting had been built. Its 'fixed' ammunition weighed 63lb; it had no loading tray; the recoil

length was 15in; and the maximum elevation was 80°. Although its all-up weight was about 3 tons more than a single 4.7, it was more than 11 tons lighter than the twin and was altogether an admirable weapon. The Admiralty, however, would not accept it for a destroyer's main armament because the destructive power of the 35lb 4in projectile did not compare with that of the 50lb 4.7in projectile.

The next option was to increase the trunnion height, thereby again creating more space for the breech end as the muzzle elevated. This scheme was perfectly feasible and it was, indeed, in this way that purely AA mountings – like the 90° 4.7in Mk XII on *Nelson* and *Rodney* – were designed. Their drawback was that they were difficult to load at *low* angles of elevation and were thus unsuited to the need for a good rate of fire in surface engagements at the closer ranges.

The fourth option was to meet the problem squarely, and build a destroyer big enough and strong enough to take power operated turrets, complete with revolving structure ammunition hoists; a gun well to allow for high elevation; and power rammers. Had such a proposal been made in peacetime it would almost certainly have been thrown out by the Exchequer: but in any case many

felt, with some justification, that a destroyer was an unstable gun platform and required not just the mounting but the fire control, automatic stabilisation, and remote power control to go with it. All these features were later to be incorporated, but the mounting destined for the 'L' and 'M' classes was a far cry from the 4.5in Mk IV mountings of the 'Battle' class destroyers.

Above: A single 4in HA has replaced the after set of torpedo tubes in this photo of HMS *Laforey*, taken in 1941. She has the radar Type 286M fixed 'bedstead' aerial at the masthead and wears the 'one white over two red' funnel bands of the 13th Flotilla.
MoD

Left:
Lookout was the only 'L' still running when the war ended, but had gone for scrap by February 1948. In November 1945 she was lying quietly to a buoy at Devonport, dwarfing the 'Bay' class frigate alongside. Notice the single 20mm Oerlikons on the quarterdeck.
P A Vicary

THE 4.7IN MK XI GUN ON THE TWIN MK XX MOUNTING

In this mounting the designers sought to provide all the features of a miniature 'turret' while preserving its 'upper deck' characteristics. They achieved an extra 10° of elevation above the 40° of the open-shield twin 4.7 Mk XIX, but size, weight, cost and complexity rose frighteningly. It was the adoption of the new twin Mk XX mounting more than any other single factor that necessitated an increase in ship size.

GUN WEIGHTS AND DESTROYER DISPLACEMENT

Mounting	Weight in tons	No fitted	Standard displacement of typical class	Shaft horsepower (shp) for 36kts (nominal) (2 shafts)
Handworked single 4.7in Mk VIII	10.6	4	'I' – 1400 tons	34 000
Power worked twin 4.7in Mk XIX	25.5	3	'J' – 1700 tons	40 000
Power worked twin 4.7in Mk XX	34	3	'M' – 1900 tons	48 000

The 50 calibre Mk XI gun was a departure from all earlier 4.7s in that it fired a 62lb shell and in this respect was much superior. It provided a powerful anti-ship capability and excellent support in the bombardment role – although more brawn was required to handle its heavy shells. Once a totally enclosed gunhouse on a basically 'upper deck' style mounting was decided upon, the features which followed progressed along a ruthlessly logical path. Ammunition had to be supplied to the gunhouse from below at any angle of training, and thus, in the absence of a revolving turret trunk within the ship, the centre of rotation was the only suitable position.

Delivering ammunition into the gunhouse at this point meant that all the loading numbers had to stand *between* the guns, which were therefore widely spaced and needed individual elevation arrangements. Hence two elevation drives and two gunlayers were required, and with weight already rising, power elevation was ruled out and the big guns were hand worked in this motion. All the problems of hand-follow (matching pointers) against aircraft targets were thereby re-introduced, although in mitigation, power training was provided. However, it could scarcely have been otherwise, for hand-follow in this motion would have been too slow if heavily geared down and too laborious with a higher ratio.

On the face of it, the ammunition supply system was cleverly arranged. A vertical tube was sub-divided into four quadrants, each containing a hoist, one pair providing shell and the other cartridge cases. The tube functioned as a central pivot and the mounting revolved around it. When a forward mounting was trained to its stowed position, the two shell hoists were conveniently positioned towards the muzzles of each gun, but when the mounting moved around the non-rotating hoist trunk, the path of the loading numbers from hoist to gunloading tray was less straightforward. The schematic sketch should make the difficulties clear. This somewhat tortuous path tended to slow down the rate of fire, especially as the shell loaders were carrying over half a hundredweight at a time.

From the maximum elevation point of view, the fact that all the loading numbers were borne on the rotating platform of the gunhouse, instead of standing on the ship's deck, allowed the design to include a shallow gun-well beneath the loading trays. It was principally in this way that the extra 10° of elevation was achieved. Empty cartridge case disposal from the gunhouse was effected by chutes in the rear of both guns down which the spent cylinders were ejected on to the deck outside.

In general appearance, the Mk XX mounting somewhat resembled the contemporary capital ship and cruiser 5.25in twin, and destroyer men were staggered by its imposing size. It was undoubtedly an excellent anti-ship weapon, but could not cope with dive bombers any more than could the 40° mountings. The uninitiated were therefore non-plussed by the institution of a 4in HA gun in place of the after tubes in these otherwise heavily armed ships.

The big twin 4.7in Mk XX mounting leaving the gun shops. Note the widely spaced individually elevating barrels, the sighting ports between them, and the ventilation trunking on the gunhouse side.
MoD

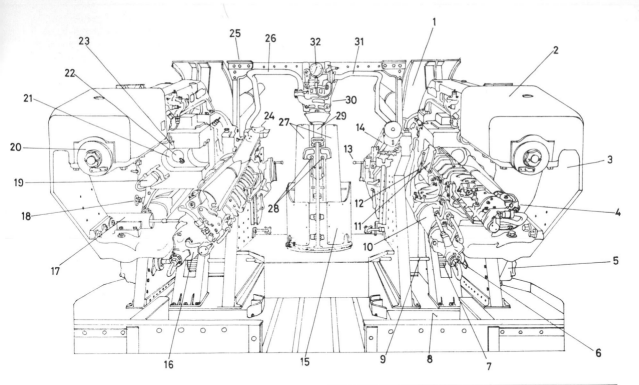

4.7 IN MK XX MOUNTING

1   Mantlet plate
2   Balance weight
3   Balance weight support frame
4   Loading tray in line with chamber
5   Right gun elevation gear box
6   Hydraulic swivel connection to loading tray
7   Elevation pinion
8   Gun well
9   Drive shaft to elevation receiver 'mechanical' pointer
10 Support tube for loading tray
11 Loading tray unlocking palm lever
12 Power rammer control lever
13 Fuze setting hand crank
14 Loaded tilting tray aligned to fuze setting machine
15 Non rotating ammunition trunking
16 Loading tray in 'out' position
17 Loading tray buffer box
18 Air blast stop valve
19 Loading tray stop pad
20 Recuperator cylinder
21 Breech block in closed position
22 Electric firing lock
23 Loading lamp
24 Tilting tray in line with loading tray
25 Gunhouse roof support plates
26 Mounting hydraulic exhaust main
27 Cartridges at top of hoists
28 Cartridge hoist starting levers
29 Co-axial hydraulic pressure and exhaust pipe at centre of rotation
30 Main hydraulic pressure and exhaust swivel connection
31 Mounting hydraulic pressure main
32 Gunhouse pressure gauge

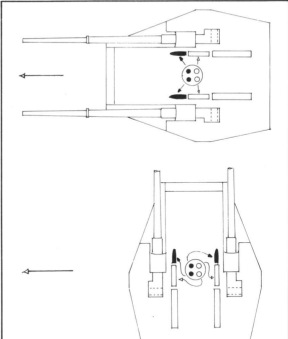

PLAN VIEW OF THE TWIN 4.7IN MK XX GUNHOUSE

The arrow between the barrels indicates the fore-and-aft stowed position. The short arrows from the ammunition trunking show the passage of shell (black) and cartridge (white) to the tilting trays. The passage is straightforward in the upper sketch, but in the lower, where the mounting is trained on the beam to 90 degrees Green, the routes from the ammunition trunking are extended and become more difficult still when the mounting trains abaft the beam.

THE 'ANTI-AIRCRAFT' 'L' CLASS

Although both classes were designed for the twin Mk XX mounting, the rate of shipbuilding outstripped that of the gun mounting manufacturers, resulting in four of the 'L' class being modified to take four 4in HA Mk XIXs. All-round weight saving permitted an enlargement of the after superstructure and the fitting of four of these most versatile weapons. Despite the aversion of the Naval Staff towards 4in guns as the main armament of destroyers – later in any case to be contradicted in the 'O' and 'P' classes – the four 'anti-aircraft' variants were very useful ships. With little real loss in terms of maximum gun range, the higher rate of fire from eight 4in guns more than compensated for their reduced hitting power. Above all, needless to say, the ships had an 80° main armament, as well as a full torpedo outfit. In addition, they were given twin overstern depth charge rails and eight throwers, and were able to deliver the devastating '14 pattern' depth charge attack.

FIRE CONTROL

Perhaps encouraged by the special combined rangefinder/DCT installed in the 'export' destroyers for Brazil and Turkey, the Admiralty produced a new director for those of the 'L' and 'M' classes which were to have the 4.7in armament. It was designated the HA/LA Director, Mk IV, Type TP, and was a reduced version of the cruiser and capital ship DCT. It carried a rangefinder in a rear compartment, had radar Type 285 added on top, was power operated* and was provided with the latest gyro director sight. This, the 'P' sight, had a master gyroscope with a power follow-up capable of stabilising the layer's and trainer's binoculars, a sight arm holding the control and rate officers' binoculars, and the rangefinder. It could not, however, accept the additional load of the radar aerial

array, to which a hand drive was fitted. In surface fire, the aerial was locked at 10° elevation, and in AA the then unemployed cross-level operator kept the 'fishbone' at the correct elevation by matching pointers on a small receiver within the tower.

The 'P' sight had been devised for surface control, and although most successful when so employed, it was less so when used in the anti-aircraft mode. Coupled with the difficulties of using the

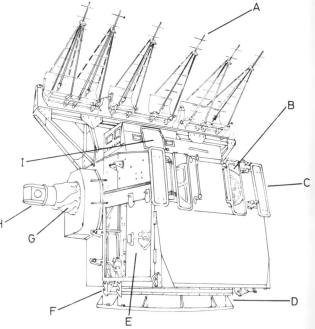

THE MK IV TYPE TP HA/LA DIRECTOR

A Radar Type 285 aerial array	
B Layer's sighting port	**F** Hangers for access ladder
C Sighting port door	**G** Flexible gaiter
D Training Base	**H** Rangefinder
E Right hand sliding access door	**I** Control Officer's sight port

*Hand training only in *Lookout*, *Laforey* and *Marne*, as first fitted.

4.7in Mk XX mountings against aircraft targets, it made the 'L' and 'M' classes a disappointment to many. Imposing they may have been, but the 4in HA abaft the searchlight was evidence enough of their limitations.

The 'Anti-aircraft' 'L' class were a little better off in having a dual purpose Rangefinder-Director – described in more detail later – instead of the rather cumbersome Mk IV, but unhappily, all four were sunk or otherwise put permanently out of action by the attentions of the enemy.

OTHER WEAPONS

Both classes took advantage of the availability of 20mm Oerlikons and followed the usual pattern of firstly having singles to supplement their machine guns, then replacing the latter, and finally doubling up to twin mountings.

By the end of 1942 the ranks of twin 4.7in armed British destroyers had been decimated. They went down fighting, but the simple table below makes sad – and sobering – reading.

Class and original numbers	Lost from all causes by 31.12.42	Final number of survivors
'Tribal' (16)	12	4
'J' (8)	5	2
'K' (8)	6	2
'L' (8)	4	1
'M' (8)	1	5
'N' (8)	1	7
Totals (56)	29	21

1. The heavy losses in the first four classes should be noted.
2. Comparative totals for the 'A' to 'I' classes (including the ex-Brazilian and Turkish) were: 85/45/31.

Left: The extended after superstructure and its two twin 4in Mk XIX mountings is clearly shown in this shot of HMS *Gurkha* (ex-*Larne*). She has multiple machine guns on the bridge wings and the usual pompom abaft the funnel, but no Oerlikons. With an exclusively HA main armament, the 'anti-aircraft' 'L' class had no need to forfeit one set of torpedo tubes and retained both. The tubes were power-operated QR Mk Xs, recognisable by the streamlined fairing over the Tube Trainer's position. *MoD*

Below: HMS *Loyal* on 30 October 1942, wearing an Admiralty Light Type camouflage scheme. She has the early 'five stick' radar, ie Type 285, aerial on the DCT, 285P at the masthead, single Oerlikons on the bridge wings, amidships and on the quarterdeck, and two sets of torpedo tubes. *MoD*

LOYAL

LATER DEVELOPMENTS IN THE PRE-EMERGENCY PROGRAMME CLASSES

Only two 'J's, two 'K's and one 'L' class were still operational in 1945, and none lasted very long thereafter. The war-weary *Jervis*, *Javelin*, *Kelvin* and *Kimberley* were all scrapped in 1949 and *Lookout* had already gone to the breakers in 1948. Of the Australian-named 'N's, *Nestor* was sunk in 1942; the other three, *Napier*, *Nizam* and *Norman* were returned to the RN after the war, and were scrapped in the mid–1950s, along with the Polish *Piorun* (ex-*Nerissa*).

Noble (I), turned over to the Royal Netherlands Navy in 1942 and renamed *Van Galen*, was active in the United Nations force during the Korean War. In company with the British Commonwealth 'Tribals', she was like an echo from the past when viewed from an RN 'Co' class destroyer, reviving many memories, particularly among the reservists who had been recalled to service with the Fleet. *Nonpareil*, which fought under the Dutch flag in WWII as *Tjerk Hiddes* lasted longest of all, ending her days as a unit of the Indonesian Navy in 1961.

The 'M' class – which missed the early war years – fared somewhat better, for five of them were still going strong in 1946. *Martin* sank in 1942; *Myrmidon*, under the Polish flag as *Orkan*, was lost in 1943; and *Mahratta* went down in 1944. *Musketeer* was scrapped in 1955 but meanwhile the remaining four were sold to Turkey, after being laid up in reserve for a number of years. Their twin Mk XX mountings were ever eyebrow-raisers, for only six of the original twelve ships to carry them were still operational in 1946, and comparatively few people knew of the Mk XX's existence.

The four ships sold abroad were all extensively refitted. The after superstructure was extended forward over the old site of the torpedo tubes to make a 'Squid' mortar deck; the close range armament was tidied up to four single Bofors Mk VII and a twin Bofors Mk V; new radars were added; and the twin 4.7s were modified for power elevation. For sheet *presence* nothing ever equalled 'The Magnificent Ms' and they remained the most imposing destroyers in the world until they faded from sight in the early 1970s.

The 'individual elevation' characteristic of the twin 4.7in Mk XX mounting is clearly seen in this shot of *Lookout* taken off Greenock in January 1942. Note the complex Admiralty Disruptive camouflage scheme and the comparatively larger size of the 4in HA when compared with the 12pdr HA fitted in the same position on the earlier classes. *MoD by courtesy of John Roberts*

5. O and P Classes
The First and Second Emergency Flotillas

THE WAR EMERGENCY PROGRAMME

When the Second World War broke out in September 1939, nothing later than the 'K' class had been completed and it was not until the end of 1942 that the last of the ships ordered under pre-war Estimates was in commission. The 'L' class had been laid down in its entirety in 1938 but with the building time already extending, in early 1939, the Admiralty decided to divide future construction into two types of destroyer. One would be a continuation of the big twin-gun ships (once existing orders had been fulfilled); the other was to be a smaller type of vessel, with less complex weapons, whose total building time could be reduced to a tolerable span, thus meeting the expected 'crie de coeur' from all quarters for 'More destroyers'.

The outcome of this 1939 decision was that, from January 1941 onwards, the launching of the new 'Emergency' classes ran in parallel with the backlog of pre-war Estimates vessels. Their shortened building time allowed them so to overhaul the earlier destroyers that *Onslow*, for example, was actually completed in October 1941 on the same day that *Loyal* moved down the slip at Scott's of Greenock, leaving five 'M' class and one 'N' elsewhere still to take to the water.

The first two classes, designated the First and Second Emergency Flotillas, continued the pre-war sequential letter theme and were allocated names beginning with O and P. The process continued without alphabetical omission up to X, which was not used for fairly obvious reasons. Less obviously, Y was also omitted, the progression reaching a natural conclusion with Z. That Y was not used is a little strange. Admittedly, words beginning with this letter occupy few pages in either a dictionary or the British gazetteer; but more than enough for a flotilla exist between the two, including *Yeoman*, *Yarrow* and *Yelverton*. If *Tally-ho* can be adopted for a submarine, why not *Yoicks* for a destroyer? One can imagine the signal traffic that would have developed between two such ships in company with a group of 'Hunt' class destroyers!

Since four more Emergency Flotillas were to follow the 'Z's one might have supposed that, logically, the process of allocating ship-names would have reverted to A, but in the event neither this letter, nor the initial B, were used.

The 11th Emergency Flotilla, ordered in 1942, was initially earmarked to receive eight almost random names, but late in that year, it was given eight beginning with 'Ca', to be followed by eight 'Ch', eight 'Co' and eight 'Cr' names. At the same time, the established practice of naming the lead ship after a naval personage was given up. *Capel* might conceivably have been used; *Codrington*, an original Leader lost in 1940 could well have been remembered; and *Cranstoun* was a suitable 'Cr' name. For the 'Ch' class, *Chequers* herself – or even *Chartwell* – would have alluded to the one-time First Lord of the Admiralty, Winston Churchill. (The name 'Churchill' had already been allocated to an ex-American 'four-stacker').

Partridge, March 1942
MoD

The Emergency Flotillas each consisted of eight ships, the special ninth 'Leader' concept having long been abandoned, but the lead ship of each class was fitted out internally to act in that capacity. Prior to the large 'C' group, the 'naval personage' theme was continued and presented no problems up to *Troubridge* (although *Rotherham* was, in fact, mis-spelt if *Rotheram* was intended) but with U, V, W and Z no suitable names could be conjured up. Hence *Grenville* (still running in early 1974) became the leader of the 'U's, taking the name of the 'G' class leader, lost in January 1940, and *Hardy* became 'Leader' of the 'V' class – again after an earlier ship lost in the same year. Similarly *Kempenfelt* was leader of the 'W' class and *Myngs* of the 'Z' class.

Towards the end of the Emergency Programme a similar 'overlap' as had occurred in 1940 began to take shape, for a new generation of big, twin-gunned fleet destroyers – the 1942 'Battles' (ordered in that year) – were being built and launched concurrently with the later Emergency Flotillas. It was popularly supposed at the time that the sixteen ships of the first two 'Battle' flotillas had, in effect, taken the place of the non-existent 'A' and 'B' classes.

THE FIRST AND SECOND EMERGENCY FLOTILLAS

The 'O' and 'P' classes showed a very clear combination of certain features of earlier destroyer classes. The profile of the hull closely resembled that of the 'J' class, even to the steep sheer of the fo'c's'le deck, and was similarly longitudinally framed. Standard displacement was, however, slightly less, as were the main hull dimensions which, coupled to the same pattern of main machinery, gave a marginal improvement in speed of about one knot at full load.

The engine and boiler installation remained standard for all fourteen Emergency flotillas, although slightly increased dimensions in the later classes fractionally reduced the best speed. On the other hand, their bunkerage was increased from 500 to 615 tons and endurance at 20 knots rose proportionally to about 4700 miles.

ARMAMENT LAYOUT AND DETAILS

The main gun armament of the first – and indeed all – of the Emergency classes copied the established 'A' to 'I' layout in having two single mountings forward, two aft, and two sets of quadruple torpedo tubes separated by the engine room vent trunking/searchlight platform. They differed in close range AA arrangements, however, in adopting the 'J' class quad pompom position immediately abaft the funnel.

OBEDIENT

1. 4in HA Mk III* mounting
2. MF/DF aerial
3. Radar Type 285 aerial on Rangefinder Director Mk V**
4. Radar Type 291 aerial
5. Main roof yard
6. Signal yard
7. 2pdr Mk VII* P mounting
8. QR Mk VIII*** torpedo tube mounting
9. Main roof yard
10. Mk II throwers
11. Unshielded 4in HA
12. Minelaying 'fantail'
13. Single 20mm Oerlikon mounting
14. Single 20mm Oerlikon mounting
15. Single 20mm Oerlikon mounting

ORIBI

1. MF/DF aerial
2. Radar Type 285 aerial on Rangefinder Director Mk V**
3. Radar Type 291 aerial
4. Main roof radio aerial yard
5. Signal yard
6. 2pdr Mk VII* P pompom
7. Main roof radio aerial 'goalpost'
8. Single 20mm Oerlikon mountings
9. Single 4in HA Mk IV mounting
10. Mk II thrower
11. Radar Type 271 aerial 'lantern'
12. Radar 'office'
13. Single 20mm Oerlikon mounting
14. 4.7in Mk XVIII mounting

PENN

1. 4in HA Mk III** mounting
2. Radar Type 285 on Rangefinder Director Mk V**
3. Radar Type 291 aerial
4. 2pdr Mk VII* P mounting
5. QR Mk VIII*** torpedo tube mounting
6. Single 20mm Oerlikon mountings
7. Stump mainmast
8. Unshielded 4in HA mounting in 'Q' position
9. Gundeck 'bandstand'
10. 4in HA MK III** mounting, stowed forward
11. Unshielded 4in HA mounting
12. Mk II throwers
13. Radar 'office'
14. Single 20mm Oerlikon mounting

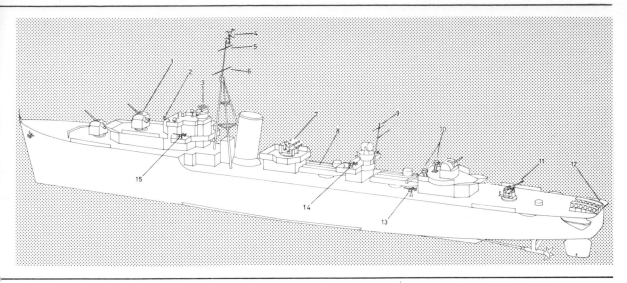

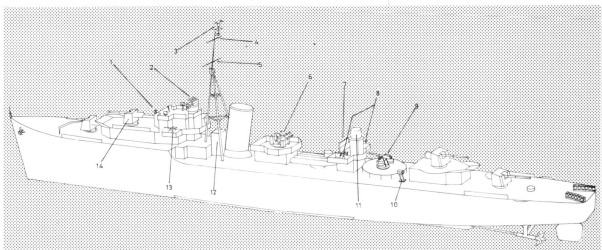

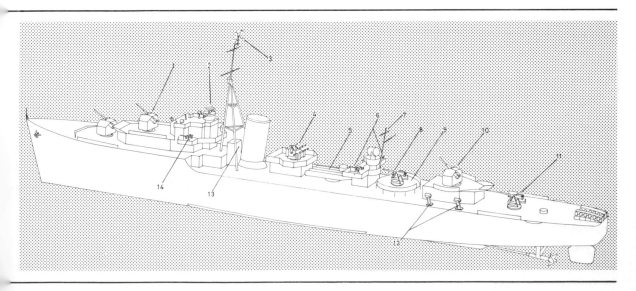

THE QF 4.7IN MK IX GUN ON THE CP MK XVIII MOUNTING

This mounting had been first installed in the 'H' class and was a development of the 30° Mk XIV of the 'A' to 'D' classes. Most of the detail can be seen in the drawing and photograph, but the training base design of a CP (central pivot) mounting needs a little explanation because it was about this feature that most of the problems of high angle capability – literally – revolved.

The circular mounting base plate was bolted directly to the deck and was supported beneath by a ring-shaped bulkhead called the 'gun support'. It was mostly used as a stowage for spare gear and stores. A lower roller path was machined on the base ring, with a similar upper roller path on the underside of the mounting turntable platform. Between the two machined paths, a ring of horizontal rollers carried the weight of the mounting, and at the centre of rotation it was located by a light cage containing vertical thrust rollers. This was known as the 'central pivot' to which the abbreviation 'CP' referred. The electric cabling conveying fire control and illumination circuits ran up through the central pivot from the gun support, with sufficient 'slack' to allow the mounting to train to its limit stops. The barrel of 'X' mounting in destroyers was alone unobstructed by ship's structure, but it still had to be fitted with training limit stops; otherwise, unrestricted rotation would eventually have resulted in the cabling being wrenched out.

The merit of the CP mounting was that it was comparatively easy to remove it complete, and it was therefore categorised as 'Transferable'. When it carried a 4.7in gun, the very nature of its design made it difficult to adapt for the dual purpose role, but, with the unspoken philosophy 'Needs must when the Devil drives', it was chosen for the first of the new destroyers. Thus, as far as the main guns of the Emergency classes were concerned, they were exactly as they had been in the pre-'Tribal' flotillas.

When the first sixteen ships were ordered, it was intended that all should receive this Mk XVIII mounting, but the events of 1940 – by which time almost all were under construction – clearly demonstrated what many already felt: that British destroyers were extremely vulnerable to air attack. The best alternative armament would without question have been the twin 4in HA Mk XIX, but everyone wanted 'twin four inch' (or as some chose to phrase it, 'four-inch twins'). Many of the larger units of the Fleet had been up-gunned with this weapon before the war, but there was still a backlog of ships waiting to land their single 4in HA in favour of the twin. These included *Exeter,*

PETARD DECEMBER 1944

1 4in twin HA Mk XIX mounting in 'B' position
2 Radar Type 285 aerial on Mk V** R/F Director
3 Radar Type 293 aerial
4 HF/DF aerial
5 IFF 243 aerial
6 2pdr Mk VII* P pompom
7 Single 20mm Oerlikon mountings
8 Radar Type 291 aerial
9 Yard on stump mainmast for Main Roof radio aerial
10 4in twin HA Mk XIX mounting in 'X' position
11 Mk IV Depth Charge throwers and 'Parbuckle' stowages repositioned abreast disarmed 'Y' gundeck
12 Twin 20mm Oerlikon Mk V mounting

Arethusa, Achilles, Shropshire, Sussex, Devonshire and *Canberra* as well as the aircraft carrier *Hermes.* The 'Tribals' were earmarked to receive it in 'X' position (in lieu, significantly of a twin 4.7in) and it was needed for 'Hunt' class escorts, *Black Swan* class sloops and half the 'L' class. But none was available. A weapon in plentiful supply was the discarded single 4in HA, whose place in the capital ships and cruisers had been taken by the Mk XIX, and in the event twelve of the first sixteen ships were armed solely with this gun.

Several policy changes took place in rapid succession. *Pakenham* and *Pathfinder,* earmarked to get 4.7s, changed names with *Onslow* and *Onslaught* while still on the stocks, to join *Offa* and *Oribi* as straightforward 4.7in destroyers. Six 'P's, already destined to be armed with single 4in HAs, were joined by the two ex-'O's and all eight ships were similarly equipped. Next, the remaining four 'O' class were made adaptable for conversion to minelayers, and to compensate for the additional topweight of 60 mines were also armed with the lighter 4in mountings. These four ships – *Obdurate, Obedient, Opportune* and *Orwell* – temporarily landed 'Y' mounting and the after set of torpedo tubes to undertake minelaying practice, but then re-embarked their weapons.

The four 'O' class ships with 4.7in guns now found themselves as ill-equipped for AA fire as the rest of the Royal Navy's destroyers, and all omitted their after set of tubes, installing a single 4in HA in lieu. In due course, the after tubes were replaced, except in *Oribi,* which retained her HA mounting until 1946. In the 4in armed ships of both classes, 'A', 'B' and 'X' mountings were given substantial gunshields but 'Y' (and 'Q' when fitted) were open unshielded weapons. *Paladin* and *Pakenham,*

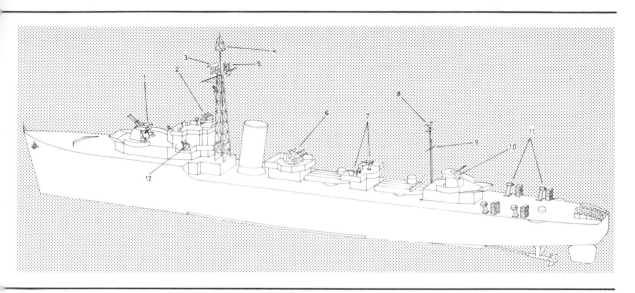

exceptionally, transposed their after mountings and had shielded 'Y' guns and unshielded 'X' guns.

An interesting feature of the four 'O' class minelayers was the special location of their port and starboard depth charge throwers. The normal position for these was on the Iron Deck in the general area of the after superstructure, but this conflicted with the run of the mine rails if and when they were fitted. Hence the minelayers' depth charge throwers were moved up one deck level and were sited on

the forward corners of 'X' gundeck much as they originally had been in the 'Tribal' class ships. The throwers are often very difficult to detect in photographs, but an indication of their position is given by the pair of depth charge handling davits which rise prominently from nearby. The davits were used both to top up the depth charge ready-use stowages and to transfer charges from them to the thrower trays. The layout drawing of HMS *Obedient* shows these high-sited arrangements and also

Pathfinder MoD

the extra single Oerlikon mountings which were added on the Iron Deck in the more usual thrower positions. Here, the deck was almost certainly strengthened (to take a thrower) and was thus suited for the weight of a single Oerlikon mounting.

By and large, the main armament of the 'O's and 'P's was nothing if not extempore in the extreme, which more than anything else, perhaps, is an indication of the urgency of the hour when they came to be fitted out.

THE 4IN QF MK V SERIES GUN ON THE HA MK III SERIES AND MK IV MOUNTINGS

There were several variants of the Mk V gun, distinguished by a suffix of asterisks after the roman numeral, but the differences were merely those of barrel construction. This changed over the years from the earliest 'A' Mk V, wire-wound in the old–fashioned way, to the final version, the Mk VC, with a modern exchangeable 'loose barrel'.

The HA mountings in which the guns were fitted were the Mks III, III*, III** and IV, all of them generally similar. The main differences were in the design of the recoil and run-out cylinders and in the position of the fuze setting platforms. The Mk III mounting had a rather unsuccessful hydro-pneumatic run-out cylinder and two small plat-

A gunshop photo of the 4.7in Mk XVIII without its shield *MoD*

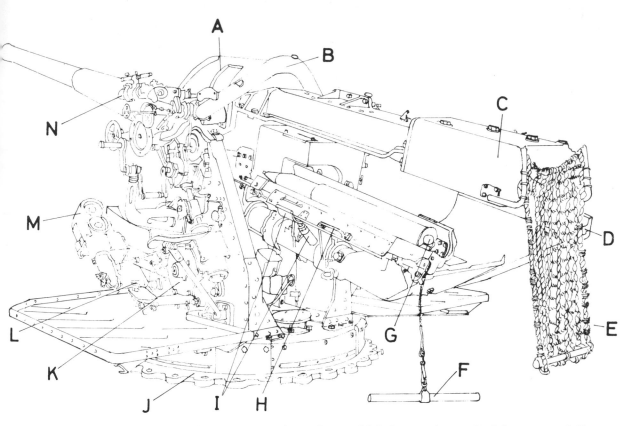

forms on each side of the trunnion supports; the Mk III* was much the same but with 'dry' pneumatic run-out arrangements; and the Mk III** had a pair of large run-out springs in prominent twin cylinders above the gun cradle and a double hand-fuze setting platform on the left hand side. The final Mk IV version (mostly from the 8in 'County' class cruisers) had an improved pneumatic run-out cylinder – otherwise known as the 'recuperator' – and a mechanical fuze setting machine on the left hand side.

The gun was 'naturally' balanced, with a conventional Quick-Fire breech block opening to the right. It utilised 'fixed' ammunition and fired a 31lb shell. The mounting was typical of the specifically anti-aircraft equipment in having a high trunnion axis – some 2ft above that of the 4.7in Mk XVIII – and was provided with a loader's platform to ease the problem of loading at low angles of elevation.

During the 1920s these weapons had a most complex High Angle geared gunsight, but it was never very successful and was removed with the advent of the High Angle Control System. The guns later had a simplified sight for local surface control, although aiming against high level bombers and surface targets was normally by 'follow-the-pointer' in director control. Against dive bom-

bers, which frequently attacked from several directions at once, the guns went into local barrage fire, for which a simple 'cartwheel' sight was fitted.

The differences in the fuze setting arrangements altered the overall width of the revolving structure, so that although to the casual observer the shielded guns in the 'O' and 'P' classes looked much the same as each other, they were wider and of different profile on the front face in the 'P's.

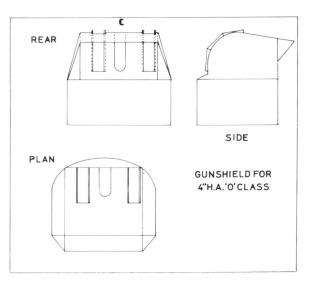

CLOSE RANGE WEAPONS

A Mk VII ('Quad') 2pdr pompom was positioned on a gundeck built over the boiler room vents abaft the funnel, and initially it was proposed to fit a quadruple Vickers .5 inch Mk III machine gun mounting on sponsons on each side of the bridge. Fortunately, by the time the ships were fitting out, the 20mm Oerlikon had become available and a single took the place of each machine gun mounting. A further pair were worked in amidships by building a platform outwards from the searchlight position. Later in the war, two of the single Oerlikons were replaced by two twin Mk V mountings, mostly on the bridge sponsons. The contrary *Paladin*, however, had twins amidships and retained her singles forward.

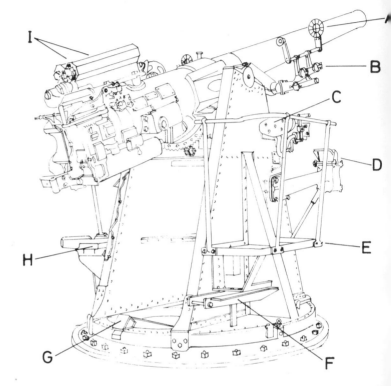

4IN HA MK III MOUNTING

A   Trainer's open sight
B   Trainer's telescope clamps
C   Trainer's body rest
D   Training receiver
E   Trainer's platform
F   Support for breech worker's platform
G   Spent cartridge deflector
H   Sight setter's platform
I   Hydro-pneumatic recuperator

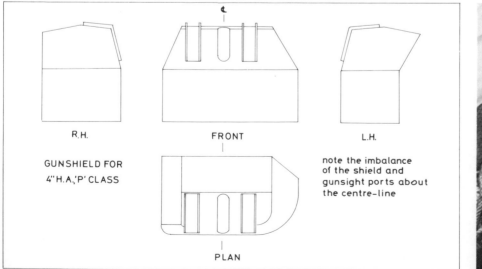

R.H.   FRONT   L.H.

GUNSHIELD FOR
4" H.A.'P' CLASS

note the imbalance
of the shield and
gunsight ports about
the centre-line

PLAN

FIRE CONTROL

The Fuze Keeping Clock, designed before the war as a small-ship anti-aircraft predictor, was associated with a lightweight Rangefinder Director and a surface calculator. The Mk II and III directors had an electrical data transmission system linking them to the Transmitting Station (TS) housing the calculators, and were for destroyer and sloop fitting respectively. They will be met with later. The Mk IV and V directors had mechanical shaft transmissions and differed in that the Mk IV had a rigidly mounted rangefinder, whereas in the Mk V it was carried in an anti-vibration cradle. Both fulfilled a dual purpose role, controlling the main armament in surface and AA fire.

The 'O's and 'P's were equipped with the Mk V** version, whose rangefinder mounting had been specially developed to withstand the vibration likely to be felt in a high speed ship. The first 'star' indicated that a windscreen was fitted, and the second that the director had a radar Type 285 aerial. To keep the length of the transmission shafting to a minimum, the 'mechanical' directors were characteristically low-set on the bridge, with the TS immediately below. The scheme had the merit of being at once compact and easy to install, but had the disadvantage of placing the TS in a rather vulnerable position. Within it were the Fuze Keeping Clock (FKC), and Admiralty Fire Control Box (AFCB) as the surface control predictor and a Gyro Level Corrector (GLC). A change-over lever on the AFCB selected the appropriate calculator.

The old 4in HA mounting appeared in several forms, some fully shielded, some open, and some, like the one shown, with a part-shield. This is the Mk III***, with twin run-out spring boxes on top of the cradle. Note the high trunnion axis and the angled trunnion cap, to take downthrusts at high elevation.
IWM

The director was hand operated, but most of the Mk V series were eventually fitted with the additional refinement of a power follow-up in elevation, controlled by the stabiliser. The latter was trained around in sympathy with the director by a shaft drive so that it always 'looked' along the line of sight to the target and its gyro measured ship movements in this plane. Relative movements between the gyroscope and its gimbals were detected and relayed to an electric motor (in the director) whose output shaft drove into the layer's hand drive via a differential. All the sights were thus automatically stabilised in the elevation plane by the superimposed power drive.

A marked feature of the mechanical transmission directors was the presence of a fixed drum-shaped wind shield around the moving platform, supported by strengthening ribs. A shallow extension screen attached to the rotating structure slid over the fixed component when the director trained. It was this windscreen assembly to which the first 'star' after the mark number referred, because the original mounting was completely open and resembled a simple rangefinder.

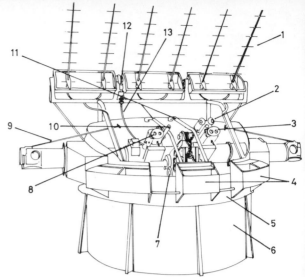

MK V RANGEFINDER DIRECTOR**

1 Radar Type 285/M3 aerial array
2 Control officer's binoculars
3 Director trainer's binocular sight
4 Wind deflectors
5 Revolving windshield
6 Fixed windshield
7 Director layer's elevating handwheel
8 Director layer's binocular sight
9 Operating rod for rangefinder shutter
10 Director layer's barrage fire telescope
11 Support frames for director cover
12 Aerial array elevating worm and wormwheel gearbox
13 Flexible cable drive to aerial array gearbox

4IN HA MK IV MOUNTING

A Pneumatic recuperator
B Breech worker's platform
C Hinged support for breech worker's platform
D Projectile supports of fuze-setting machine
E Fuze-setter's footrest
F Set fuze number hand crank
G Fuze-setting head, revolved by F
H Lever, ejecting round from fuze-setting head
I Fuze number receiver motor
J Fuze number dial of HA gunsight

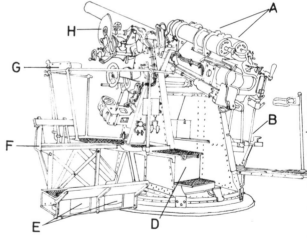

4IN HA MKIII MOUNTING**

A Twin run-out spring boxes
B Trainer's platform
C Breech worker's backrest stanchion
D Loading steps
E Twin rotating fuze-setting positions
F Fuze-setters bench seat
G Sight-setters backrest
H HA gunsight

Note:
on this mounting, the 'fixed' projectiles were placed base downwards on the fuze-setting positions and rotated by hand, while the fuse-setting numbers in the gun's crew, holding the shell nosecap, set the appropriate fuze, called out by the sight-setter.

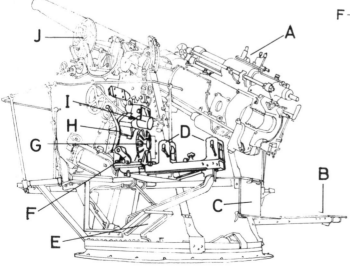

In the 4.7in armed ships, the system was linked to these guns in both forms of control, the 4in (when fitted) being used in barrage fire either with the main armament or alone at high angles of elevation. In the totally 4in fitted ships, the system was identical, except that the FKC and AFCB were adapted internally to take account of the different ballistic characteristics of the smaller calibre.

A device called the Auto Barrage Unit (ABU) formed part of the radar Type 285 set and provided the means of firing a once-only controlled barrage. Having loaded the guns with shells fuzed for a particular barrage range, the unit was then switched in and automatically completed the firing circuit at the correct time with respect to the radar range.

TORPEDO TUBE MOUNTINGS

The Quadruple Revolving (QR) and Pentad Revolving (PR) series of torpedo tube mountings were pre-war developments and stemmed in the first instance from the QR Mk I, designed for the cruisers *Emerald* and *Enterprise* of 1926. In fact, as was so often the case with weapon equipments, the two ships were completed ahead of their proper tubes and temporarily shipped Triple Revolving (TR) Mk Is. The QR II and II* mountings went to the *Kent* and *London* class 8in cruisers and all were similar in having a distinct gap between the two centre tubes where the mounting trainer's crankshaft handles were sited. These 'tube mountings' had a self-locking single-start worm and wormwheel training drive, but because it could be damaged by the shock of discharge, a lever-operated locking bolt was also provided. The training hand drive could be de-clutched from the worm shaft and coupled to 'launching-in' drums on top of the torpedo tubes. The drums, in conjunction with cables and fairleads, were used to haul the torpedo into its tube.

The first quadruple mounting for destroyers was the QR Mk III in the 'A' class ships of 1929-30. It was followed by the QR Mk III* mounting in the 'B', 'C', and 'D' classes, the QR IV in the 'E' class

and the QR VI* in the 'F' class. The 'G' class of 1935-36 was fitted with QR Mk VIIIs* and by the 'H' class the QR VIII* had appeared. These 'quads' had gun mounting style training drives with a training pinion meshing into an 'internal' training rack machined on the inside of the training base and a training stop bolt to lock the mounting on the fixed firing bearing of 90° Red or Green. There was also a 'housing' position at 180° and special arrangemements to train the tubes past the 90° position (called the 'semi-permanent' stop) to the loading position at 45° off the bow on each side. The sideways 'kick' on discharge from wing tubes was considerable and all the contemporary handbooks stressed the need to ensure that the mounting was locked before it was fired. Operator's instructions also warned that at any angle other than 90° from the bow, there was a danger that the torpedo might strike the deck. The weight of the mounting was taken by 14 tapered rollers running on a machined path and it revolved about a central pivot fitted with roller bearings.

Meanwhile, the Naval Staff were contemplating a five-fold – or 'Pentad' – mounting for future destroyers and early designs show a two-tier arrangement of two-on-three tubes. However, a more conventional side-by-side style was eventually adopted. It was fitted experimentally in HMS *Glowworm*, and subsequently made its appearance as the PR Mk I in the 'I' class destroyers.

These ships were followed by the 'Tribals' and because the new 'super destroyers' were to ship only one set of tubes, it was deemed necessary to provide power training so that they could bring them to the action position as quickly as possible. Their tubes were QR Mk IXs and had a new style of self-locking training drive incorporating twin worm shafts set at 90° from a common bevel wheel

One of the 4.7in armed 'O' class, HMS *Onslow* in December 1942, screening merchantmen in convoy. She is painted to the special Home Fleet Destroyers' camouflage scheme.
MoD

assembly such that the shafts made tangents to the fixed wormwheel training base. The powering system was hydraulic with Variable Speed Gear control, but the design soon gave trouble. In HMS *Afridi*, it was found that the twin worm shafts were, if anything, too 'self-locking' and tended to jam if the mounting was suddenly stopped, or even when it was slowly trained – as happened when it was approaching the firing bearing in 'follow the pointer' control. Modifications were put in hand to overcome the problems and these resulted in the Mk IX* which was fitted (or modified from Mk IX) in all the 'Tribals', including the Australian and Tyne-built Canadian ships. In all, the training control and Operator's positions were on a platform on the right hand side of the mounting as had been the case in the earlier Mk VIII series.

By 1938, sprayshields had been experimentally fitted to one mounting in the cruiser HMS *Aurora* with such success that the idea was generally adopted for future designs, and at the same time, the outboard siting of the operating positions in the Mk VIIIs and Mk VIII*s was found to be subject to excessive vibration. Hence, from the 'J' class onwards, it was decided to place the Operator's position centrally between the tubes and to provide him with a sprayshield on the forward mounting and an enclosed blast screen (or 'cupola') on the after. This difference did not alter the mark of mounting, which was designated the PR Mk II and employed the same hand worked rack-and-pinion training gear as had featured in the Mk VIII and Mk VIII*.

An objection that the Torpedo specialists had to this arrangement was that while the Operator was protected, the trainers were still exposed as they manned their handcranks at each end of the long cross-shaft that traversed the tubes. Thus, with the ambitious 'L' class, not only was the Operator housed in a blast screen but the trainer – with a power training control – was similarly protected (in his position in the centre of the mounting immediately in front of the blast screen) by an enclosed fairing. Its streamlined appearance became the recognition feature of the QR Mk X torpedo tube mounting.

The 'N' class followed the 'J's and 'K's with minor modifications to their tubes making them PR Mk II*s, but with the 'M's and the Emergency Flotillas, the simplest and most successful quadruple mounting was chosen as standard. This was the Mk VIII** and Mk VIII***. Both were virtually identical and some ships – like *Obedient*, *Petard*, and *Undaunted* – even had one of each. They were hand-worked by cranks on each end of the usual cross-shaft over the tubes driving the rack and pin-

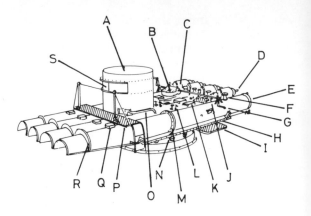

THE QR MK VIII* TORPEDO TUBE MOUNTING**

A Enclosed blast screen, housing Torpedo Deflection Sight and percussion firing levers. (Access door in rear)
B Transfer gearbox to training pinion shaft
C Explosion chamber
D Cordite valve
E Rear door
F Set gyro angling handwheel
G Tube training handcrank
H 'Tube feet' girders, supporting torpedo tube
I Trainer's platform
J Set torpedo running depth handle
K Distribution box for tube heater circuits
L 'Top stop' and spring catch holding torpedo
M Flange securing Rear and Lip Ends
N Training roller
O Cable trunking to Operator's position
P Servicing platform
Q Access flaps for torpedo pistols
R Stiffening flange over Lip End
S Sighting port shutters

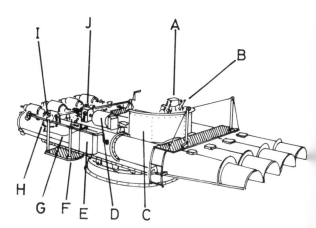

THE QR MK IX* TORPEDO TUBE MOUNTING**

A Pedestal for Local Torpedo Deflection Sight
B Percussion firing levers
C Open-topped spray shield
D Electric training motor
E Motor starter
F Hand training platform
G Flexible cable from percussion firing lever to breech
H Firing mechanism bell-crank lever and re-cocking lever
I Breech
J Hand/power gear box and change clutch

ion gear, and had a blast screen sited over the inner right hand tube, immediately forward of the centre of rotation. The Mk VIII*** outnumbered the 'two star' variant (only fitted in 15 individual ships) and was spread between the 'M' class and the 'Ca's. Elsewhere it has been said that the 'U' class – and perhaps the 'V' class 'Emergencies' – utilised spare PR Mk II* mountings with the centre tube removed, but the author has found no official record of this, and certainly, both classes are listed as having QR Mk VIII (series) mountings in the appropriate Torpedo Tube Handbook. This is not to say that modified mountings did not exist, however, for such was the eventual outcome of the first Pentad tubes in the survivors of the 'I' class, which were then known as 'PQR Mk I*' mountings. It is difficult to gainsay an official handbook, but in deference to other authors, it is conceded that perhaps the 'U's and 'V's were earmarked for, or actually received, the mysterious 'PQR Mk II' and either were not, in the event, fitted with it or were subsequently given QR Mk VIII*** mountings during refit.

The topweight problems of the 'Ch', 'Co', and 'Cr' groups are related later in this book, but on the particular subject of torpedo tubes, it is interesting to note that since for topweight reasons they could only carry one set, the philosophy evidenced in the 'Tribals' was echoed in the final three Emergency Programme Flotillas. In other words, if they could only have one set of tubes, at least they would be capable of power operation. Thus, an 'electrified' version of the original Mk IX mounting evolved. Four Mk IX** mountings were developed for the Canadian-built 'Tribals' *Micmac*, *Nootka Cayuga* and *Athabaskan*(II), having blast shields, and the Mk IX*** and Mk IX**** versions were designed for the final three 'C' classes. These had spray shields, electric power training and worm/worm-wheel training drives. The only difference between the 'three star' and 'four star' variants was in the speed of the electric driving motor and the gear ratio of the training drive. The earlier problems of the worm drives were ingeniously solved by designing the worms to 'float' on their shafts. They were linked by a 'compensating' rod which automatically balanced out the thrusts and ensured that the worms locked the mounting when it was stationary, but at no time could they jam. As a bonus, the 'compensating' rod also balanced out any backlash in the worm and wormwheel mesh.

TORPEDO TUBES

Once the Mk IX torpedo became the standard – even though it was modified through the Mk IX* to the Mk IX** – the construction of the actual tube itself scarcely altered. It was made from rolled steel plate and comprised a Rear End and a Lip End, bolted together by flanges either riveted or welded to the tube. The rear section was cylindrical and the Lip End was cylindrical for about three feet and was then cut away underneath. The torpedo was supported by side lugs, running in channels called Side Strips inside the tube. A cylindrical Explosion Chamber with a percussion or electric breech held a cordite charge and was connected to the tube by an inlet pipe. The chamber incorporated a spring-loaded cordite valve that only opened after a predetermined gas pressure had been generated. This forced the torpedo from the tube at about 45fs; but as the pressure fell the valve reclosed, making the discharge 'flashless'.

The torpedo was held by a 'top stop', itself released by the gas pressure of the explosion chamber, and all settings to the torpedo could be applied by spring-loaded setting handles whilst it was within the tube. Thus, immediately before firing, running depth, gyro angling, speed and 'pattern running' (zig-zag) characteristics could be determined. The 'tube ready' switch was closed, and the torpedo was fired either electrically from the torpedo firing pistol on the bridge, in percussion from the tube operator's firing levers, or, as a last resort, at the breech itself. As it left the tube, the torpedo engine automatically started and the gyro impeller wheel blasted off to control the course. If gyro angling had been set, the torpedo entered the water at 90° to the ship's track but then turned automatically through 60°. If 'pattern running' had been applied, the torpedo proceeded on a zig-zag course, produced by the 'W' gear in the gyro control. This reduced the maximum range, of course, but was sometimes tactically advantageous, since the torpedo track constantly changed.

TORPEDO CONTROL

Torpedo Deflection Sights, Tube Ready lamps and Firing Pistols (for each tube) were mounted on either side of the bridge. The sight was quite simple and had three 'foresights' to give the required spread. The attacking ship turned away from the target on a set turn and the tubes were fired in succession from aft to forward as the 'outer' foresight came on to the target. Each tube was distinguished by a letter (usually in brass on the rear door), the standard arrangement being F I R E (M) for the forward mounting and (P) Q X Y Z for the after – the letters in brackets being applicable to the Pentad mountings. The sequence of discharge depended on the bearing on which the torpedoes were fired: on the port beam, aft to forward, it would be Z Y X Q (P), (M) E R I F, but on the starboard it was (P) Q X Y Z, F I R E (M).

British destroyers carried no reloads for their tubes but their destructive potential was very high while they retained their 'tin fish'. Quite often a feint attack against major enemy units was sufficient to cause the targets to make a tactically disadvantageous alteration of course – a device superbly demonstrated by the British 'O' class destroyers against the German cruiser *Hipper* in the Battle of the Barents Sea.

ANTI-SUBMARINE WEAPONS

The Emergency classes were intended more for escort than fleet duties and thus omitted the TSDS in favour of an improved AS armament. The short quarterdeck and close proximity of 'Y' mounting ruled out lengthy oversterm racks and at the same time made it necessary to site any depth charge throwers well clear of the gundeck. Nevertheless, twin racks were fitted, with two throwers on each side, abreast the after superstructure.

DEPTH CHARGES

The standard depth charge consisted of a steel drum 18in in diameter and 30in long, with an all-up weight of more than 400lb. It was filled with 300lb of high explosive – often TNT – and was coded with coloured bands to indicate the type of filling. A hollow tube ran through the axis of the charge, one end containing a removable primer and the other a removable 'pistol'. The latter was triggered hydrostatically by water pressure and could be adjusted while on the discharger – either throwers or rails – to operate at various depths.

The primer was spring loaded towards the pistol but was held clear of it by a safety device until the charge was released. When the charge reached the set depth, water pressure operated the pistol to set off a detonator. This in turn exploded the primer which detonated the main charge. Primed depth charges on deck presented an extreme hazard to survivors if their own ship sank and were therefore always set to 'safe' immediately before abandoning ship. This had the effect of blocking the passage through which sea-water passed to the pistol diaphragm, so rendering it inoperative.

A modified type of standard depth charge was developed during the war, known as the Deep Depth Charge. It was similar to the original but with an extra ballast weight added, bringing its all-up weight to about 550lb. The increase caused it to sink faster, and thus a 'standard' and a 'heavy' dropped together (but with different depth settings) would explode at two levels at the same time. The 'heavy's' depth setting calibration was altered to suit its range and it could also be used if the submarine had gone very deep.

The twin rail/four thrower set up allowed the 'Ten Pattern' attack to be carried out. It was usual to load the port rails and forward throwers with 'heavies' and the other group with standard charges, with the object of sandwiching the target between two layers of five explosions.

One of the 4in armed 'O' class destroyers, HMS *Obedient*, in 1942, painted, like *Onslow*, to the 'special' pattern. The high-sited depth charge throwers and their handling davits forward of 'X' gun are clearly visible in the original print. She has single Oerlikons on the Iron Deck abreast the after superstructure in the positions more usually occupied by DC throwers.
MoD

DISCHARGE ARRANGEMENTS

A normal set of WWII overstern rails held six charges. The outboard section terminated in the 'trap', held three DCs and was inclined downwards at 10°. The next section inboard held three more charges and was inclined at 1½°. The trap gear is shown in the sketch, from which it will be seen that the mechanism allowed one charge at a time to be dropped. To prevent unnecessary strain on the outer trap lever, a removable stop-bar was inserted between the first and second trios. Wooden wedges were often knocked between the stop bars and adjacent charges to prevent them from bumping a seaway.

In other classes (like escort frigates) the rails could be extended inboard by 3-charge 1½° sections to a maximum capacity of 18 charges, but there was never room for such extensive arrangements on destroyers with a 'Y' mounting. Some specialised ships, particularly those involved in the Battle of the Atlantic, had twin double-tiered rails holding a total of 72 DCs and four throwers on each side. Destroyers had re-loads on deck chocks close to the rails, into which they were handled by davits, and carried further charges below in the DC magazine.

The throwers were developed by Thornycroft of Southampton to give some means of achieving a 'spread' of explosion. They functioned like mortars, and, again, the details can be seen in the sketch. The explosion forced the carrier outwards like a piston, flinging the depth charge from the trough-shaped tray. In the early throwers the carrier was discharged with the DC – a rather wasteful procedure alleviated by the introduction of the Mk IV thrower. On this, the carrier was brought to rest by hydraulic buffer cylinders and returned to its original position by gravity. Immediate re-loads were stowed in adjacent chocks and were davit-handled into position on the carrier. Re-loading at speed called for considerable effort and Depth Charge crews worked very hard in an AS action.

Later in the war, each thrower had a rack stowage arranged in such a way that re-loads could be slid sideways directly on to the tray. The six stowed charges were manoeuvred in sequence to the transfer position adjacent to the thrower, lifting within the stowage tiers being carried out by a windlass working on the 'parbuckle' principle. This generic name was adopted for the arrangement which became known as a 'parbuckle stowage'.

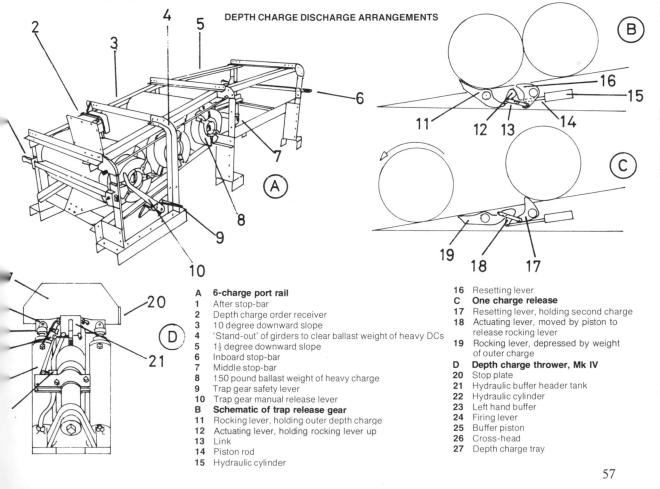

DEPTH CHARGE DISCHARGE ARRANGEMENTS

A **6-charge port rail**
1. After stop-bar
2. Depth charge order receiver
3. 10 degree downward slope
4. 'Stand-out' of girders to clear ballast weight of heavy DCs
5. 1½ degree downward slope
6. Inboard stop-bar
7. Middle stop-bar
8. 150 pound ballast weight of heavy charge
9. Trap gear safety lever
10. Trap gear manual release lever
B **Schematic of trap release gear**
11. Rocking lever, holding outer depth charge
12. Actuating lever, holding rocking lever up
13. Link
14. Piston rod
15. Hydraulic cylinder

16. Resetting lever
C **One charge release**
17. Resetting lever, holding second charge
18. Actuating lever, moved by piston to release rocking lever
19. Rocking lever, depressed by weight of outer charge
D **Depth charge thrower, Mk IV**
20. Stop plate
21. Hydraulic buffer header tank
22. Hydraulic cylinder
23. Left hand buffer
24. Firing lever
25. Buffer piston
26. Cross-head
27. Depth charge tray

Having detected the submarine by Asdic, the attacking ship steered a course to pass over it, a master firing circuit being automatically initiated by the Asdic range recorder. The firing mechanism on throwers and traps alike was electro-hydraulic and the firing circuit, once initiated, caused ten charges to be released in the correct sequence. This was two from the traps, the four from the throwers with a second pair from the traps, and then a final pair. In the event of equipment failure, local firing was carried out, timed by stopwatch. Because half the pattern comprised Heavy charges, the target ideally would be caught between two roughly cross-shaped bursts of five.

To regularise manufacture, the automatic firing equipment was designed for particular plan distances between the traps and quarter-deck mounted throwers, for an optimum 15 knot attack. When throwers had to be positioned further forward than this – as in the Emergency classes – they were angled astern in compensation.

BOATS

The usual outfit for all the flotillas was a 25ft motor cutter at the break of the fo'c's'le on the starboard side, balanced by a whaler to port. A second whaler was carried abaft the cutter opposite a 16ft motor dinghy on a wheeled cradle. The latter craft was referred to as the 'Skimming Dish' or 'skimmer' and at speed careered around in a most alarming manner. It had a diminutive cockpit forward, manned by the sole crew member – the skimmer driver – who had engine controls and a motor car style steering wheel. Towards the stern there was a second, small canopied cockpit for the intrepid passenger. Manoeuvring a skimmer alongside at slow speed was a desperately difficult business. With only the driver aboard, the boat adopted a distinctly nose-down attitude and its small rudders made it almost unsteerable. A 'skimmer' trip was nothing if not hair-raising.

RADARS

The problem of providing a warning radar set for destroyers and small ships was very severe. The few sets that were in service in the Fleet – in battleships and cruisers – were in the 7.5m wavelength band and, for technical reasons, their associated aerial systems were very large. To give the best possible coverage, the aerial was set at masthead height; but destroyers could not tolerate the topweight penalties involved. All the aerials were of the dipole type – in other words, basically similar to the 'H' shaped household television aerial – so an obvious step was to reduce the aerial size. This, however, was governed by the wavelength of the set, whose reduction could only be achieved by the design, development and production of new thermionic valves. Work was proceeding in this direction, but meanwhile destroyers, and small ships generally, had no radar at all.

Fortunately the Royal Air Force had a small Air/Surface Vessel (ASV) set in service with Coastal Command and this was found to be suitable for small ship fitting. The RAF generously released a number of sets to the Royal Navy, where they were given the Type number 286. Its wave length of about 1.4m brought a significant reduction in aerial size but it was still a quite large affair of complex struts and dipoles.

The first model was Type 286M, whose aerial was a fixture at the masthead, and because of its shape it was soon referred to as the 'bedstead'. It gave coverage over an arc of about 120° centred on the bow and was disliked by commanding officers

The refitted *Petard*, flying her paying-off pendant in May 1946, with twin 4in guns in 'A' and 'X' positions. The forward mounting has triple rocket flare launchers on each side of the gunshield.
Wright & Logan

because they had to 'swing' their ship to obtain the bearing of a target. In any case its accuracy and range were weak and it was replaced by 286P with the refinement of a rotating aerial. The beam was narrowed, making it more accurate in the all-important determination of target bearing, and all round cover was now available. Type 286PQ followed, with increased power for longer range, but none of the 286 series was very successful afloat, in an environment for which they had not been designed. In addition, to maintain and test a complex electronic gadget like a radar set on shore, with maximum support services, is one thing; to carry out the same duty at sea in a small ship is quite another. The aerial for this Radar was fitted at the mastheads of ships of the first two flotillas in which it functioned as a Combined Warning – ie Air/Surface – set. No provision had been made in the original designs for the associated radar 'office', so this was added as a box-shaped compartment between the bipod supporting legs of the mast.

The next Combined Warning set was Type 290 but this, too, was not very efficient. Its successor, on the other hand, gave excellent results: surface detection out to ten miles with good accuracy, and aircraft cover out to 50 miles. Type 291, as it was called, had a neat, distinctive aerial of basically cruciform shape and remained in service – principally in the Air Warning role – until well into the 1950s. *Onslow* and *Oribi* ended the war with 291 at the foremast head, but others like *Onslaught*, *Offa* and *Petard* carried it on a stump mainmast stepped on the after superstructure.

The next warning set was a world-beater and a break-through for the British designers and scientists ashore. Spurred on by the urgent need to provide small escorts with the means of detecting a U-boat on the surface at night, they came up with Type 271. They drove the wavelength down to 10cm, pushed up the power and condensed the radar transmission into a probing 'searchlight' beam which even on a corvette could 'see' a surfaced U-boat at 3–4 miles and a capital ship out to about 16. The considerable reduction in wavelength allowed a reflector instead of a dipole array to be employed and thus the aerial took on

the now familiar 'cheese' form. It was contained within a protective cover, physically rather like a lighthouse top, and this, allied to the 'searchlight' beam of the radar, made 'lantern' a fairly natural descriptive term. The one drawback of Type 271 was that power was seriously dissipated between the set and its aerial, so both had to be as near to each other as possible. To keep them in close proximity, the radar office and aerial were built as a combined structure, and the most practical position for its site (with due regard to topweight) was amidships at the old searchlight position. Thus it appeared in *Oribi*.

The next improvement allowed for the office to be divorced from the aerial, so that the latter could be positioned at a more advantageous height, with the consequent benefit of increased maximum range. The set was then known as Type 272 and again employed a 'lantern'. Depending on the all-important topweight considerations, its aerial appeared either on a pylon amidships, or on a foremast platform (where it was sited in *Onslow*).

While work was proceeding apace on the Combined Warning and Surface Warning sets, radar for gunnery ranging purposes was also progressing. If the radar beam was to be sent along the master line of sight to the target, its aerial had to be carried on the director and carried in such a way that it could be elevated to range on an aircraft. The rangefinder directors already existed and could accept only limited extra loading, so nothing could be achieved until the electronics conducive to short wavelength – and small aerials – had been developed.

Once these components became available, a reflector could be employed as it had been in 271, but instead of the 'cheese' shape, a curved 'pig-trough' was employed. To help direct the beam, wooden struts were added, each with a series of short cross-bars, the whole array quickly being termed a 'fishbone' aerial. In the 'transmit' phase, the assembly helped to direct the radar beam; in the 'receive', it helped to gather the echo towards the reflector. The more modern TV receiver aerials are often of similar design. The gunnery set with these features was Type 285 and was widely fitted throughout the fleet. All the marks of rangefinder director were modified to accept it, together with the separate breed of High Angle Control System directors found in larger ships. It was also sometimes mounted on secondary DCTs in cruisers and capital ships and survived well into the 1950s.

Two other important aerials (not radar) were to be found in individual vessels. One was the 'talk between ships' TBS radio aerial added at the masthead, and the other, the pyramid-on-cube HF/DF frame. The former provided a 'voice' link which made for rapid communication between

ships in company, and the latter had been developed as a means of finding the direction of high frequency radio messages transmitted by surfaced U-boars to their headquarters and to each other. *Paladin* had TBS on the foremast and HF/DF on a pole mast aft, while *Orwell* had the direction-finder on a lattice pylon.

MINELAYING GEAR

The minelaying gear essentially consisted of a rail of trackway on each side of the Iron Deck, running from the quarters to a point approximately abreast the forward torpedo tube position, and a power operated conveyor for each trackway. The conventional spherical contact mine with detonator 'horns' was carried on a sinker in the form of a box-shaped four-rollered bogie and it was the latter that ran on the trackways. Within the sinker was a drum with a cable attached to the mine proper, and on reaching the seabed, the mechanism was released. The mine then rose to a predetermined level, whereupon the cable drum locked, leaving the mine moored. A special time delay device was incorporated in the design of the cable drum so that the mine could, if necessary, be held on its sinker at the seabed, to rise automatically as before when the preset timing device was triggered.

The trackways were of 'U' section girders turned inwards towards each other to constrain the bogie rollers, and near their after end (approximately at 'Y' gun's position) there were hinged sections in the upper part of the rails which could be opened to allow the mines to be loaded. A similar loading position was provided at the forward end of the rails. The power units were fitted in the steering gear compartment (or 'tiller flat', as it was usually called) and consisted of an electric motor driven hydraulic pump unit (with variable directional and delivery control) linked to a hydraulic engine. The drive from the engine was led through shafts, gear boxes and clutches to either or both of the quarter-deck conveyors and also to a quarterdeck capstan.

A 'dummy bogie', fitted with two guide sheaves, was free to run the length of the mine rails, and to load mines from the after position the dummy bogie was run to the foward end. The first mine was then lowered into the loading gap and rolled forward by hand until it was close up to the dummy bogie. The rest of the mines were loaded in succession and each was coupled to its neighbour by a simple drop-pin, so that the mines formed a complete train. However, when they were coupled together they were too heavy to be moved by hand, and so to bring the train aft towards the conveyor, a wire cable was led via snatch blocks from the capstan to the dummy bogie in order to 'shunt' the mines. A conveyor had a pair of sprocket wheels driving an endless chain, bicycle-fashion, the chain having large spaced teeth which exactly matched the pitch of the coupled mines. The conveyors were recessed into the existing deck in the 'C' class minelayers (which had a square stern), but in the round-sterned 'O's and 'P's a 'fantail' had to be added on to allow a straight run for the mine rails.

To prepare for laying, the train of mines was first shunted by the capstan until the aftermost came up to the conveyor teeth. Then the conveyor was clutched to the power drive, and when the hydraulic unit was started the endless chain began to revolve, drawing the train of mines towards the quarters. Here, the rails curved downwards, so that as each mine and sinker tipped over the stern its linking pin was pulled out, uncoupling it from the

DIAGRAMMATIC ARRANGEMENT OF DESTROYER MINELAYING GEAR

1   Starboard 'U'-section mine rails
2   Mine on sinker
3   Linking drop-pin
4   Sinker bogie
5   Rollers, running in mine rails
6   Motor starter
7   Electric driving motor for hydraulic pump
8   Hydraulic pump
9   Pump output and directional control handwheel
10 Oil header tank
11 Oil delivery and return lines
12 Hydraulic motor
13 Worm and wormwheel gearbox
14 Worm and wormwheel drive to capstan
15 Quarterdeck capstan
16 Final drive gear to cross-shaft
17 Dog-clutch box for starboard conveyor
18 'In-out' clutch handle
19 Starboard conveyor driving sprocket
20 Endless chain
21 Conveyor well
22 Idler sprocket
23 Curved final section of mine rail
24 Conveyor teeth, matching pitch of coupled mines
25 Dog-clutch for port conveyor

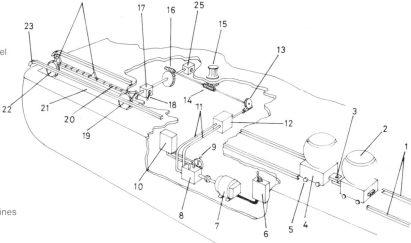

DIAGRAMMATIC ARRANGEMENT OF CABLE LEAD FROM CAPSTAN TO DUMMY BOGIE

1   Port mine conveyor
2   After mine loading position
3   Cable securing eyebolt
4   Mine coupling drop-pin
5   Forward mine loading position
6   Mine rail end stops
7   Dummy bogie wire cable sheaves
8   Wire cable
9   Capstan

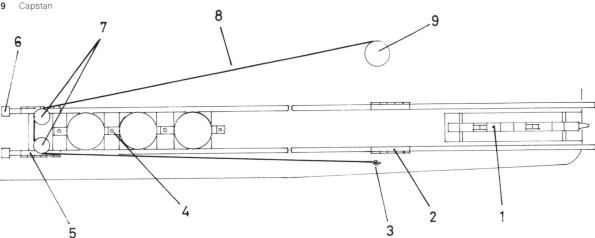

next mine. The variable speed control of the hydraulic gear allowed for various dropping rates which were decided by a combination of the ship's speed when laying and the required 'spread' of the mines. Both conveyors could be clutched in at the same time to lay a double row or, perhaps, used in succession to lay one continuous line.

The conversion of a destroyer to minelaying duties could be carried out reasonably quickly (provided, of course, that she had been so designed in the first instance) because the conveyor gear and its powering units were always retained, leaving only the actual mine rails to be bolted down to the prepared positions on the Iron Deck. However, there was always the need to reduce armament to compensate for the topweight of the mines themselves, and ships usually lost their torpedo tubes, 'Y' gun and 'Q', too, if applicable. It is interesting to observe that in the 4in armed 'O' class – in other words, the prospective minelayers – the 'permanent' 4in mountings at 'A', 'B' and 'X' positions had gunshields, whereas the 'removable' mountings did not. In the 'C' class post-war minelayers, the 4.5in in 'Y' position and the single set of torpedo tubes were temporarily landed – the whole exercise being a matter of taking bits off the ship and adding bits on in the fastest possible time.

In minelaying it was vitally important, needless to say, to ensure that the proposed 'lay' was placed in the correct position, and because minefields were frequently laid at night, the *exact* position might be very difficult to ascertain. For this reason, 'taut wire' gear was employed. The minelayer, having obtained a positive 'fix' of her position well away from the laying area, then dropped a sinker to which a fine piano-wire was attached. She set off on a very carefully calculated course, streaming the wire astern from a large reel on the quarterdeck. Because it was taut and therefore did not appreciably sag, the wire gave the minelayer a very precise measure of her distance run from the known starting point.

In peacetime, a minelaying exercise was naturally followed by a *minesweeping* exercise, in which case a marker was dropped in place of the first mine to indicate the actual position of the dummy field, but although extensive 'sweeping' after both World Wars gathered up the majority of these potentially most dangerous devices, they are still occasionally trawled up by fishing vessels, or drift up to the surface when corrosion eventually eats through their mooring cables.

LATER DEVELOPMENTS

The advantages of the twin 4in Mk XIX have already been remarked upon, but only one ship was finally so refitted. This was *Petard*, whose forward and after armament was contracted to one of these mountings in 'B' and 'X' positions, backed up by twin Oerlikons in the bridge wings, singles amidships and two sets of torpedo tubes.

After the war, several ships were sold abroad. *Offa*, *Onslow* and *Onslaught* went to Pakistan (as destroyers), the latter pair being subsequently converted to Type 16 AS Frigates. *Oribi* was transferred to Turkey, leaving *Obedient*, *Obdurate*, *Opportune* and *Orwell* still under the White Ensign. To meet a strategic requirement in the 1950s for a group of fast minelayers, the RN units took up the rôle for which they were originally earmarked, and had mine rails on each side of the Iron Deck, terminating in power operated conveyors carried on 'fantail' projections on each quarter. The RN ships (less *Opportune*) were scheduled to undergo conversion to Type 16 AS Frigates, but in the end only *Orwell* underwent this major change – apart, of course, from the Pakistani units already mentioned.

The 'P's were the hardest hit of any of the Emergency classes, only three of them surviving the war. By 1948, *Penn*'s armament amounted to only single 4in in 'B' and 'X' positions, and she ran as a Submarine Escort and Target Vessel for a few years, until going to the breakers in 1950. *Paladin* and *Petard* both became Type 16 AS Frigates (the latter being the last ship to be so converted) and the former also had the minelaying 'fantail'.

The 'Type 16' conversion gave the ships something of an anti-submarine rôle, but the modifications were not so extensive as those received by other classes : the destroyer profile was retained, as was the after set of torpedo tubes, but the armament layout was considerably revised. A twin 4in, modified for electric Remote Power Control (RPC), and controlled from a Simple Tachymetric Director (STD) on the bridge, formed the main gun armament. There were single 40mm Mk 7 Bofors on the bridge wings, with a third on the otherwise empty quarterdeck, and a twin electric-powered 40mm Mk 5 mounting – also STD controlled – amidships. The old 'X' gundeck and after superstructure were rebuilt to carry a pair of AS mortars Mk 4 – more familiarly called 'Squids' – together with a mortar bomb handing room. Other changes included a lattice foremast for modern radars and additional compartments on the original site of the forward torpedo tubes. The Type 16 conversion produced an attractive and remarkably flexible unit, combining a reasonable gun, torpedo, and AS armament as well as a minelaying capability, within the confines of a destroyer hull. As AS frigates, they, and the more extensively converted Type 15s, formed an important stop-gap until the advent of the purpose-built Type 12s and their successors.

6. Q to W Classes
The Third to Ninth Emergency Flotillas

THE THIRD AND FOURTH EMERGENCY FLOTILLAS

The more one considers the armament of the 'O' and 'P' class ships, the odder it becomes. Whatever may have been said at the time, in retrospect the fact that only four of the sixteen received their designed armament of 4.7in Mk XVIII mountings seems to indicate that it was more a shortage of weapons that dictated a change in the remaining twelve than anything else. That there was a need to improve the AA defence of destroyers is undeniable, but it would appear a little inconsistent to accept that four ships would have only one 4in HA each, while the remainder would have this calibre alone. It is almost as though the 'gungeneers' needed time to pick up the threads of Mk XVIII production (apart from the ship building for Brazil and Turkey, it had last been fitted in the 'I' class of 1937-38), and that as a matter of expediency the Admiralty took what guns were quickly available for the first two flotillas.

Be that as it may, the next sixteen ships all received their allocated armament of four 4.7in Mk XVIII mountings and although the first intention was to forfeit the after set of tubes and include a 4in HA in the fashion of the day, this was not in fact implemented. A pompom was again fitted abaft the funnel and the increasing output of 20mm Oerlikons allowed for four singles to be sited on an enlarged platform around the searchlight, backed up by singles on the bridge wings.

The big HA/LA DCT of the 'L' and 'M' classes was neither easy to manufacture nor successful in the HA mode, the Destroyer DCT and Three-man Rangefinder combination in the 'J', 'K', and 'N' classes left a good deal to be desired, and so the 'Q' and 'R' classes reverted to the 'Tribal' class arrangements. These comprised a Destroyer DCT, a Rangefinder Director Mk II(W), an Admiralty Fire Control Clock (AFCC) Mk I – for surface control – an FKC Mk II* and a Gyro Level Corrector (GLC).

The Mk II(W) director differed from the Mk IV and V series in several ways. It had a windshield attached to the *rotating* structure (signified by the 'W'); it was one of the family with electrical data transmissions; it had no power stabilisation; and it was high-set on a pedestal to overlook the DCT. Radar Type 285 was fitted as standard, but the 'fishbone' aerials were often erased from contemporary photographs by the wartime censor.

Redoubt (appropriately to seaward off Fort St Elmo at the entrance to Grand Harbour, Valletta) in October 1945 with her attractive 'candystripe' funnel flotilla marks and the standard camouflage panel on the hull. Typical of the variations of weapon fit in a particular class, she has four single Oerlikons amidships, has retained her searchlight, and has surface warning radar Type 272 on the foremast. *A & J Pavia*

There were several proposed AS weapon fits, but eventually most ships had the 'ten pattern' arrangements. Radar Type 290, with its masthead cruciform aerial, took over from the obsolescent 286 series, and was itself superseded by 291. The 272 'lantern', when fitted, appeared on a pylon above the searchlight position (*Quality, Rocket, Roebuck, Rotherham, Relentless*) or on a foremast platform (*Racehorse, Redoubt*). *Raider*, apparently more slanted towards AS work, had no masthead Combined Warning (but TBS instead), 271 between the tubes and HF/DF on a pylon aft. With the exception of the foremast fit of 272, what radars there were could be carried on a tripod mast, with which the first four Emergency flotillas were fitted. Several of the 'O' class, however, were later given lattice replacements, as were *Racehorse* and *Redoubt*.

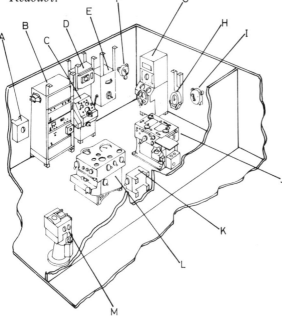

TYPICAL TRANSMITTING STATION LAYOUT FOR 'Q' TO 'W' CLASS DESTROYERS

A Gun Elevation Synchronous Unit
Received Gun Elevation from either FKC or AFCC and drove transmitter banks to the gun mounting elevation receivers

B Radar 285 Panel L 24
With coarse and fine range tubes

C Range Transmission Unit
Measured Radar range as indicated by the coarse and fine tubes in the Radar Panel and transmitted it to the FKC and the Matching Receiver. Also produced Range Rate for the FKC

D Emergency Training Tube linked to Radar 285
Duplicate of a similar tube in the R/F director. The director trainer could keep the director trained on a 'blind' target by centering the target echo in his Training Tube. In the event of the Director tube failing, the director could be conned on to the target from a Bearing handwheel in the TS transmitting to a Radar Bearing Receiver in the R/F Director

E Interlinking Unit
Received Target bearing from Warning Radar and transmitted it to the Radar Bearing receiver in the R/F Director. A change clutch disconnected the Warning Radar input and substituted a local Bearing handwheel used in association with the Emergency Bearing Tube

F Normal/Blind Training Change of Switch for Surface Fire
In Normal, switched DCT training directly to the AFCC Mk I, and R/F director followed DCT. In Blind, received R/F Director training as determined by Training Tube or Warning Radar Bearing, and DCT followed R/F Director

G Auto Barrage Unit
Controlled the firing circuits to the guns for a once-only Radar controlled barrage broadside

H Matching Receiver (Suspended from the deck-head over the AFCC)
Received Radar Range from the RTU on one pointer for comparison with the calculated Range from the AFCC to indicate the accuracy of AFCC settings of Target Speed and Indication

I HA/LA Changeover switch
Selected circuits for AA fire or surface Fire Control

J Admiralty Fire Control Clock Mk 1
Continuously calculated Gun Training, Gun Elevation, Gun Range and Gun Deflection and transmitted them to the gun receivers for surface fire

K Fuze Number transmitter
Transmitted fuzes as predicted by the FKC to the fuze number receivers at the gun mountings

L Fuze Keeping Clock Mk II
Continuously calculated Gun Elevation. Total Training Corrections and Fuze Number for AA fire

M Gyro level corrector
Trained electrically to follow the R/F Director. Received Director Elevation and stabilised it to produce Angle of Sight for the FKC

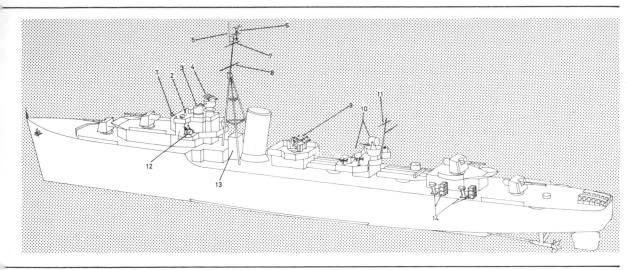

An important domestic re-arrangement came with the 'R' class, when the traditional after position of the wardroom was changed to a new location under the bridge superstructure. This had proved to be a most successful scheme in the 'Hunt' class and once introduced, remained unaltered thenceforth. Most of the officers' cabins were shifted forward too, leaving three unfortunates in the dreaded 'Triple Cabin' aft, next to a single cabin usually occupied by the Torpedo Officer. The old officers' galley was retained as a secondary unit, and the remaining accommodation spaces were taken up by mess decks and messes. The forward seamen's messdeck was in the fo'c's'le under 'A' gun, with the stokers one deck below. The POs lived under 'B' gun, with the wardroom immediately abaft and the Captain's Day Cabin in close proximity. (He also had a Sea Cabin near the wheelhouse). There were officers' cabins at two levels under the fo'c's'le

deck, mostly on the starboard side, together with a separate mess for the cooks and stewards.

The after seamen's messdeck under 'Y' gun was often called the 'TAS' (Torpedo, Anti-Submarine) mess because it was mostly populated by the torpedo tube and depth charge crews. The Chief Petty Officers, Engine Room Artificers and Stoker Petty Officers each had their own enclosed messes under the after superstructure, the senior member becoming Mess President. In the case of the Chief's mess, this was always the Coxswain who was automatically regarded as the senior CPO, irrespective of his actual seniority, because in small ships he functioned as the Master-at-Arms. The shift of the wardroom forward was motivated by the need for the officers to get to the bridge as quickly as possible. Before 'catwalks' were introduced to bridge the torpedo tubes and thus link 'X' gundeck to the pompom deck and the fo'c's'le, negotiating the

Iron Deck in bad weather was hazardous in the extreme. It was no joke having to fight one's way forward in pitch darkness along a deck swept by seas, to relieve a weary officer of the watch on the bridge, and then stand the Middle Watch, with probably Dawn Action Stations to follow. Wire 'lifelines' were strung overhead above the Iron Deck, with sliding hand-holds spliced to them, so one became a sort of sea-going 'strap-hanger'. For the erstwhile bank clerk, it was a far cry from the Piccadilly Underground Line.

In both the 'Q's and 'R's, the hull dimensions were slightly increased to conform exactly to the 'J' class, with the result that the contour of the bow and fo'c's'le changed. The extra hull volume allowed for more oil fuel bunkerage with the proportional improvement in endurance related earlier in the book. Another feature was the 'squaring-off' of the earlier round stern.

During wartime refits, there was a gradual improvement in the close range weaponry. Twin Mk V power Oerlikons commonly replaced the singles on the bridge wings, and in some cases, hand-worked Land Service (Army pattern) Mk III* Bofors superseded existing Oerlikons amidships. As always, topweight was the overriding consideration and it is interesting to observe that ships with Type 272 on a heavy lattice foremast kept their original Oerlikons around the searchlight platform, while *Raider*, with a low-set 271, could afford to mount four single Bofors.

If British destroyers had gone to war in 1939 with as many close range weapons as had *Raider* in 1946, they would undoubtedly have fared much better. In this photo, she has a quad pompom, four single Bofors and two twin Oerlikons. Her radars include 271 amidships, and Air Warning 291 at the foremast head. She also has a lattice mainmast carrying the HF/DF aerial.
Wright & Logan

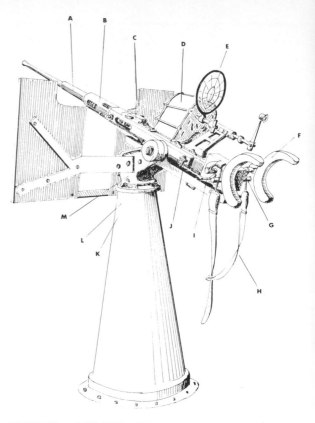

SINGLE 20mm OERLIKON MOUNTING

A   Non-recoiling barrel
B   Recoiling barrel spring casing
C   Double loading interlock
D   58-round magazine
E   Foresight, with 300, 200 and 100 kt rings
F   Shoulder rests
G   Hand grips
H   Aimer's body strap
I   Trigger
J   Cotter, connecting recoiling side plates to gun bolt
K   Trunnion
L   Fixed pedestal
M   Training cradle

LATER DEVELOPMENTS

All the 'R' class survived the war, but *Racehorse* had gone for scrap by 1949. *Rotherham*, *Raider* and *Redoubt* were transferred to the Indian Navy in the same year, and the remaining four ships were among the first of the Type 15 AS frigate conversions. Three of the RN frigates had been scrapped by 1971 and only *Rapid* remained afloat as a tender to HMS *Caledonia*, the artificer apprentices' training establishment at Rosyth on the Firth of Forth.

THE FIFTH AND SIXTH EMERGENCY FLOTILLAS

These two flotillas introduced the modified bow form that became standard for all the later Emergency classes. The fo'c's'le deck was extended, while maintaining the same length between perpendiculars, resulting in a more gentle sheer forward and an attractively raked stem. Several other important changes distinguished the ships from their predecessors. For the comparatively simple mass-produced type of destroyer envisaged in 1939, no better 4.7in mounting than the Mk XVIII existed but the need for an improved weapon was recognised and development on it started concurrently with the building programme of the first Emergency flotillas. Somehow, the designers had to come up with a mounting having significantly greater elevation and yet remaining hand-worked, and it had to be easy to load at all angles and take in a 4.7in calibre gun – all without an unacceptable increase in weight.

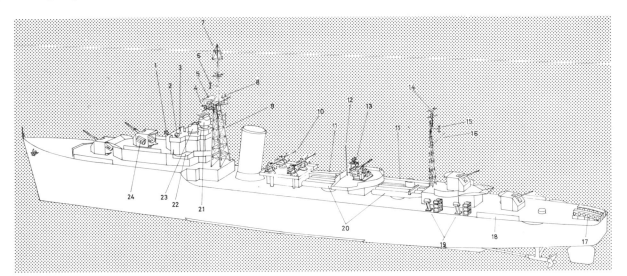

SAUMAREZ APRIL 1946

1 MF/DF Aerial
2 Port signal/searchlight
3 Captain's sight
4 Combined wind speed and wind direction unit
5 Radar Type 293 Aerial
6 IFF Type 253 aerial
7 HF/DF Aerial
8 IFF Type 241 'pitchfork' aerial
9 Short type lattice mast
10 40mm Bofors Mk III mountings
11 Catwalks over torpedo tubes
12 Redundant stump mast
13 Radar Type 282 aerial on 40mm Bofors Mk IV ('Hazemeyer') mounting
14 Radar Type 291 aerial
15 IFF Type 253 aerial
16 Ensign gaff (sea position)
17 Twin 6-charge DC rails/traps
18 Deck-edge splinter screen
19 Mk IV throwers and 'parbuckle' stowages
20 QR Mk VIII** torpedo tube mountings
21 Radar Type 285 aerial on Rangefinder Director Mk II(W)
22 Disarmed bridge wing close range weapon sponsons
23 Destroyer DCT
24 Left triple 2in Rocket Flare Launcher on 'B' gunshield

The single 20mm Oerlikon, surrounded by a 'safety-firing' rail to prevent the gun from firing into its own ship's structure. Notice the wooden wedge knocked between the inboard depth charge and its stop-bar. *IWM*

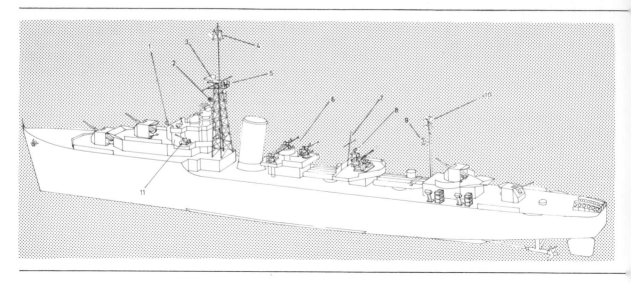

Above: The run of 4.7in Central Pivot mountings culminated in the Mk XXII, shown here at maximum elevation. The Tray worker is now accommodated on-mounting, but observe how he has to lean over his body rest above the fuze-setting machine to push the loading trays inwards. The later automatic tray operation was an obvious advantage, but it needed very careful adjustment to ensure that the rammer head tripped at the correct time. This mounting was virtually indistinguishable from the 4.5in Mk V, but is revealed as the 4.7in in this photo by the 'V'-shaped machined grooves on the upper face of the open breech block.
IWM

Right: The 'U' class followed the pattern set by the 'T's, and some, like *Ursa* here, mounted an extra Bofors on the searchlight platform abaft the funnel.
Wright & Logan

THE 4.7IN MK IX** GUN ON THE SINGLE CP MK XXII MOUNTING

The considerable labours of the design teams resulted in an extremely viable weapon. By setting the trunnions as high as was compatible with ease of loading for low angle firing, 'breech-trunnioning' to the absolute limit, and shortening the recoil from $26\frac{1}{2}$ to 18in, they produced a mounting with 55° maximum elevation at an all-up weight of 13.3 tons.

Some sort of power ramming was required at the higher angles of elevation, and how this was to be achieved in a hand-worked mounting was initially problematical. However, Messrs Vickers Armstrong's Barrow-in-Furness works had developed a spring-loaded rammer for the single 4.5in gun, originally designed for the Admiralty and then taken up by the War Office. This device proved to be most successful and was immediately built into the new naval mounting. It was a most ingenious arrangement, utilising the powerful recoil action of the gun to cock a heavy rammer spring. When the loading tray was pushed across into line with the chamber, the spring tripped automatically and operated a power rammer head. This then moved forward at high speed, so ramming the shell and cartridge, at the same time compressing a lighter 'rammer return spring'. When the tray was moved outwards, ready for reloading, the return spring reset the rammer head to the rear, the main rammer spring being re-cocked when the gun next recoiled.

The extra 3 tons in weight above the 4.7in Mk XVIII was taken up by the increased structural strength required to accommodate the additional shock resulting from the short recoil, the heavier balance weight arising from the breech trunnioning, and the much more substantial gun shield. This was sharply angled on the front face, a feature which, allied to the splendid bow, gave the ships a thrusting, rakish look. Special stop gear was designed for 'X' mounting to allow it to train through a total arc of approximately 580°, so that it appeared – as a matter of choice within the ship or flotilla – with the muzzle stowed either at zero or at 180°.

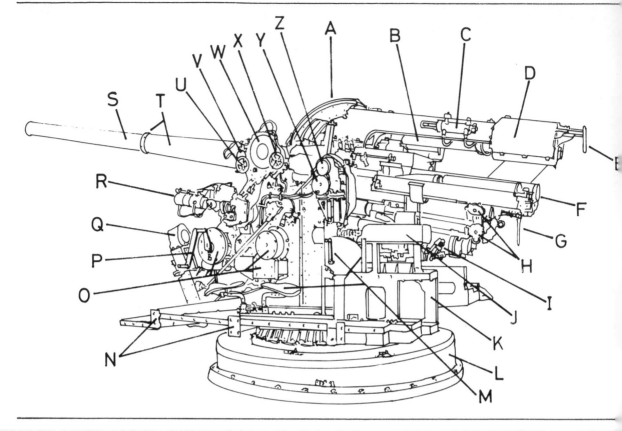

A   Mantlet plate
B   Recuperator ram
C   Intensifier
D   Balance weight
E   Frame for cartridge catch-net
F   Loading tray
G   Wire strop of secondary hand-rammer
H   Lead sheaves for spring rammer cable
I   Spring rammer trip adjustment
J   Shell loader/tray worker's body rest
K   Support for fuze-setting machine
L   Mounting training base
M   Fuze-setter's seat and fuze-setting hand crank
N   Gun shield rib securing positions
O   Elevation drive gear boxes
P   Layer's hand cranks
Q   Elevation receiver
R   Layer's monocular gunsight telescope
S   'Loose' barrel
T   Jacket and jacket sealing collar
U   Set deflection handwheel
V   Deflection dial
W   Range dial
X   Set range handwheel
Y   Set fuze number handwheel
Z   Fuze number receiver

CLOSE RANGE GUN DECKS

Another obvious profile change was apparent with
the shift of the searchlight from its almost traditional position between the torpedo tubes to the
gundeck abaft the funnel, this to allow the principal close range weapon to be sited amidships where
it enjoyed better sky-arcs. The planned armament
was a twin Bofors Mk IV (Hazemeyer) mounting at
the new location, with a staggered pair of twin Oerlikons abaft the funnel and a further pair on each
side of the bridge. Inevitably, insufficient
Hazemeyers were available, and the 'S' class took
what they could. *Scorpion* had a quad pompom and
Savage two twin Oerlikons on the midship gun
deck, but all received the intended twins elsewhere.

Five ships were quickly turned over to our allies
– three to the Netherlands and two to Norway –
and *Swift* was lost off Normandy in June 1944.

Left: The markedly 'breech-trunnioned' 4.7in Mk XXII mounting. Note
the 'Fuze-setter' number's low seat facing toward the Mk V fuze-setting
machine and the padded body-rest for the shell loading number.
MoD

Right: The cab side and door have been removed in this photo of the twin
20mm Mk V mounting to show the hydraulic piping leading to the
aimer's 'joystick' controller. Key features of the mounting are itemised in
the drawing.
MoD

Only *Saumarez* and *Savage* survived to run under
the White Ensign in the immediate post-war years.
The former was up-gunned to four single Bofors
abaft the funnel with empty bridge sponsons in
topweight compensation, and the latter retained a
layout so distinctive as to be worthy of special mention.

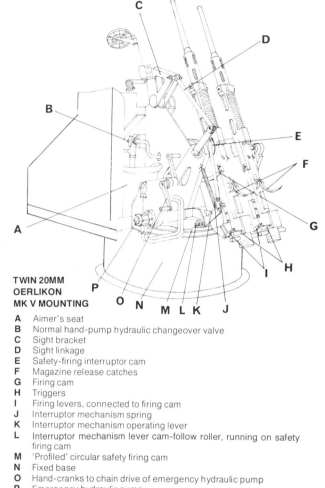

**TWIN 20MM
OERLIKON
MK V MOUNTING**

A   Aimer's seat
B   Normal hand-pump hydraulic changeover valve
C   Sight bracket
D   Sight linkage
E   Safety-firing interrupter cam
F   Magazine release catches
G   Firing cam
H   Triggers
I   Firing levers, connected to firing cam
J   Interruptor mechanism spring
K   Interruptor mechanism operating lever
L   Interruptor mechanism lever cam-follow roller, running on safety
    firing cam
M   'Profiled' circular safety firing cam
N   Fixed base
O   Hand-cranks to chain drive of emergency hydraulic pump
P   Emergency hydraulic pump

HMS SAVAGE AND THE 4.5IN GUN

The 4.5in had been developed in about 1935 as a new anti-aircraft gun, and made its first appearance in the fleet as a prototype twin mounting in the gunnery training ship *Iron Duke* in 1936. The gun mounting evolved in two forms. The first was the 4.5in Mk II, described as a 'Between Decks' or 'BD' mounting, and the second was the Mk III (which differed only in that it had an open gunshield) and was known as a 'UD' or 'Upper Deck' mounting. The Mk III was principally for centre line fitting but, exceptionally, was 'sided' in the wartime *Ark Royal*, where – because of the blast considerations – the Mk IIIs were more widely spaced than was the case with the Mk IIs of the later fleet carriers. Elsewhere it became the standard mounting for depôt ships and also appeared in *Scylla* and *Charybdis*. Both were nominally *Dido* class 5.25in cruisers but suffered from the same mounting supply problems as had the 'L' class destroyers.

The Mk II was totally enclosed by a circular gun shield with only a proportion of the gun mounting above deck level – giving rise to the 'Between Decks' description. It was essentially for 'sided' fitting in the modernised capital ships (*Queen Elizabeth*, *Valiant* and *Renown*) and in new-construction aircraft carriers. In order to preserve an unobstructed width of flight deck, the Mk IIs in carriers were supported by sponsons angled outboard from the ships' sides, with the mounting tops just above flight deck level. But because the centre of rotation of the mounting was outside the confines of the hull, it was impossible to provide it directly with ammunition through a conventional revolving 'turret trunk' linking the gunhouse to the magazine. Thus, in the carriers, a 'fixed structure' hoist brought ammunition up within the hull, whence it was transferred outwards by hand into the sponson below the gunhouse. Here, it was stowed in large revolving cylinders – exactly like a scaled-up version of the cylinder of the familiar revolver – and from these it was passed upwards by hand into the gunhouse. Because of its configuration, the space below the gunhouse was called the 'gunbay', a term later adopted to describe an ammunition handing area beneath any gun mounting.

In passing, it is worth remarking that the twin 4in followed an almost identical pattern of development, split between BD and UD installations. The BD variant (4in twin Mk XVIII) went temporarily into the battlecruiser *Repulse* but was not proceeded with; the UD type became the ubiquitous 4in Mk XIX.

At the same time, a *single* 4.5in HA mounting

had been designed for the Admiralty but was subsequently taken up by the War Office. (It was for this gun that Vickers had designed the spring rammer previously mentioned.) The 4.5in gun was chosen in the belief that it was the largest calibre that could employ fixed ammunition with an all-up weight that could be handled by the crew loading numbers. The weight of the combined shell and cartridge was 85lb, on a total length of just over 4ft.

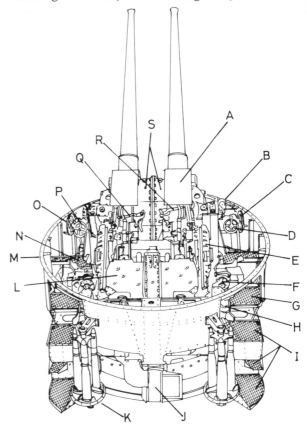

THE 4.5 IN MK II BD MOUNTING

A Mantlet plate
B Training receiver
C Trainer's manual handwheel
D Trainer's power drive handwheel
E Right gun loading tray
F Right gun fuze-setting machine
G Gunhouse deck level
H Fuze-setting tray
I Loading access steps
J Ventilation fan and trunking
K Revolving 3-round scuttle
L Balance weight
M Securing flange for upper portion of gunhouse (at gundeck level)
N Breech-worker's platform
O Layer's manual handwheel
P Layer's power drive handwheel
Q Left gun QF/SA lever in 'Quick-fire' position
R Right gun QF/SA lever in 'Semi-automatic' position
S Left and right sections of common gun cradle

The decision to adopt it on this count was strangely contradictory for two reasons. Firstly, the slightly lighter destroyer 4.7in ammunition had always been made 'separate' to relieve the task of the loading numbers, and secondly, a comparable fixed round had been designed in the 1920s for the 4.7in Mk XII anti-aircraft gun, having an all-up weight of 74lb. The shell itself weighed 45lb, and had been deliberately made 5lb lighter than the standard 4.7in projectile in an attempt to reduce the fatigue of loading. The Mk XII was unpopular – at least among the loading numbers – because, in fact, its fixed round was still too heavy for comfort. It is a little odd that, if by the early 1930s a 74lb 4.7in round was already showing itself to be unhandy, in the middle of the same decade an 85lb round was deemed acceptable. The lesson learnt on the 4.7in had to be re-learnt on the 4.5in.

The principal arguments in favour of the 4.5in projectile were that it was 5lb heavier than the old 50lb 4.7in shell and at the same time ballistically better. Against this was the fact that 4.7in ammunition had been stockpiled at British naval bases all round the world, and to rebuild the stocks with a new calibre would be difficult, particularly in wartime. However, in February 1942, the decision was taken not only to adopt the 4.5in calibre for all future destroyer classes but also to provide a twin power mounting for the successors to the 'L's and 'M's. The totally enclosed nature of the existing 4.5in BD Mk II, allied to the fact that it had no revolving 'turret trunk', made it a suitable vehicle for modification to meet the Staff Requirement for the new destroyer mounting. As it happened, a BD Mk II was in the early stages of construction at Barrow-in-Furness as an aircraft carrier spare, upon which work was halted to allow the necessary re-design to commence.

The outcome was the prototype twin Mk IV mounting, whose front face showed the same circular configuration and 'bevelled' junction with the gunhouse roof that had featured in the BD Mk II but whose gunhouse rear was 'squared-off' with access doors to the left and right. A short trunk, extending one deck downwards and containing power operated ammunition hoists and a 'spent cylinder' compartment, was suspended below the gunhouse floor, and at the same time provided a gun well to permit a maximum gun elevation of 80°. The Naval Staff also called for full RPC facilities which entailed considerable modification to the existing hydraulic elevation and training systems. Initially, it was intended that the Mk IV should employ the standard 'fixed' 4.5in ammunition (which, incidentally, was already very unpopular) but before the design had progressed beyond

the point of no return, reports from the cruisers *Scylla* and *Charybdis* indicated that their loading numbers were experiencing difficulties in handling the fixed 4.5in ammunition in bad weather. If loading was causing problems in a 6000 ton cruiser, they clearly would not be any the less in a much livlier 2000 ton destroyer. The Admiralty took a bold and imaginative step. Notwithstanding that there was no such ammunition in existence as 'separate loading' 4.5in, the decision was made that this style was to be produced for the new destroyer gun. Thus was the lesson learnt a second time.

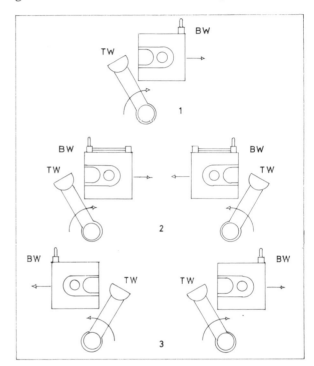

LOADING TRAY AND BREECH DISPOSITIONS VIEWED FROM THE REAR

1 Basic arrangement of loading tray and breech for single 4.7in Mk XVIII, single 4.7in Mk XXII and single 4.5in Mk V mountings. Breech Worker (BW) on the right and Tray Worker (TW) on the left. Arrows show the directions to open the breech and swing the tray to the loading position. The breech mechanism lever is coupled directly to the (internal) breech actuating shaft

2 Arrangement for a twin mounting with guns in a common elevating cradle (twin 4.7in Mk XIX and twin 4.5in Mk IV mountings). The breech mechanism lever is connected by a link rod to the breech actuating shaft. The breech opens towards the Breech Worker, who is on the same side as the Tray Worker

3 Arrangement for a twin mounting with guns in individual elevating cradles (twin 4.7in Mk XX mounting). Note that the right gun corresponds to the dispositions of a single mounting

The twin barrels, which elevated together in a common cradle, had individual ammunition supply arrangements. Shells, in a 'pusher' hoist, were conveyed horizontally to the gunhouse, outboard of the loading trays, where they were delivered directly into line with the fuze-setting machines, and cartridges were lifted in a single-stroke hoist to emerge close to the rear of the trays. Both hoists automatically stopped operating when the 'top of the hoist' position was full, but immediately recommenced as soon as the ammunition was removed. Provided that the ammunition numbers in the gunbay below kept the bottom of the hoists replenished, shell and cartridge were always available in the gunhouse. The loading trays could be charged at any angle of depression or elevation and the hydraulic powered rammers, with a single self-resetting lever control, gave a rate of fire of about 20 rounds per minute per gun.

To provide the essential test-bed for the prototype twin, *Savage* (then under construction) was altered to accept it in 'A' position in lieu of her two forward single 4.7in Mk XXIIs, and at the same time her two after mountings were re-barrelled with 4.5in guns, both to preserve uniformity of ammunition and to evaluate the single 4.5in Mk V. HMS *Savage*, therefore, has a very special place in the history of Royal Naval gun mountings, introducing both the single and the twin to British destroyers. The 'production' twin Mk IV rendered excellent service for many years thereafter in the 'Battle' class destroyers, and the single Mk 5 survives to this day in the 'Tribal' class General Purpose frigates (albeit in a much improved form). Eventually 'separate' 4.5in ammunition became the standard form and thus the final variant of the original BD Mk II – the Mk 2***, in *Eagle* and *Ark Royal* – was modified for 'separate' ammunition.

WEAPON ARRANGEMENTS IN THE 'T' CLASS

The 'T' class kept the same fire control, torpedo tube and depth charge arrangements introduced by the 'R' class and continued in the 'S's; but their close range midship gundeck fit varied from ship to ship, just as it had done in the past. The earliest units mounted a pair of single Oerlikons between the tubes, *Terpsichore* had a pair of Mk V twin Oerlikons, and the remainder had the intended Hazemeyer. The searchlight immediately abaft the funnel soon became redundant, and was often replaced by a single Mk III* Bofors. In 1946, *Tumult* had a Hazemeyer amidships, three Mk III* Bofors abaft the funnel and 'Boffins' on the bridge wings. Concurrently, *Tuscan* had the same twin Bofors, a Mk III* Bofors on the searchlight plat-

form and 'Boffins' in the other four close range weapon locations.

The nickname 'Boffin' was given to a hybrid piece of equipment created by adapting a twin Mk V Oerlikon mounting to carry a single 40mm Bofors barrel. The alteration to the cradle was reasonably easy to implement and produced a very good weapon at little cost in extra weight, and an actual reduction in the gun's crew because the duties of the layer and trainer on the Mk III* were combined in the aimer's 'scooter' control column on the 'Boffin'.

RADARS

Type 285 was, of course, standard on the RF director, and its small cousin 282 went with the Hazemeyer Bofors. Type 291 had become a normal fitting – either on the fore topmast or on a stump mainmast or lattice aft. A gradual introduction of lattice foremasts came with the sixteen ships, about half having the new style structure and the remainder being given the earlier tripod. All the RN units eventually received lattice masts, with the exception of the unique *Savage*, which retained her original tripod to the end of her working life.

The complexity of the Hazemeyer is easily seen from this photo of the original Mk IV mounting. Note the small independent rangefinder on the extreme right front, the hand-worked calculator and the shaft-drives to the radar aerial.
MoD

TWIN 40MM BOFORS MK IV* ('HAZEMEYER') MOUNTING

A	Stowage box
B	Range unit
C	Range taker's footrest
D	Range taker's seat
E	Barrel water cooling header tank
F	Telephone stowage boxes
G	Spent cartridge chutes
H	Water circulating pump
I	Radar switching unit
J	Radar aerial gearbox
K	Ready-use ammunition lockers
L	Radar Type 282 aerial array
M	Cross-rolling aerial gantry
N	Aerial elevation and lateral deflection drives
O	Gun ammunition auto loaders
P	'Safe-Automatic-Single shot' selector lever
Q	Cocking lever
R	Layer's binocular sight
S	Barrel run-out springs
T	Water-cooling jackets
U	Flame guards
V	Elevation toothed arc
W	Layer's elevation handwheel
X	Layer's manual hand cranks
Y	Ranging handwheel
Z	Cross-roll frame counterbalance weight

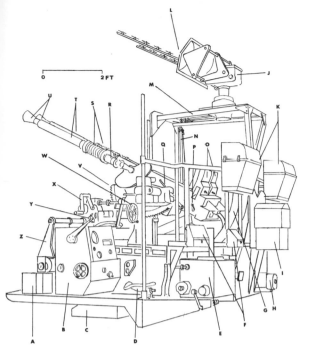

:win Mk IV* was a later version of the Hazemeyer. A second balance
it has replaced the rangefinder, the aerial support structure has been
ned by a second rear-support girder and radar 'tubes' in consoles,
been added to the left and right. The cross-roll axis can be seen in
ıid-point of the balance weight beam.

The 2pdr Mk VII (P) mounting, which was hydraulic powered, with the
wartime splinter shield. The 'joystick' control column can be seen
through the open access door.
MoD

LATER DEVELOPMENTS

The ships serving under the Dutch and Norwegian flags had all been scrapped by mid-1963 (one having already been lost off Normandy in the same month as HMS *Swift*), *Saumarez* went to the breakers in 1950, and only *Savage* ran for any appreciable time under the White Ensign after the war. She was progressively disarmed but retained her prototype twin Mk IV mounting – and her tripod mast – to the last. She ended her days as an experimental ship evaluating advanced screw propeller designs.

The 'T's were all rejuvenated after the war when they were altered to AS Frigates, seven to the 'Limited Conversion' Type 16 and *Troubridge* to the 'Full Conversion', Type 15. The Type 16s had all gone for scrap by mid-1966, and *Troubridge* was declared 'for disposal' in 1970.

THE SEVENTH AND EIGHTH EMERGENCY FLOTILLAS

This group of ships was a repeat of the 'S' and 'T' classes in almost all respects. The supply of Hazemeyer mountings improved to the extent that thirteen of the sixteen vessels shipped their designed close range armament (one Hazemeyer and four twin Oerlikons), leaving only *Ulysses* and *Volage* with a midship quad pompom, and *Urchin* with two extra twin 20mms in lieu.

Grenville, *Ulster* and *Venus* were completed with tripod masts. The others all had a short lattice structure to carry an ever increasing weight of radar aerials, and sometimes a topmast for the HF/DF frame. *Grenville* initially had no Surface Warning set but was fitted with a lattice mainmast for HF/DF; *Ulster* had the Type 272 lantern on the foremast; but elsewhere, a new Surface Warning set's aerial – Type 276 – appeared on a foremast platform. As has been said, 272 was hidden and protected by a 'lantern', but in fact its aerial was a 'double cheese' – one part for the transmitter and the other for the receiver. With Type 276, the aerial now revealed itself as a 'single cheese' combining both functions. An IFF 'candelabra' Type 243 aerial was also mounted on the foremast, usually on a platform abaft the single yardarm. It was rotatable and functioned to detect friendly aircraft echoes on the warning radar screens.

The radar offices were by now designed into the ship's structure (rather than added as boxes on the deck) and it was the concentration of radars forward that created the need for a more substantial lattice mast to carry their aerials. The three tripod-masted ships later received a lattice structure too, but were given a taller rig.

UNDAUNTED MAY 1944

1 MF/DF aerial
2 Destroyer DCT
3 Radar Type 285 aerial on Rangefinder Director Mk II(W)
4 Combined wind speed and direction unit
5 Radar Type 293 aerial
6 HF/DF aerial
7 IFF Type 243 aerial
8 Twin 20mm Oerlikon Mk V mountings
9 Radar Type 282 on 40mm Bofors Mk IV ('Hazemeyer') mounting
10 Twin 20mm Oerlikon Mk V mounting

VOLAGE DECEMBER 1945

1 Left triple 2in Rocket Flare Launcher on 4.7in Mk XXII gunshield
2 MF/DF aerial
3 Radar Type 285 aerial on Rangefinder Director Mk II(W)
4 Combined wind speed and direction unit
5 Radar Type 293 aerial
6 HF/DF aerial
7 IFF Type 243 aerial
8 Starboard forward single 40mm Bofors Mk III* mounting
9 Centre line 40mm Bofors Mk III* mounting
10 Stump mast for main roof aerial
11 2pdr Mk VII* P pompom mounting
12 IFF Type 253 aerial
13 Radar Type 291 aerial
14 Ensign gaff
15 Staggered 40mm Bofors Mk III* mountings
16 Disarmed bridge wing sponsons

WIZARD JUNE 1947

1 Radar Type 285 aerial on Rangefinder Director Mk III (W)
2 Radar Type 293 aerial
3 Stump topmast for main roof aerial yard
4 IFF Type 241 aerial
5 Two single 40mm Bofors Mk III* mountings
6 Stump mast for main roof aerial
7 Radar Type 282 on 40mm Bofors Mk IV ('Hazemeyer') mounting
8 IFF Type 253 aerial on pole mast
9 Radar Type 291 aerial
10 Single 2pdr Mk XVI pompom mounting

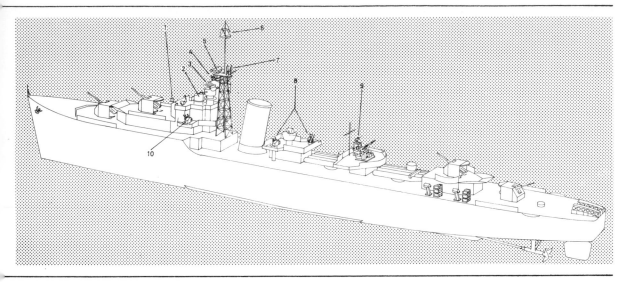

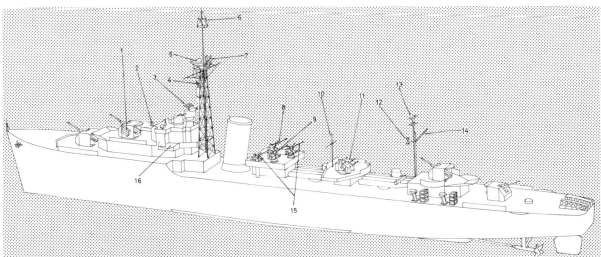

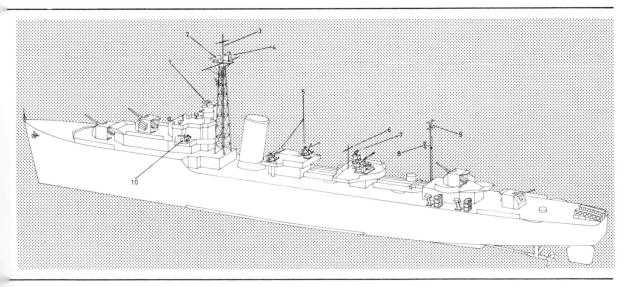

Both classes were upgunned with 40mm Bofors in the place of the existing Oerlikons. The 'U's often shipped the extra gun on the redundant searchlight platform to give them a 40mm trio abaft the funnel, but this was not a feature of the 'V's, which landed their searchlight platforms completely. *Volage*, as a special case, compensated for her obsolete midship pompom by having a cluster of four single Bofors abaft the funnel, *Saumarez* fashion.

The launch dates of the Emergency Classes were as variable as their individual close range weapon fits and a good deal of overlapping occurred. An extract from completion dates shows:

Rotherham	August 1942
Tuscan	March 1943
Grenville	March 1943
Ulster	June 1943
Rocket	August 1943
Urchin	September 1943
Terpsichore	January 1944

Operationally, too, the ships usually ran in a pretty mixed bunch, although sister ships were frequently in company. In the *Scharnhorst* action, the two destroyer groups were disposed as follows:

Force 'Z': *Duke of York*, *Jamaica*, *Savage*, *Scorpion*, *Saumarez*, *Stord* (RNN – ex-*Success*).

36th Destroyer Division: *Musketeer*, *Opportune*, *Virago*, *Matchless*.

The convoy escort for Russian Convoy JW 55B comprised: *Onslow* (Senior Officer), *Onslaught*, *Orwell*, *Scourge*, *Impulsive* (RN 'I' class), *Haida*, *Iroquois*, *Huron*, (RCN 'Tribals').

LATER DEVELOPMENTS

All the 'U' class were converted to Type 15 AS frigates and at the time of writing *Grenville* is still running as a trials ship in the Second Frigate Squadron. In July 1966, history repeated itself when part of one ship was used to replace a damaged section of another. This had occurred in WWI, when the old 'Tribal' class ships *Nubian* and *Zulu* were combined and re-emerged as HMS *Zubian*. It now happened again, when part of the stern of *Urchin* was built on to the previously damaged *Ulster* in Devonport, but no *Urster* or *Ulchin* found its way into the records, and *Ulster* retained her original name.

The leader of the 'V's, *Hardy*, was torpedoed in January 1944 and *Valentine* and *Vixen* both went to the Royal Canadian Navy from building, adopting the names *Algonquin* and *Sioux* respectively. The remaining five were converted to Type 15s, the last runner, *Verulam*, going for scrap in 1971. The 'U'

class as a whole had twin Mk 10 AS mortars linked to the advanced Mortar Control System, Mk 10, but the 'V's had the simpler twin 'Squid' installation. The bulk of both classes had gone for scrap by the mid-1960s, although *Volage* went on in a non-operational capacity as a Harbour Training ship for Royal Marines.

Above: April 1946 saw the arrival of *Tuscan* at Portsmouth with her Paying Off pendant floating from the masthead. She is tidily armed with a Hazemeyer, four power operated single Bofors, and a hand worked single replacing the searchlight abaft the funnel.
Wright & Logan

Below: The 'S' class introduced the single 4.7in Mk XXII mounting with its characteristic gunshield. The twin Bofors Mk IV (Hazemeyer) began to appear amidships although in insufficient numbers for all ships. *Scourge*, with a Spit Fort in the background, was one of her class to get this novel and – at the time – futuristic weapon, obscured here by its large windshield.
IWM

THE NINTH EMERGENCY FLOTILLA

This class marked a break-point in British destroyer armament in being the last to carry the long-lived 4.7in calibre gun. The 'W's also heralded the dual purpose director concept of the future in omitting the Destroyer DCT, giving their bridges an appearance somewhat reminiscent of the extempore 'O's and 'P's. It was, however, a totally different fire control installation, employing a Mk III(W) rangefinder director (with electrical transmissions) in association with the same calculating instruments as the 3rd to 8th Emergency Flotillas. The Mk III(W) differed from the Mk II(W) only in that it was designed for the dual purpose rôle and had an extra position for the Rate Officer, who had previously been accommodated in the DCT. His job was to estimate the course and speed of a surface target and relay them to the Transmitting Station, where they were set on to the surface predictor.

With the supply of the very complex Hazemeyer mounting still not meeting the demand, two ships had to accept the faithful quad pompom, and although the first-fit of supplementary close range weapons pursued the same policy as before, all vessels were later up-gunned to 40mm calibre. As if deliberately to confound the student of naval technical history, the practice of mounting a Bofors on the searchlight platform was re-adopted. It was invariably a hand-worked Mk III, but elsewhere twin Oerlikons remained, or were transformed into 'Boffins'. All eight ships received the 'tall' variety of lattice mast from building, with the 'cheese' aerial and IFF platforms and HF/DF on the topmast.

A standard fit of 291 was carried on a pole mainmast on the after superstructure. The now-established 'ten pattern' AS and torpedo tube fit completed the armament.

'Catwalks' over the tubes were now a normal feature and were retrospectively fitted to earlier flotillas which then wondered how they had ever managed without them. Like so many other admirably simple ideas, the 'catwalk' was an obvious fitting – once someone had thought of it.

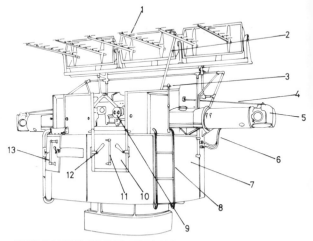

MK III (W) RANGEFINDER DIRECTOR

1   Radar Type 285/M3 aerial array
2   Detachable elevating link
3   Aerial elevating link securing bolt
4   Rangefinder shutter operating rod
5   Rangefinder shutter
6   Rangefinder desiccator pipes
7   Revolving windscreen
8   Trainer's access ladder
9   Trainer's binocular sight
10 Trainer's sighting port, clipped open
11 Trainer's sighting port closing handgrip
12 Sighting port clip
13 Layer's sighting port, clipped open

LATER DEVELOPMENTS

In the early 1950s *Wessex* and *Whelp* (whose First Lieutenant in the Pacific Theatre had been the Duke of Edinburgh) were transferred to the South African Navy, followed by *Wrangler* in 1957. The first pair had a special Type 16 Frigate conversion which included a second 4in twin on the quarterdeck, and ran as *Jan van Riebeeck* and *Simon van der Stel*, while the third was converted to a 'Squid-fitted' Type 15 and became *Vrystaat*. A year later, *Kempenfelt* (*Kotor*) and *Wagner* (*Pula*) were sold to Yugoslavia, leaving only three in the RN as Type 15 frigates. One of them, *Wakeful*, lasted until 1971, having had a modern-style bridge fitted in a 1959 refit.

A useful close-up of *Virago* in 1947, recovering her whaler after it had been swamped. Note the Mk II R/F director on its tall pedestal.
P A Vicary

7. Z and C Classes

The Tenth to Fourteenth Emergency Flotillas

THE TENTH AND ELEVENTH EMERGENCY FLOTILLAS

Consequent upon the Admiralty's decision to adopt the 4.5in calibre for future destroyer classes, and the successful outcome of the trials on the modified after mountings in HMS *Savage*, production of the 4.5in Mk IV gun was put in hand. Following the Mark number sequence which had reached IV in the prototype twin, the new single became the Mk V mounting. The 'Z's were the first to receive it as a class, followed by the nearly identical 'Ca's.

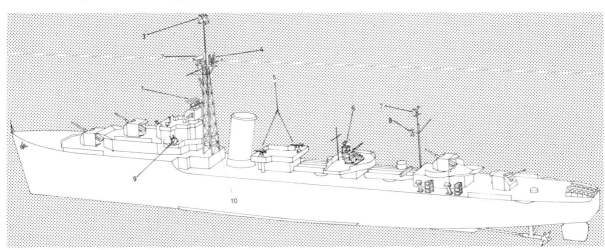

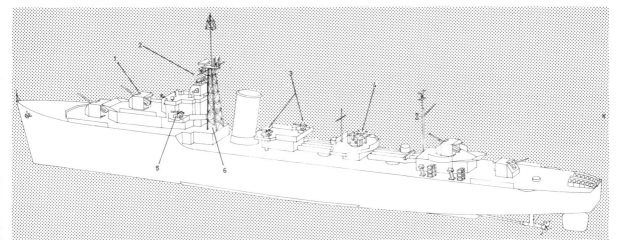

ZODIAC

1	Radar Type 285 aerial on K Director
2	Radar Type 293 aerial
3	HF/DF aerial
4	IFF Type 243 aerial
5	Single 20mm Oerlikon mountings
6	Radar Type 282 on 40mm Bofors Mk IV ('Hazemeyer') mounting
7	Radar Type 291 aerial
8	IFF Type 253 aerial
9	Twin 20mm Oerlikon Mk V mounting
10	'Tall' type lattice mast

CAPRICE

1	4.5in CP Mk V mounting
2	Radar Type 285 aerial on 'K' Director
3	Single 2pdr Mk XVI pompom mounting
4	2pdr Mk VII* P pompom mounting
5	Single 2pdr Mk XVI pompom mounting
6	'Short' type lattice mast

THE 4.5IN MK IV GUN ON THE CP MK V MOUNTING

The gun and parent mounting mark numbers had got out of step very early in the 'four-five' story. The navalised version of the military 4.5in gun was the Mk I(N) which utilised certain breech mechanism components of the 4.7in and was directly interchangeable with the Mk III(N) gun with its 'own' breech parts; either gun could be fitted into the Mk II BD or Mk III UD mounting and both types used fixed ammunition. The next development was the 'straight' Mk III, utilising separate ammunition to suit the Staff requirement for the new Mk IV twin mounting, but for the single Mk V mounting a new breech mechanism was required and this resulted in the production of the Mk IV gun. The double numbering continued after the war, when the now-familiar twin 4.5in Mk 6 mounting first entered service in the *Daring* class carrying Mk 5 guns. (It should be made clear that in the early 1950s the old scheme of roman numerals was replaced by arabic.)

Apart from the modifications necessary to allow the new barrel to be fitted, the 4.5in Mk V mounting was identical to the 4.7in Mk XXII and even shared the same technical handbook. It was handworked, and although heralded as a 'Dual Purpose' weapon its similar upper elevation limit of 55° made it no more so than the 4.7in.

FIRE CONTROL

Major changes were made to the fire control arrangements in these two classes. It had been hoped that the advanced Mk VI HA/LA director would be available, but production difficulties necessitated an interim system for the sixteen ships, to allow the first production models of the new equipment to go to the '1942 Battle' class.

The stop-gap director was designated the Mk I Type K HA/LA and was soon referred to simply as 'The K tower'. In less complimentary terms it was called 'Kay's Folly' by those closely associated with it. A large structure by contemporary standards, it was in many ways a re-hash of the DCT of the 'M' and 4.7in-fitted 'L' classes. A conventional type of gyro stabilised sight was carried for LA control, having a type letter 'K', from which the director took its name. Additionally, and unlike the earlier tower, it had a high angle sight, which in fact could elevate well above the 55° upper limit for the associated 4.5in calibre guns. To enable it to do so, however, the complete roof had to be wound open to the rear by a rack-and-pinion drive. Expensive noises were generated if the de-clutchable HA sight was accidentally elevated with the hood closed.

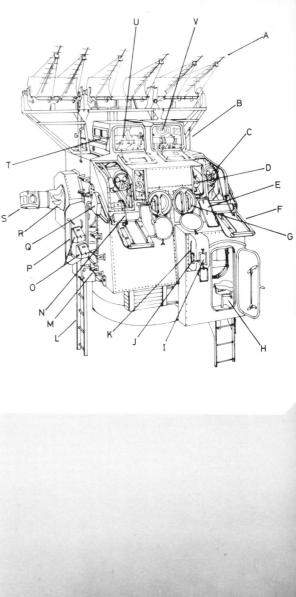

THE MK 1 TYPE 'K' HA/LA DIRECTOR

A Radar Type 285 aerial array
B Hand-grip
C Layer's HA binocular sight
D Layer's unstabilised LA binocular sight
E Unstabilised sighting port door
F Folding HA sighting port door
G Layer's stabilised sighting port
H Cross level operator's position
I Port providing light to cross level sight
J Cross level sighting port
K Manual sighting port wiper
L Access ladder
M Access rungs
N Closing lever for HA sighting port doors
O Communication headset stowage boxes
P Link between access door securing clips
Q HA sighting port door counterbalance weight
R Flexible gaiter
S Rangefinder
T Sliding hood over control and Rate Officer's position
U Rate Officer's binocular mounting plate
V Control Officer's Angle of Presentation binoculars

Oscillating seats were provided for the layer and trainer to permit them to sit behind whichever sight was in use, and in the HA mode a take-off drive elevated a sight beam with binoculars for the Control Officer and Rate Officer. Similar drives were linked to the rangefinder and radar Type 285 aerial. An extra frontal compartment housed a cross level unit providing aiming corrections in surface fire for ship movements across the line of sight. If, for example, the director was trained dead ahead, pitch movements of the ship were taken care of by the stabilised 'K' sight and the cross level unit measured roll. The converse was the case if the director was trained on the beam.

There was no 'X' or 'Y' class, so the 'Z' class followed the 'W's, and this is *Zest* soon after her completion in July 1944. She has the special Home Fleet Destroyers camouflage pattern, and like so many contemporary ships has an extempore close range armament of twin Oerlikons on the bridge wings, single Oerlikons abaft the funnel and a Hazemeyer amidships.
IWM

The tower had a hydraulic power follow system (with alternative hand drives), 'scooter' column control for the Control Officer, and remote power control from the radar panels in the TS. Radar 285 was not versatile enough to allow for full 'Blind Follow' but this could be carried out in the training motion to permit radar tracking of unseen surface argets. Nevertheless, the facility of RPC from the Transmitting Station in both motions allowed the director to be pointed at targets designated by the Gun Direction System.

The fire control calculators for both surface and AA fire remained as before but were adapted for the ballistics of the 4.5. An additional stabiliser called the Cross Level Corrector together with the existing Level Corrector provided automatic stabilisation to the director in the AA mode. For the first time, the duties of the director layer and trainer were duplicated by two of the TS crew who functioned as the 'Below Layer' and 'Below Trainer' in the Target Acquisition and Training Blind Follow forms of control. They sat at a large console called a 'Tallboy' with a Constant Prediction Unit for radar controlled firing between them.

The hydraulic power control gear of 'The Folly' was extremely sensitive and the tower was very prone to violent surging as it trained around at high speed. Riding in it was rather akin to the skimmer trip previously related, and the director rather deserved its unkind nickname.

CLOSE RANGE WEAPONS

With the exception of *Caprice* (which had a quad pompom), all had a Hazemeyer amidships and the usual mixed fit of close range weapons elsewhere. The onset of the Kamikaze attacks in the Pacific Theatre showed that even a twin Oerlikon had insufficient power to destroy an aircraft in the sky. The Japanese pilots who had dedicated their lives to their Emperor intended to die anyway, and would not be diverted from their suicidal course by mere gunfire, and even supposing a pilot were killed in his cockpit by a lucky shot there was every likelihood that the plane would continue on its dive and crash into the defending ship as was the Japanese intention. There was, therefore, an urgent need for heavier calibre close range weapons, for the 20mm Oerlikon found itself in precisely the same position as had the Vickers .5in machine gun in 1939.

Right: The first of the extensive 'C' class were the 'Ca's, and they alone among the later ships had the normal two sets of quadruple torpedo tubes. With pendant numbers flying from the starboard yardarm and the 'Right of Way' hoist on the port, *Carysfort* enters Portsmouth to pay off in May 1946.
Wright & Logan

Below: By the end of the war, the 20mm Oerlikon had become as ineffective against current aircraft as had been the Vickers machine gun in 1939. In the absence of sufficient 40mm Bofors, the single pompom was reintroduced in a power mounting, and *Zephyr* has these mountings on the bridge wings and abaft the funnel.
Wright & Logan

There were not enough 40mm Bofors available as a ready alternative and thus it was that the single pompom re-emerged. It was fitted in a hydraulic-powered mounting closely resembling the Oerlikon Mk V, with a mark number to distinguish the type of 2pdr gun that it carried. The original 2pdr Mk II went into the Mk XV mounting and the later 2pdr Mk VIII into the Mk XVI. (These two mountings were quite different, of course, from the *hand-worked* Mk VIII* that were fitted as anti E-boat bowchasers in some of the 'Hunt' class escort destroyers.) Close range weapon fits now became even more variable than hitherto, but *Caprice* was at least tidy, with a quad and four single pompoms.

The first three 'Z's to complete – *Myngs* in June 1944 and *Zambesi* and *Zest* in July – had the short-style lattice mast but the other thirteen ships all received the taller rig. Radars included Type 285 on the director, 282 on the Hazemeyer, 293 surface warning/gun direction on the foremast (with HF/DF on the topmast), 242 and 253 IFF and 291 combined warning radar on a pole mainmast. Both classes had the now familiar 'ten pattern' DC discharge arrangements and a pair of quadruple torpedo tube mountings.

In main armament gunnery, the two flotillas were very much a compromise, for although they had a power operated and stabilised director, their hand-worked 4.5in guns presented the same problems of accurate target tracking – particularly against aircraft – as had been apparent for several years.

LATER DEVELOPMENTS

With a careful eye towards the balance of power in the Eastern Mediterranean, Britain sold two 'Z' class ships to Egypt and two to Israel. In October 1967, *Eilat* (ex-*Zealous*) was sunk by missile attack from an Egyptian Fast Patrol Boat – an event that clearly demonstrated the potency of the small ship surface-to-surface guided weapon system. In 1971, Israel squared the account when her aircraft sank the Egyptian *El Qahar* (ex-*Myngs*). The remaining four ran in the RN as destroyers, and finally *Zest*, alone in the class, was converted to a Type 15 frigate. She was scrapped in 1970, having outlived the other three by some ten years.

The 'Ca's went into reserve on their return from the Far East in 1946. (with, on the whole, few miles on the clock), and so they remained until the mid-1950s, when the complete flotilla was brought forward for modernisation. There were several variants among the eight. *Carron*, *Carysfort*, *Cavalier* and *Cavendish* were given bridges patterned on the *Daring* class, while the other four had the enclosed structure that featured in the contemporary new construction frigates. All had twin 'Squids' in place of 'X' mounting, one set of torpedo tubes and three 4.5in Mk 5 RP 50 mountings. The ill-favoured 'K Tower' was removed and replaced by a Mk 6M director linked to the Flyplane Mk 5 fire control system (as in the new construction frigates) and the long-term intention was to arm the ships with a quadruple Seacat launcher amidships. In the event, six of the 'Ca's had nothing better than Bofors amidships and the accompanying photographs demonstrate the various fits more clearly than any verbal description.

Four were scrapped in 1967, *Carysfort* was for disposal in 1970, *Cambrian* went in 1971, leaving *Caprice* and *Cavalier* as the sole survivors of the war-time Emergency destroyer – although, of course, ex-destroyers were still running as Type 15 frigates and others continued to run under foreign and Commonwealth flags.

Their 40000 shp gave them a fair turn of speed, and in 1972 *Cavalier* and *Rapid* competed in a light-hearted race to establish which was the faster ship. Doubtless both were heavily backed and it seems a pity that *Wager* wasn't on hand to hold the stake money. The two contestants lined up at the start and sped southwards down the North Sea over a forty mile course. *Rapid,* with clearly a name to live up to, held off her rival, but *Cavalier,* perhaps rather appropriately, had the last laugh, for the Type 15's steam safety valves lifted, she lost pressure at a critical point, and was beaten at the post by about 40yds. The winner then claimed the title of 'Fastest ship in the Fleet' – to derisive comment from the Fast Patrol Boat men.

THE TWELTH, THIRTEENTH AND FOURTEENTH EMERGENCY FLOTILLAS

The 'Ch' and 'Co' classes were both laid down in 1943 (some units as early as March of that year) followed by the 'Cr's in 1944, but such were the weapon equipment production difficulties met with that none saw war service. *Chevron* and *Chaplet* completed in late August 1945 and the others joined the fleet through 1946 until April 1947, when RNN *Oslo* (ex-*Crown*) joined the Norwegian Navy. It was not these difficulties alone that delayed their emergence, but also the fact that the complications of the new weapon system extended the 'setting to work' time and it is probably true to say also that once the Second World War had ended, the work-pace in the various shipyards slackened considerably.

The three classes were near-identical (at least at first fit) and were easily distinguishable from the previous flotillas by their large Mk VI HA/LA director with its 'searchlight' style radar Type 275 transmitter and receiver aerials. The increase in weight of gunmounts has already been noted and much the same progression occurred with the directors themselves, as the following list shows:

Director types	Approx total weight
Destroyer DCT and Three-man Rangefinder	2.9 tons
Destroyer DCT and Rangefinder Director Mk II(W)	3.5 tons
'K' Director	6 tons
Mk VI Director	10 tons

CHEVRON MAY 1956

1. 'Lookout' hood on local control position of 4.5in Mk V RP 50 mounting
2. Radar Type 275 aerial nacelle on Mk VI AA/SU Director
3. Independent 'Searcher' sight hatch
4. Blanked-off rangefinder housing
5. Single 40mm Bofors Mk VII mountings
6. Main roof aerial yard
7. Type 6 gyro gunsight on Simple Tachymetric Director ('STD')
8. Twin 40mm Bofors Mk V RP 50 mounting on enlarged midship gundeck
9. Windshield on QR Mk IX*** torpedo tube mounting
10. Two AS Mortar Mk IV ('Squid') mountings
11. Mortar bomb handing room on extended after superstructure
12. Single 40mm Bofors Mk VII mounting*

COCKADE JANUARY 1949

1. Rangefinder Mk VI in Mk VI AA/SU Director
2. Stump topmast
3. IFF Type 253 aerial
4. Single 2pdr Mk XVI pompom mountings
5. 'Goalpost' frame for main roof aerial
6. Twin 40mm Bofors Mk IV ('Hazemeyer') mounting
7. Mk IV thrower and 'parbuckle' stowage
8. Single 20mm Oerlikon mounting

BERGEN (EX-CROMWELL) APRIL 1950

1. Single 40mm Bofors Mk 7 mountings
2. Radar Type 291 aerial on stump mainmast
3. Type 6 gyro gunsight on STD
4. Twin 40mm Bofors Mk 5 RP 50 mounting on original 'Hazemeyer' gundeck
5. Single 20mm Oerlikon mounting

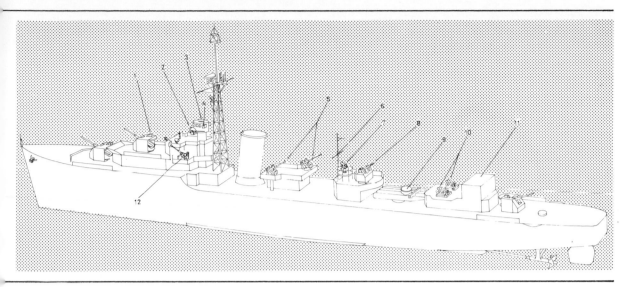

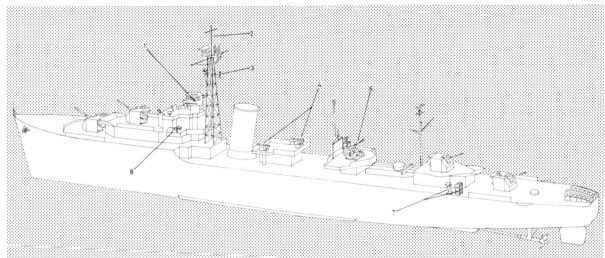

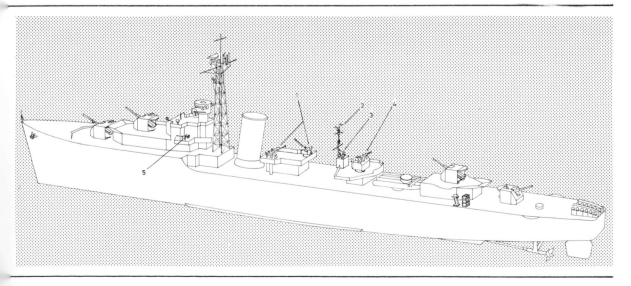

The full potential of the Mk VI director, with its electric RPC system providing for complete blind-fire procedure from the 'Tallboy' in the TS, would have been largely negated had the gun mountings not been given RPC too. The modifications to the 4.5in Mk V – principally electric drive motors and their associated gearboxes – pushed up the mounting weight, and on the now standard Emergency class hull dimensions sufficient topweight compensation could only be achieved by the omission of the forward set of torpedo tubes and other equipment reductions.

THE 4.5IN Mk V RP 50 SERIES MOUNTINGS

After its introduction as a re-gunned version of the 4.7in Mk XXII, the 4.5in Mk V progressed through four improvement programmes, developing through the 4.5in Mk V RP 50, the 4.5 Mk V*, the Mk 5* Mod 1, and finally the Mk 5* Mod 2. The addition of electric powering was by far the most important change, giving the mounting automatic follow capabilities in both motions up to 20° per second. Alternative local power control was provided by adding a 'scooter' control column on the right hand side, manned by the Captain of the Turret. His lookout hood was the only outward and visible sign that the mounting was the RP 50 version – 'RP' standing for Remote Power and the number signifying that it employed electric and electronic units developed by Messrs Metropolitan Vickers. The extra equipment increased the mounting weight by 1.7 tons to approximately 15 tons.

The next variant was the Mk V*, whose special feature was an improved loading tray mechanism. Previously, although spring power ramming was available, the tray itself had to be pushed into line with the chamber and manually withdrawn. In the Mk V*, extra spring mechanisms were incorporated and the complete cycle was automatically initiated by a single control lever, close to the breech. When put to 'Ram', the sequence was:

1. Tray moved inwards into line with chamber
2. Rammer advanced, ramming round
3. Rammer retracted
4. Tray moved outwards, breech closed, 'Ram' lever reset.

On gunfire, the recoil action recocked all the spring mechanisms. This particular single 4.5 was fitted in 'Q' position on the 1943 'Battle' class and, like its predecessor and immediate successor, it retained alternative hand drives for elevation and training, sighting ports in the gunshield, a conventional geared gunsight and lanyard-operated hand ramming – all in case of power or equipment failure.

No further major changes were made until the 'Ca' class modernisation programme, when refinements to the RPC components created the Mk 5* Mod 1, followed by the Mod 2 in the new construction 'Tribal' class frigates.

CLOSE RANGE WEAPONS

The omission of the forward torpedo tubes did not entirely compensate for the increased top weight created by the heavier mountings and director, and further compensation could only be achieved by limiting the close range armament (particularly in the bridge wings), reducing the AS armament to two instead of four throwers, and cutting down on the number of stowed depth charges.

Twin Bofors were available for first fitting in all ships, commonly supplemented by two single pompoms abaft the funnel and single Oerlikons on the bridge wings. The complex twin Mk IV Hazemeyer began to be phased out, and several ships – *Chivalrous*, *Comus*, *Concord*, *Crispin* and *Creole* – had the twin Bofors Mk V RP 50 mounting instead. This weapon employed an RPC system almost identical with that of the 4.5in Mk V, and was controlled in the primary mode by its own Simple Tachymetric Director, sited on a pedestal on the forward edge of the midship gundeck.

This single 2pdr – the Mk VIII gun on the Mk XVI mounting – appeared in the early 'Battle' and final Emergency classes. It closely resembled its relative, the Mk XVI.
MoD

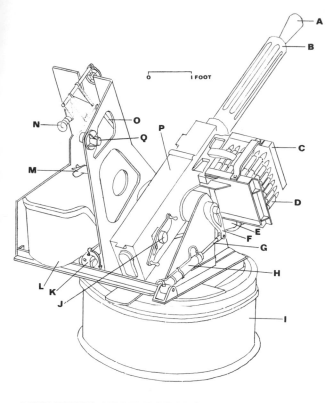

SINGLE 2PDR MK XV MOUNTING

A Flame guard
B Water jacket
C 56-round ammunition tray
D Articulated steel link
E Elevation balance spring box
F Elevating crank, right hand
G Elevating piston, right hand
H Elevating cylinder, right hand
I Fixed base
J Hand operating crank
K Elevating cylinder, left hand
L Aimer's seat
M Left-hand grip of aimer's joystick
N Eyepiece of back sight
O Link arm to sight
P Sight trunnion

THE TWIN 40MM BOFORS MK V RP 50 MOUNTING

The Dutch-designed Hazemeyer control system was the most advanced of its kind anywhere in the world, but far-sighted as its basic concept was the Mk IV was a difficult mounting to maintain under the arduous conditions of war. In 1943, the British began the development of an even more complex twin Bofors, which in post-war years was to emerge as the STAAG mounting, but meanwhile, the United States (to whom the British had introduced the 40mm Bofors) already had their Mk I (twin) Bofors mount and a Mk II (quad) entering service. Their vast resources allowed for large numbers of both pieces of equipment to be built, and many were supplied under Lease-Lend to the Royal and Allied navies. The appearance of the USN Bofors mounts in RN vessels usually indicated a North American wartime refit.

Comus, of the third 'C' class group, was lucky enough to get a Bofors Mk V soon after being built as well as single Bofors abaft the funnel, but has Oerlikons on the bridge wings in this 1946 shot of her leaving Portsmouth for duty with the 8th DF in the Far East.
Wright & Logan

The British Mk V Bofors was based on the design of the American twin, but utilised suitable components of the 2pdr pompom mounting (as well as the 4.5 Mk V RPC). It was very much a 'utility' weapon, but none the worse for that, and in fact outlived the vast 17 ton STAAG. When controlled remotely from a pedestal-mounted gyro gunsight (hence 'Simple Tachymetric Director') the Mk V was as accurate as the STAAG under visual aiming conditions but lacked a blind fire capability. A fully automatic, self-contained, radar-controlled weapon had obvious attractions, but they were largely outweighed, so to speak, by the 17 tons of equipment that grew around what were, after all, only two 40mm Bofors barrels. The 5½ton Bofors Mk V was altogether a much better proposition and proved to be a popular and efficient mounting.

A sprinkling of single 40mm Mk VII mountings began to appear (abaft the funnel) in later ships of the general group, but single Oerlikons remained on the bridge wings until the ships were modernised in the early 1950s.

FIRE CONTROL

The three Flotillas were identically equipped with what was known as the 'Battle System' – taking its name from the '1942 Battle class' installation. This comprised the Mk VI director, AFCC MkI** (the first asterisk signifying 4.5in calibre and the second that a Bearing Clock for Indirect Bombardment procedures was fitted), FKC Mk II**(S), Gyro Level Corrector, Gyro Cross Level Corrector and radar Type 275 'Tallboy'. The weakest link in an otherwise quite efficient chain was the limited ability of the Fuze Keeping Clock as an AA predictor, but this was to be remedied in the later Modernisation programme.

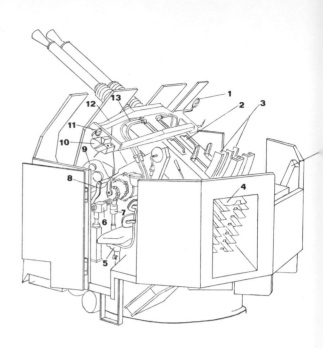

TWIN 40MM BOFORS MK V MOUNTING

1. Trainer's open sight
2. Breech cover plate
3. Gun auto-loaders
4. Ready-use ammunition 'letter box' stowages
5. Layer's seat
6. Local control joystick column
7. Elevating shaft drive
8. Layer's manual control hand-cranks
9. Elevation receiver
10. Gyro gunsight
11. Layer's open sight
12. Sight beam
13. Water cooling pipes

RADARS

Type 275 supplanted 285 as the main gunnery set, although 282 remained as long as its parent mounting, the Hazemeyer, existed. Type 293 on the foremast was fitted throughout, but while some ships had a pole mainmast for Type 291 and HF/DF on a foretopmast, others omitted either or both. All followed the arrangements introduced in the 'S' class by rigging their main roof radio aerials between the foreyard and a diminutive stump mast on the forward edge of the twin Bofors gundeck to give clear sky-arcs astern and abeam.

LATER DEVELOPMENTS

The post-war years found the 'Ca' class in reserve, the 'Ch's in the Mediterranean, the 'Co's in the Far East, and only two of the 'Crs' – *Creole* and *Crispin* – under the White Ensign. Four of the 14th Emergency Flotilla were taken over from building by the Royal Norwegian Navy and two by the RCN, and in 1956 the two RN units were purchased by Pakistan, becoming *Alamgir* and *Jahangir*.

Above: The durable twin 40mm Mk V mounting. Developed as a 'utility' weapon, it rendered sterling service from its inception and deserved its high reputation.
MoD

Left: The American Mk I (Twin) Bofors mount, upon which the British Mk V was based. It rather looks as though there has been a jam on the right gun, for the rating on the extreme right has removed the spent cartridge deflector. This turned the empty case downwards as it was ejected, and directed it into the curved chute which led to the gun deck in front of the mounting.
IWM

Below: The 'Ch' class introduced the Remote Powered version of the 4.5in Mk V coupled to a Mk VI Director and the same fire control system as the '1942 Battle' class. Shortages of close range weapons added to new top weight problems still made for very mixed armaments – *Cheviot* in December 1945 has a Hazemeyer, two single pompoms and two single Oerlikons.
Wright & Logan

After a few years of service in their 'as first fitted' state, the 'Ch' and 'Co' classes were modernised during longish refits (as indeed were the two 'Cr's before being taken over by Pakistan). The obsolete FKC was replaced by an electronic AA computer, when the fire control system became known as 'MRS 7' (Medium Range System 7). The gun in 'X' position was landed to make way for a twin Squid set-up identical with that already described for the modernised 'Ca's. Close range armament was standardised as a twin Mk V Bofors amidships and four single Mk VIIs, two abaft the funnel and a pair on the bridge wings. There were of course, the inevitable exceptions. *Chieftain*, *Chaplet* and *Comet* were given mine-rails reminiscent of the 'O' class and had the same type of 'fantail' quarters to house the power-operated dropping gear, losing the two Mk VIIs abaft the funnel and their only set of torpedo tubes in compensation for the additional weight of a full mine load. A particularly odd-looking weapon layout existed for a short time in the Far East, where some of the 'Co's had already landed their 'X' gun in preparation for the Squid deck rebuild. When the Korean war broke out in 1950, a single 40mm Bofors Mk III* was fitted on the vacant space and looked rather lonely on what was a surprisingly large gundeck.

The 'Co's, led by *Cossack*, formed the 8th Destroyer Flotilla (less *Comet*, plus *Charity*). The latter had been detached from the 1st DF in the Mediterranean and arrived in Hong Kong still wearing the '1' of her flotilla on her funnel. A signal lamp flashed from Captain(D) in *Cossack*, stages were hastily rigged, the '1' was painted out and an '8' very quickly appeared in its place. The 8th Flotilla had a busy time in the Far East and saw a good deal of action in the Korean war, as well as being involved in the earlier Yangtse Patrols and the *Amethyst* incident.

In the same way that the 'Co's moved out to the Far East soon after completion, so did the 'Ch's go to the Mediterranean as a re-juvenated 14th Destroyer Flotilla. Like their sisters in the 'Far Flung', they spent most of their working lives on the one foreign station. *Constance* led a procession to the scrapyard in 1956 and, apart from the sales to the Commonwealth navies, most had gone by the mid-1960s, although *Chevron* survived until 1969 as an overflow accommodation ship for HMS *Cochrane* in Rosyth Dockyard. Having served in her in 1955-56, it was a sad experience for me to walk her neglected decks towards the end of her days.

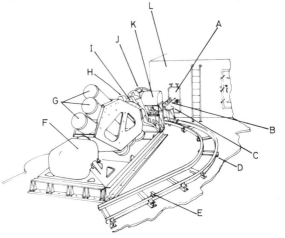

STARBOARD 'SQUID' MORTAR ON 'X' GUNDECK, AS IN TYPE 16 FRIGATES AND 'C' CLASS DESTROYERS

A Bomb scuttle
B Swivelling tray
C Bomb trolley
D Trolley rails
E Permanent trolley stops
F Forward trunnion and firing switch housing
G Barrels of differing lengths and planes to give bomb pattern
H Roll receiver
I Roll drive-pinion cover
J Follow roll and loading handwheel
K Roll power follow-up motor
L Mortar bomb handing room

The Royal Canadian Navy took *Crescent* and *Crusader* from building and retained the names. The former ship enters Portsmouth on a visit in May 1951, painted to the distinctive Canadian two-tone scheme and with the red 'Maple Leaf' emblem on the funnel.
Wright & Logan

8. Battle Class

THE '1942 BATTLES'

The completion of the final pre-war designed destroyers ran on well into 1942, with the earlier Emergency Classes, as has been related, building in parallel with them. The inadequate anti-aircraft defence of destroyers both at long and close range had clearly been demonstrated, so that when the designs for the 1942 building programme were being considered a much more powerful vessel was envisaged. The result was the '1942 Battle' class, so called from their programme year. Most handsome in appearance, they embraced all the features that had been sought after, but the complications of their weapon fits so extended their building time that only one – *Barfleur* – had been completed by September 1944. A further six joined the Fleet in the summer of 1945 within weeks of the end of the War, but the majority of the total of 24 ships were not completed until after the cessation of hostilities. In fact, it was not until May 1948 that the last RN unit – *Alamein* – was commissioned, while the Australian pair were even later.

The sixteen '1942' ships were split into two sub-groups. In the first, a 4in Mk XXIII 'Starshell' gun was to be fitted abaft the funnel, while in the second, this was to be omitted in favour of a further two close-range weapons.

The 4in concept proved unsuccessful, and was abandoned after the fifth fit in *Hogue*. Subsequently, all the early ships exchanged it for a standard layout of two 'sided' single Bofors Mk 7 mountings.

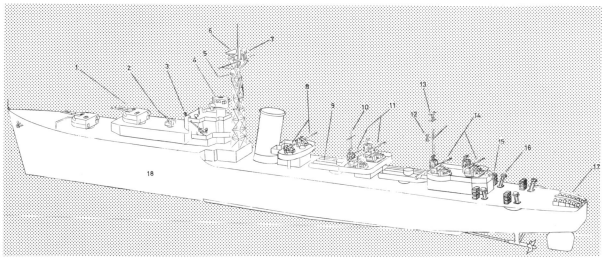

ST KITTS NOVEMBER 1948

1   Twin 4.5in Mk IV RP 10 mounting
2   Single 40mm Bofors Mk VII mounting
3   HF/DF aerial
4   Mk VI HA/LA Director
5   Combined Wind speed and Wind Direction Unit
6   Gun Direction/Surface Warning Radar Type 293 aerial
7   IFF aerial
8   'Sided' 40mm Bofors Mk VII mountings
9   Quadruple Torpedo tube mounting QR Mk VIII***
10 Stump mast for main roof aerial
11 'Sided' Twin 40mm Bofors Mk IV ('Hazemeyer') mountings
12 IFF aerial
13 Air Warning Radar Type 291 aerial
14 Twin 40mm Bofors Mk IV ('Hazemeyer') mountings *en echelon*
15 'Parbuckle' DC stowage
16 DC thrower
17 Twin 6-DC overstern rails and traps
18 Port single 40mm Bofors Mk VII mounting

THE 4.5IN TWIN MK IV RP 10 MOUNTING

The background to the twin 4.5in Mk IV RP 10 mounting has already been dealt with, but the disposition of the two mountings in 'A' and 'B' positions was both interesting and, at the time of their appearance in the 'Battles', contentious. In the early classes, only 'X' gun was clear enough from ship's structure to allow all-round training (if the stop design was suitable), but in the 'Battles' 'A' mounting was set sufficiently far forward for its barrels to clear the forward screen. Similarly, 'B' gundeck projected so far forward as to allow not only all-round training for 'B' mounting, but also the inclusion of a close range weapon on the centreline between the twin 4.5in guns and the bridge. Both 'A' and 'B' could make one and a half revolutions in each direction from the mid (fore-and-aft) position – a total of 1080°. No conventional mechanical stops were fitted, the flow to the hydraulic training motor being automatically throttled to a 'creep' speed at the limits of normal movement. If this were allowed to continue in the same direction, a limit switch broke power to the pump motor and the mounting came to rest. It was then necessary to clutch-in the training hand drive and bring the mounting back to its safe arc before the mounting pump motor power could be restored.

One school of thought deplored the lack of 4.5in coverage for the after arcs and this lobby may have been instrumental in the fitting of a single 4.5in Mk V mounting in the 'Starshell' gun position in the third group of ships.

FUZE-SETTING ARRANGEMENTS

In the single 4in HA Mk III mounting, fuze-setting was carried out by hand, the 'fixed' ammunition being placed with its base on a revolvable turntable on the mounting platform. The fuze-setting device was shaped rather like a large egg-cup and was placed over the nose cap until internal knife edges cut into the fuze body. Twisting the shell on the revolving turntable in one direction and twisting the fuze-setting tool in the other, set the index (or 'fuze') number against an engraved line.

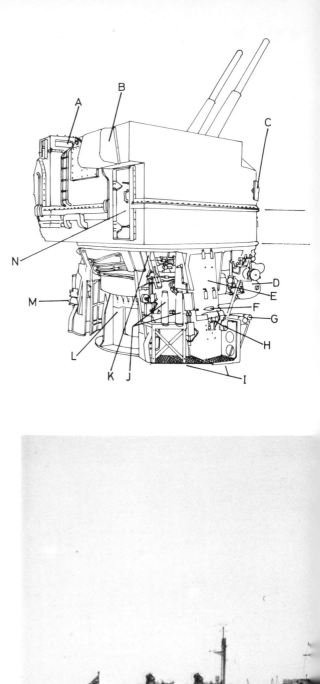

The fourteenth 'Battle' class destroyer to complete, *Sluys* was one of the 1942 group with two single Mk 7 Bofors abaft the funnel. She was modernised by Vosper Thornycroft for the Iranian Navy and recommissioned as INS *Artemiz* in 1970, and is still serving, thirty years after this photo was taken.
Wright & Logan

THE 4.5IN RP MK IV MOUNTING

A Captain of turret's lookout hood
B Exhaust fan trunking
C Trainer's sighting port door
D HP air bottle for air blast
E Right gun shell hoist trunking
F Shell 'legend' at foot of shell hoist, to ensure correct projectile position, nose to the rear
G Waiting shell
H Automatic shell release, synchronised with hoist movement
I Right gun shell and cordite hoist operators' platform
J Waiting cartridge
K Single-stroke cartridge hoist
L Fixed mounting training base
M Left gun shell and cordite hoist structures
N Right hand gunhouse access door
1 Original gundeck level in Mk II mountings
2 Revised gundeck level for Mk IV mountings

Because there was obviously a time-delay between setting the fuze and then loading and firing the round carrying it, the predicted fuze number had to take into account the rate of fire. This time-delay period was known as 'Dead Time', and was set according to the capability of the slowest gun's crew – for all guns received the same fuze number. The fuzing and firing was programmed by a unit within the Fuze Keeping Clock called the Fuze and Firing Interval Clock. This burnt a lamp to indicate when the fuze should be set, and after the 'Dead Time' period had elapsed automatically sounded the firing buzzer to indicate to the Director Layer when he should press the trigger.

Fuze-setting arrangements on the twin 4.7in Mk XIX were similar, except that, because the ammunition was 'separate', a pedestal turntable was provided for the shell.

THE FUZE-SETTING MACHINE MK II

The early models of the twin 4in HA Mk XIX mounting and the single 4in HA Mk IVs were fitted with this device. The combined shell and cartridge was placed on a pair of rollers in a slightly nose-down attitude, with the fuze entered into the setting-head of the machine. One crew member (who doubled as sight-setter in local surface fire) followed the electrical pointer of the fuze number receiver with a small handwheel which set the internal mechanism. A second crew member, on seeing the 'fuze' lamp burn, operated the fuze-setting handle which spun the setting head around through the number of degrees determined by the fuze number. The ejector lever was then operated, which freed the shell from the grip of the setting head knives.

THE FUZE-SETTING MACHINE MK V

This became the standard manual fuze-setting machine for all mountings from the 4in to the 5.25in. The rollers were replaced by a trough into which the shell fitted with its nose about 1ft from the setting head. 'Follow-fuze-number' was as in the Mk II, but the operating cycle was quite different. The setting handle was capable of two complete revolutions before it locked. During the first 360° the setting head advanced outwards, at the same time revolving to a datum position to 'take-off' any previous fuze-setting angle. Two shafts from the machine, terminating in serrated dog-toothed levers, operated to jam against each side of the shell, just before the setting head passed over the nose cap, to prevent it from being pushed backwards. The second revolution of the setting handle revolved the head to set the fuze, then retracted it, and finally released the dogs. The locking after the two turns was by a detent inside the machine which was released by a short setting-handle movement in the opposite direction.

Because every fuze nose cap was always set to the 'safe' index mark while stowed in the shell room, and because the appropriate fuze number was a matter of degrees of rotation from this datum, the shell itself did not need to be rotated to any particular line-up position when it was placed on the trough. The setting-head knives were formed internally on a steel ring having a certain measure of lateral 'float' so that it was self-centring over the nose cap.

By and large the Mk V machine worked very well, the greatest problem being the precise adjustment of the jamming dogs. If too free, they did not grip the shell body; if too tight, they made the shell difficult to remove from the trough (with 'Dead Time' ticking away). After some practice, one crew member with a degree of ambidexterity was able to follow fuze number with one hand, and fuze-set with the other, thereby releasing one 'number' to back up the loading team.

CLOSE RANGE WEAPONS

The main strength of the close range AA defence relied upon four twin 'Hazemeyers' – one pair side by side amidships and a further pair *en echelon* on what would otherwise have been 'X' gundeck.

The very earliest 'Battles' had single 20mm Oerlikons in four standard positions – abaft 'B' mounting, on the bridge sponsons and on the quarterdeck – but improved deliveries of better weapons soon allowed the 20mm mountings to be phased out. Single 2pdrs appeared on some bridge wings, but the most powerful layout was six single Mk VII 40mm Bofors in these four positions with a further

sided pair on the redundant 4in 'Starshell' gundeck. Later the 'Hazemeyers' were removed and two Twin Bofors (STAAG) mountings replaced them aft, but because of their weight these were omitted from the midships position.

THE TWIN BOFORS MK IV ('HAZEMEYER') MOUNTING

This, a Dutch development, was an early attempt to produce a weapon with its own built-in fire control system, and the manufacturing drawings were rescued from enemy clutches in 1940. It was a very imaginative weapon and years ahead of its time, but was difficult to maintain. Two models were produced, the Mk IV and the Mk IV*, and it was, of course, quite widely fitted, particularly in the later Emergency Classes. The complete cradle carrying the elevation structure was driven in the 'cross-roll' direction by a toothed arc at right angles to the fore-and-aft line of the mounting. This motion was also conveyed to the aerial frame making the complete assembly triaxial in movement, which, in a ship, is the ultimate requirement for stabilisation. Target ranging was by radar Type 282 and all prediction was calculated on mounting. A slip-ring permitted continuous all-round training and the earlier model even had its own rangefinder as a secondary means of ranging. Change-clutches allowed normal hand-follow by open sight, and it has to be admitted that it was probably used more often in this way than 'in power'.

The 7-ton 'Haslemere', as it was generally known, was a brilliant concept, but unfortunately it needed more advanced technology than then existed. It cannot claim to have been the most popular of weapons but at least it provided a little light relief on occasions. When stationary in the 'power-off' mode during maintenance, a combination of training, depression and cross-roll made it look for all the world as though it was about to fall off its gundeck. Observations like 'I see the Haslemere is ill again' were common.

THE SINGLE 40MM BOFORS MK VII MOUNTING

This was the final development of the single hydraulic-powered close range weapon, and stemmed from the twin Mk V Oerlikon mounting. The latter had been adapted to carry a 2pdr (on the Mk XV and XVI mounting), a 6pdr (for Coastal Forces) and a 40mm Bofors (on the 'Boffin'), but all three were somewhat restricted in their maximum elevation. The reason for this can be seen by comparing the relative positions of the elevating trunnion axis on the drawings of the 2pdr Mk XV and the twin Oerlikon Mk V. The custom-built Bofors Mk VII on the other hand could elevate to 90° and, further, having a simple slip-ring unit on the centre of rotation for electrical power, it had continuous training without the complication of the hydraulic swivel connection previously employed. Utilising lightweight alloys, it was neat, efficient, and weighed only 1½ tons. Like its ancestors, control was by one man from a 'scooter' in the sports car style aimer's cab. In recent years it has been largely superseded by the electrically powered Mk 9 version, but it is still fitted in some MCMs and in the assault ships *Fearless* and *Intrepid*.

Developed from the Mk V Oerlikon mounting, the Mk VII Bofors was a compact and deservedly well-liked weapon and is still in service. *MoD*

SINGLE 40MM BOFORS MK VII MOUNTING

A Aimer's open sight
B Air-cooled barrel
C Casing over barrel run-out spring
D Recoil buffer
E Normal/hand-pump hydraulic changeover valve
F Elevation counterbalance spring boxes
G Spent cartridge ejector tube
H Hydraulic power unit
I Spent cartridge ejector trough
J Gyro sight regulator unit
K Hand-cranks to chain drive of emergency hydraulic pump
L Guard rail for emergency pump operator
M Ready-use ammunition 'letter-box' stowages
N Gun auto loader
O Guard rails for loading number

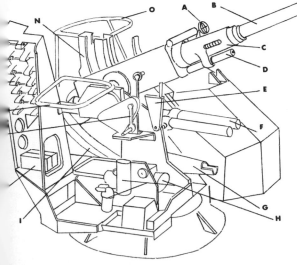

THE TWIN 40MM BOFORS STAAG MK II

This, the eventual replacement for the 'Hazemeyer', became the standard 'Battle' fit, and was carried on into the 'Weapon' and *Daring* classes. In retrospect, it was the self-contained concept carried to extremes. Not satisfied with on-mounting radar (Type 262), automatic target acquisition, in-built prediction, stabilisation and automatic target tracking from radar, the design included a secondary rangefinder and even an on-mounting diesel generator for emergency power. The result was a massive shielded weapon carrying only two Bofors barrels at the cost (in weight terms) of 17 tons. What the monetary cost was is not known, but it must have been enormous.

The mounting was hydraulic, and like the 'Hazemeyer' the barrels moved in three independent planes, although in a different manner. Training and elevation were natural movements but the third, instead of being 'cross-roll', was a lateral deflection movement. This was achieved by a vertical axis passing between the gun barrels, so that 'aim-ahead' moved them laterally with respect to the centreline of the mounting. Thus the main structure 'looked' at the target's present position, but the guns 'looked' ahead to its predicted future position.

The initial letters of the name stood for Stabilised Tachymetric Anti-Aircraft Gun; by many it was known as 'the antlered beast', and it could be a most fractious animal when so minded.

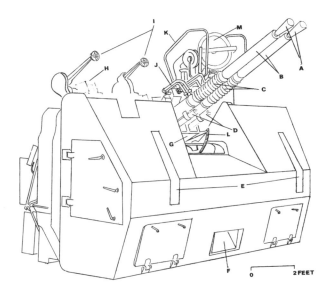

TWIN 40MM BOFORS (STAAG) MK II MOUNTING

A   Flame guards
B   Water cooling jackets
C   Barrel run-out springs
D   Recoil buffers
E   Rangefinder apertures
F   Spent cartridge ejection chutes
G   Cradle lateral deflection frame
H   Aimer's reflector sight
I   Control Officer's open sights
J   Flexible barrel water-cooling circulating pipes
K   Frame for aerial cover
L   Left gun elevation arc
M   Radar Type 262 aerial 'dish'

Left: A technical nightmare, the STAAG twin Bofors was an example of extreme over-complication. With an all-up weight of 17 tons, it was less reliable and little more effective than the 6½-ton twin Bofors Mk V.
MoD

Below: Two '1943 Battles' at anchor in the Clyde in September 1952, *Corunna* in the foreground and *Barrosa* beyond. Probably no two ships ever had their names more frequently misspelt than did this pair. Compare the size of the starboard STAAG with the twin Mk 5 Bofors amidships and observe the splinter shield to protect the 'Squid' mortar crew, the 'gash' chute over the starboard quarter and the two open escape-ports in the ship's side aft.
Conway Picture Library

Right: The two twin Mk 5 Bofors replacing the STAAGs and the quarterdeck 'Squid' are clearly seen in this shot of *Trafalgar* in reserve at Portsmouth in 1968.
John G Callis

THE 4IN MK XXIII MOUNTING

Despite its somewhat basic, not to say elderly, appearance this, the unpopular 'Starshell' gun in the first few 'Battles', was to a deliberately simple design to make it suitable for quick production and rapid fitting in merchant ships and auxiliaries. Its presence rather spoilt the new ships and, as has been said, it was quite quickly abandoned.

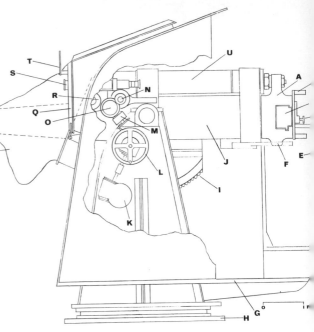

A   Breech ring
B   Breech operating lever
C   Breech block
D   Striker re-cocking handle
E   Breech-worker's platform guard rail
F   Guide for gun in recoil
G   Mounting platform
H   Mounting base
I   Elevating arc
J   Gun cradle
K   Elevation wormwheel gearbox
L   Layer's handwheel
M   Range-setting drive
N   Deflection-setting handwheel
O   Deflection dial
P   Canvas blast bag
Q   Sighting port
R   Range dial
S   Layer's telescope
T   Open barrage sight
U   Combined run-out spring and recoil buffer cover

The single AS mortar Mk 4 ('Squid') on the quarterdeck of a modernised 'Battle'. The different barrel length (for range 'spread') and the lateral alignment displacement (for horizontal 'spread') for mortar bomb trajectory is obvious. Note the combined after capstan and winch, the quarterdeck davit and the steel tripod support for the timber ensign staff.
By courtesy of Anthony Peters

FIRE CONTROL – THE 'BATTLE' SYSTEM

Mention has been made of this system in the section covering the last three Emergency classes, but unlike them, it was now allied to 80° 4.5in mountings, and so was more comprehensive in its capabilities.

The Director, the Mk VI HA/LA (later, of course, designated Mk 6 SU/AA) was electrically powered by the Melandyne System, and in the 'Blind Follow' mode was remotely controlled by radar operators seated before radar screens in the TS. As in all contemporary RN equipment, alternative means of follow were provided including 'Aloft' power, 'Hand', and 'Scooter'. Originally a rangefinder was fitted for emergency ranging, but this was later removed. Two gyro units in the TS, training in sympathy with the director, provided it with a power stabilisation input in the roll and 'cross-roll' planes; and although the Fire Control calculators (AFCC Mk I** and FKC Mk II) remained as in earlier classes, the 'Battle' system as a whole was far in advance of anything hitherto seen in a British destroyer.

TORPEDO TUBES AND ANTI-SUBMARINE WEAPONS

The 1942 'Battles' were given the usual torpedo and A/S weapon fit – two sets of QR VIII*** tubes and four DC throwers with 'parbuckle' stowages and twin overstern rails, controlled by Asdics 144Q and 147, all of which equipment has already been described.

MK VI HA/LA DIRECTOR

1 Elevation transmission unit of independent searcher sight
2 Searcher sight binoculars (shown at 90° to Director Line of Sight)
3 Searcher sight elevation link from elevation handle to binocular platform
4 Searcher sight hatch in open position
5 Fixed rangefinder shield
6 Slot for lens of Rangefinder Type UL Mk II
7 Nacelle blower motor starter
8 Roof access ladder
9 Nacelle trunnion access platform support tube
10 Forced lubrication pipe to trunnion bearing
11 Nacelle trunnion end cap
12 Nacelle air blower pipe
13 Radar Type 275 Receiver nacelle
14 Layer's window, fully open
15 Control Officers window, fully open, over layer's window
16 Twin IFF dipole aerials
17 Nacelle trunnions support beam
18 Radar Type 275 Transmitter nacelle
19 Rate Officer's position
20 Trainer's and Rate Officer's windows, fully open
21 Roof windows, fully open

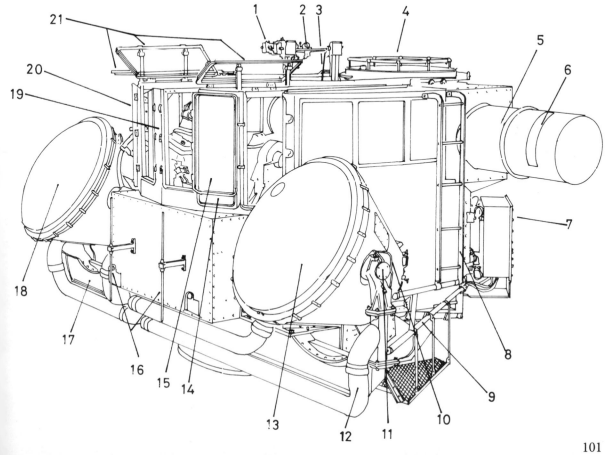

POST-WAR MODIFICATIONS

These included the exchange of four 'Hazemeyers' for two STAAG mountings, the removal of the 4in 'Starshell' gun, the suppression of the quarterdeck close range weapons, and the general adoption of single Mk VII Bofors mountings.

The fire control system was first improved by an interim modification to the FKC to cope with aircraft speeds up to 500 knots. Then in the early 1950s, the FKC was removed completely and replaced by an electronic predictor called the Simple Electric Deflection Calculator ('SEDC'). Stabilisation compensation was improved y an Electric Cross Level Calculating Unit ('ECL LU') and the old Gun Elevation Synchronous Unit was redesigned. The working name of the latter – the 'GESU' – incurred the displeasure of the Chaplain of the Fleet's Department (for obvious reasons) and its successor was officially the 'Gun Elevation Unit' (but it was still called the 'GESU' in the Fleet).

The complete system was designated 'Medium Range System Mk 7' (MRS7) and it was also fitted to the 'Ch', 'Co' and 'Cr' classes. The SEDC, an early adventure into electronic computation, was theoretically an improvement on the mechanical FKC but in practice caused the burning of much midnight oil. Adjustable potentiometers within the device, which were supposed to be set up, locked and thereafter left untouched, were found to be in need of constant re-adjustment, and in many ships (quite unofficially) the ship's staff repositioned them in more accessible positions so that they could be used as 'spotting' correctors on a 'left a bit, up a bit' basis.

On the quarterdeck, the depth charge arrangements were removed, the superstructure was increased by an extension towards the stern (as a mortar bomb handing room) and a single 'Squid' mortar was added, set off the centreline to starboard.

The final runners of the '1942s' thankfully gave up their STAAGs, and instead had a pair of STD-controlled twin Bofors Mk 5. Two, *Cadiz* and *Gabbard*, were sold to Pakistan, *Sluys* became the Iranian *Artemiz*, while the others went to the ship-breakers in batches through the early, middle and late 1960s, *Saintes* ending as a tender to the artificer's training establishment at Rosyth.

THE '1943 BATTLES'

The eight ships of this group were launched between January 1945 and February 1946 and were the remnants of a larger order, many of which were scrapped on the slipway. Whilst preserving the general outline of their older sisters, the '1943s' differed in several fundamental ways.

A single 4.5in Mk 5* RP 50 mounting appeared abaft the funnel – perhaps as a sop to the 'after-arcs' lobby; the Mk 7 Bofors was omitted from 'B' gundeck; and an STD-controlled Twin Mk 5 was added amidships between the tubes (with the usual pair of STAAGs aft). 'Squid' was included from building, and 'Pentad' PR Mk 3 hand-worked torpedo tubes replaced the QRs in the earlier group.

The two 4.5in mountings, the Mk 37 Director and the radar Type 965 'bedstead' on an AD conversion 1943 'Battle'. The larger and smaller 'cheese' aerials are for weapon direction and navigation respectively.

The fire control utilised 'Lease-Lend' American equipment. This, the USN Mk 37 system, was outstandingly good, and although having a 'mechanical' computer was superbly engineered. It could cope with aircraft speeds up to 1000 knots *and* diving targets, and the director had triaxially stabilised sights and radar. Streets ahead of contemporary British equipment, the '37 system' showed what a combination of foresight, know-how, finance and production capability could produce.

In the 4.5in mounting, the original hand-worked Mk 5 Fuze-Setting Machines were replaced by Metadyne-powered automatic Mk 7s, and various other attempts to provide automatic fuze-setting were made, including 'muzzle fuzing'. Neither the Mk 7 fuze-setters nor the experimental devices were particularly successful, but meanwhile the old 'Time/Mechanical' Fuzes had become obsolete, and thereafter 'Vicinity/Time' equipment was used for AA firings. In these the fuze was triggered by its proximity to the target, and thus obviated the need for the predictor to compute a fuze number in addition to gun orders in training and elevation.

The 'VT' fuze has now long been the standard, but it suffers from the disadvantage that if it does not 'trigger' it is extremely difficult to analyse by how much and in what path it missed the target area. Starshell ammunition is still provided with a TM fuze, but this is normally hand-set, except in one or two special cases ouside the province of this book.

LATER MODIFICATIONS
Three ships, *Alamein*, *Dunkirk* and *Jutland*, were scrapped in 1965, the last-mentioned by that time having had her two STAAGs replaced by Mk 5 Bofors, giving her three such mountings in all. *Matapan*, placed in reserve immediately after her acceptance trials, was finally brought forward and rebuilt as an experimental Sonar ship. Unrecognisable as a 'Battle', she ran until 1977, but was then withdrawn from service.

The remaining four ships, *Agincourt*, *Aisne*, *Barrosa* and *Corunna*, were modernised to the Aircraft Direction rôle. A massive lattice mast was built to carry the radar Type 965 'Double Bedstead' and the waist was taken up by new superstructure. While the vessels retained the '37' system, the 4.5in Mk 4s forward and the 'Squid' aft, both sets of torpedo tubes and all the Bofors were removed and a GWS 21 Seacat system was installed aft, with two 'junk-bashing' Oerlikons nearby. All four were placed for disposal in 1970, soon to go on the final 'one-way-ride' together with the remnants of the post-war Type 15 conversions and the modernised 'Ca's.

Happily, *Cavalier* (still laughing) is to be preserved as a museum; the Canadian 'Tribal' *Haida* lies quietly alongside on Lake Ontario; and the Iranian flag yet flutters from *Artemiz*.

'Ave atque vale, Caesar!'
P A Vicary

Part 2.
United States Navy Destroyers

The *Fletcher* class destroyer *Harrison* (DD573) refitting at Mare Island, 8 January 1945.

All photos in this part are USN official

9. Design & Development

US destroyer design and armament is best understood in the context of intended employment. From about 1919 onwards, the US Navy was developed in the expectation that the next war would be fought against Japan. US strategy in such a war would call for an advance across the Pacific by the battle fleet towards a decisive Jutland-style engagement somewhere near the Philippines. An essential element of this plan was the seizure of the Pacific islands which had fallen into Japanese hands as a result of World War I. From 1921 onwards at least, the US Navy was assured by treaty of a 5 to 3 superiority in battleships, which at that time both the US and Japanese Navies considered the primary elements of sea power. The combat theory of that time held that forces should be compared as the squares of their numbers. Thus when, after the London Naval Conference of 1930, the battle fleets of the United States and Japan had been set at 15 and 9 units respectively, the ratio of effective strengths, not counting the actual ship-for-ship superiority of some of the US vessels, could be set at 225 to 81, or a ratio of well over 2 to 1, against Japan.

American strategists reasoned that the Japanese would seek in those weapons not restricted by the Naval Treaties an 'equaliser', to reduce the American fleet at least to even terms by the time it reached Japanese home waters and the decisive fleet battle. By the early 1930s, when the United States was ready to resume destroyer construction after a gap lasting from about 1921, the US estimate was that the Japanese 'equaliser' would be a combination of submarines and naval aircraft based on the islands through which the fleet would have to come. It followed that destroyers screening the battle fleet would probably have to survive, indeed defeat, a series of air and submarine attacks before they came close to the classical destroyer rôle in a fleet action. On the other hand, there seems to have been relatively little expectation that in a future Pacific war the US Navy would have to carry out extensive convoy operations; and it is well to keep in mind that until the late 1930s the United States government had little expectation of becoming embroiled in a European or, far worse, a two-ocean war.

Pacific warfare would entail fleet movements over vast distances, in an ocean with few US bases. Although destroyers could fuel at sea, there was no expectation that they could receive ammunition, especially torpedoes, under way. In any case, the fleet of the 1920s and 1930s included no ammunition ships designed specially for replenishment at sea. However, it would have been imprudent to assume that there would be only a single major engagement as the fleet crossed the Pacific. It followed that destroyers ought to carry enough torpedoes for at least two fleet engagements; although they might have few opportunities for torpedo fire in any one battle, they might well have to carry an unusually heavy load of torpedoes merely in order to have enough aboard for two. Moreover, since torpedoes would be difficult to handle in a seaway, it was best for destroyers to carry all or most of their reserve torpedoes in tubes. Thus came about the US practice of mounting three or even four quadruple torpedo tubes in one ship, even though only eight could be fired on the broadside.

Indeed, the US Navy expected its destroyers to have relatively few opportunities to use torpedoes in combat. Japan possessed three (reduced by Treaty from four) battlecruisers fast enough, it was believed, to dominate the lanes by which US destroyers might try to approach the Japanese battle line in a fleet action. On the other hand, the US Navy suffered from a shortage of small cruisers suitable for operations against enemy destroyer forces approaching its fleet. Therefore, it was argued, even in a fleet action, US destroyers were more likely to use guns than torpedoes; and it was vital for those guns to be capable of effective anti-aircraft fire.

DESIGN THEORY

These ideas were the basis for the series of destroyers designed by the US Navy from 1930 to 1940, ie from the *Farraguts* to the *Fletchers*. They explain in particular the American insistence upon the 5in/38 DP gun and its elaborate fire control system, and the torpedo tube configuration peculiar to American designs. In fact American estimates of Japanese ideas were not far from being accurate, although they did not appreciate the degree of sophistication that the Japanese would build into their air- and sea-launched torpedoes.

The US Navy was fortunate to have emphasised anti-aircraft fire power over the more conventional concerns then current in, for example, the Royal Navy. The British concept of destroyer operations laid stress on a surface fleet action; destroyer guns were intended to defeat enemy destroyers and so emphasised weight of shell and muzzle velocity, to give a flat trajectory maximising danger space (and therefore the probability of hitting) against rapidly-manoeuvering surface ships. These considerations translated into a long weapon whose recoil would have required a deep pit (or a very tall mount) had it been required to fire at high elevations. US destroyer gun designers, on the other hand, took the high-angle requirement for granted, since the destroyers would assist the battleships they were escorting in breaking up enemy air attacks. In fact, the US 5in/38 had been lengthened from a shorter-barrel AA weapon, the 5in/25, with the aim of improving its *surface* performance; hence the dual-purpose designator. Important considerations in the design of both guns were a high rate of fire secured through the use of ammunition which individual crewmen could handle easily, and light gun weight to secure quick rates of training and elevation. Indeed, the 5in/38 was so biassed towards HA considerations that at the end of the 1930s serious consideration was being given to its replacement by a more surface-orientated weapon, the 5in/54.

On the other hand, US pre-war destroyer designs did not include provision for many automatic AA weapons, partly because the slow development of the 1.1in machine gun made this a moot point for many years. The 5in gun was considered useful for breaking up horizontal bombing formations, and perhaps for dealing with torpedo bombers flying at low level (eg by firing into the water to create splashes); but it was useless as a counter to the two other major airborne threats, the dive bomber and the strafer. Against the latter, most pre-war destroyers were armed with the .5in water-cooled machine gun. The 1.1in weapon was intended to deal with dive bombers, but pre-war destroyers generally limited by treaty to 1500 tons could not accommodate it, the only exceptions being the 1850-ton destroyer 'Leaders'. By 1937 many people in the fleet wanted the 1.1in gun aboard destroyers, but that appeared impossible until the design of the large *Fletchers*. 'Impossible' turned out by 1941 to mean rather 'impossible unless some other weapons were sacrificed', and much of the story recounted here is the story of the variety of 'trade offs' made between traditional destroyer weapons and the weapons required for close range air defence.

Pre-war US strategy also called for anti-submarine armament, which before 1941 was generally restricted to a pair of depth charge tracks and a sonar. After that date depth charge batteries increased to the point of competing with guns for topweight, and a variety of depth charge projectors appeared. However, the Navy did not convert any of its modern destroyers to specialised long-range AS escorts, largely because of the availability of large numbers of destroyer escorts for Atlantic convoy duty.

World War II did not quite correspond to pre-war US concepts; in particular the US destroyer force had been designed for fleet actions rather than for Atlantic AS warfare. Ships assigned to the Atlantic received more complete AS batteries. In addition, some of them were rearmed for AA support of the

Right: The *Farraguts* began the pattern for all US pre-war destroyers of the '1500-ton', '1570-ton' and '1620-ton' classes. Here Destroyer Squadron 20, composed entirely of *Farraguts*, emerges from a smoke-screen laid by aircraft of Patrol Squadrons VP-7, -9, and -11, off San Diego, 14 September 1936, in an exhibition for the Movietone News Company.

Below: USS *Monaghan* (DD354) of the *Farragut* class, at sea, 30 May 1937. Note the absence of depth charge tracks aft. Her bridge shows the usual US pre-war arrangement, a big DP director flanked by a pair of 2.5m navigational rangefinders. The latter represented top hamper which was eliminated soon after the outbreak of war in the Pacific. The *Farraguts* were the last class completed with no blast shields to their torpedo tubes.

Normandy invasion. Pacific fleet AA augmentation, on the other hand, did not come until after the first experiences with Kamikazes in October 1944.

Although the war was so different from pre-war concepts, it is worth noting that the outline idea of the destroyer as an AA quite as much as an anti-destroyer screen unit did prove valid, and in fact US destroyers found few opportunities to employ torpedoes after the destroyer engagements of the Solomons in 1942-43. The last such opportunity was, fittingly, at the last classical fleet action of all, Surigao Strait, on 25 October 1944.

By that time the modern concept of the fleet, in which carriers supplied the strike and much of the defensive power and surface escorts operated in support and as radar and sonar platforms for the carriers, had begun to form. After the war, those destroyers maintained in service gradually lost their torpedoes and, with them, their anti-ship rôle, while their AA and AS batteries became more sophisticated. To some considerable extent new destroyers and frigates were intended as radar pickets, to provide early warning of enemy aircraft and to direct fighters from the carriers. The forerunner of this series was the radar picket destroyer of 1945.

US DESTROYER DEVELOPMENT 1930–45

The present work is concerned with modern US destroyers, a category defined by the long gap between the 'flush deckers' of the World War I programme and the first new ships of the 1930s. Since over 500 ships were built between 1931 and 1945, and since this book is of limited length, no list of names has been provided. Rather, the brief class-by-class notes below include the hull numbers of the ships in each class, and names will be given in cases of special interest.

The United States ended World War I with a fleet of new destroyers so large that the Navy could not hope to obtain any more from Congress, no matter how favourable that body might be to further naval construction. Unfortunately, the large war programme had consisted of ships built to a design frozen in 1916 and somewhat outdated with respect to the contemporary British 'V & W' type, especially in the matter of wetness forward. Moreover, US pre-World War I policy had emphasised battleship construction over that of the kind of cruisers which might have operated in support of destroyers, so that the very large destroyer fleet in service had a desperate need of light cruisers or destroyer 'Leaders'. Neither requirement was fulfilled in the 1920s; the Navy found it easier to convince Congress to pay for capital ships (carriers and battleship refits) and for large 'Treaty cruisers'. Design studies of destroyers and destroyer 'Leaders' were pursued and designs were actually drawn up in 1927-28; they formed the basis for the first new ships, and in fact the discussion of these designs introduced the concept of a DP battery for US destroyers.

At this time US practice was for the General Board, a council of senior Admirals, to draft Characteristics (equivalent to British Staff Requirements) for new ships. The Board, and also the technical Bureaux (Construction and Repair, responsible for ship design; Engineering, for power plants; and Ordnance) were responsible only to the civilian Secretary of the Navy. Actual operations were the province of the Chief of Naval Operations, who was also

Above: USS *Porter* (DD356), lead ship of the series of 1850-ton 'Leaders' designed parallel to the *Farraguts*, on 26 April 1938. Her boxy enclosed directors were single-purpose Mk 35s to control her 5in main battery. Torpedo reload lockers are evident at the base of her second funnel and further aft, and she has depth charges aft.

Below: The second class of 1850-ton 'Leaders' had only a single funnel and three rather than two quadruple torpedo tubes. Here *Jouett* (DD396) is shown at a Naval Review in New York in 1939. Note the absence of reload lockers for her tubes, which had no blast shields in view of their remoteness from the main battery.

responsible for war planning; in his office were the Divisions of War Plans, Fleet Maintenance and Fleet Training. Usually the General Board would hold hearings on proposed Characteristics, asking the divisions of the office of the CNO for comments on their desirability, and the technical Bureaux for comments on feasibility. Towards the end of the 1930s the CNO began to gain more and more influence, and in some cases he was able to override decisions of the General Board. For most of World War II the offices of CNO and Commander-in-Chief, US Fleet (Cominch) were united in the person of Admiral Ernest J King, who was able to dominate much of the ship procurement and modification process; many major developments of the latter part of the war do not appear in General Board records at all. In 1945 a Ship Characteristics Board was formed within the CNO organisation; it took over the supervision of ship modification and then of Characteristics for new construction, edging out the General Board. Thus it was the SCB which codified the emergency AA modifications of 1945, although the General Board had performed a similar task in 1941.

There was no monolithic 'Navy' to decide policy one way or another. Policy was usually, but by no means always, suggested by the General Board and then ratified or rejected by a civilian Secretary who might or might not be particularly well informed on naval matters. Policy papers of this sort were relatively rare before World War II, and therefore their

Above: Probably the best of the 1500-tonners were the sixteen *Mahans*. Here *Downes* (DD375), later destroyed at Pearl Harbour, is shown at sea in 1936. She shows the effects of sea-going experience in the two successive cowls added to her forefunnel. Note also the two machine gun pedestals atop the gun crew shelter just abaft her No 2 gun, with two more less visible aft.

Right: Following the *Mahans*, the US Navy built 22 destroyers with four quadruple torpedo tubes and four 5in guns each: the eight *Bagleys* are representative. Here *Patterson* (DD392) is shown before the war, unfortunately in an undated photograph. Note the enclosed Mk 33 director, in contrast to the open-topped ones in the *Mahans*, and the blast shields on the after banks of torpedo tubes.
By courtesy of A D Baker III

minor details tended to be taken rather seriously. In particular, Characteristics for new designs were assumed, unless specifically modified, to be the Characteristics already approved for the previous class. This meant that some features of earlier ships tended to survive not merely unchanged but, more importantly, unexamined, since there were other changes which the relatively small naval staff considered far more important. One example of interest here may be the survival of a requirement for four reload torpedoes in destroyers after the quadruple tubes had given way to quintuple types.

THE PRE-1936 CLASSES

Perhaps the most important characteristic of pre-war destroyer development was that weapons and ships developed so quickly that there was never very much experience with any one class before the class after next or even the one after that had to be frozen in design and ordered. The sole important exception was the first new class, which most certainly was a reaction to a decade of the problems of the huge fleet of 'flush deckers'.

This *Farragut* class (DD348–355) set the pattern for succeeding pre-war types: five 5in/38 DP guns controlled by a DP director (in this case a Mk 33), and eight torpedo tubes in two quadruple mountings on the centreline. There were also four heavy (.5in) water-cooled AA machine guns, mounted two forward (before the bridge) and two aft (around the searchlight tower) to give all-round fire clear of any fore-and-aft obstacles. AS gear was limited to a sonar and a listening device, although the 'fantail' was strengthened for depth charge tracks. In the interest of weight saving under the 1500-ton limit set by treaty, shields were provided only for Nos 1 and 2 guns; they were considered to be primarily for weather protection.

The *Porter* class (DD356-363) was the first US attempt at a destroyer 'Leader', a category for which the treaty limit was 1850 tons. Although a battery of six single 5in/38 DP guns was initially planned, it proved possible to substitute eight *single-purpose* 5in/38. However, in place of the pairs of machine guns fore and aft these ships had quadruple 1.1in, as well as one .5in, machine guns. They carried only the two quadruple tubes of their destroyer contemporaries, but a hidden feature was eight reload torpedoes stowed amidships.

The *Mahan* class (DD364–379) introduced a high-pressure steam plant, which was to be of great importance in Pacific operations, and a new battery arrangement. During the *Farragut* design process, the Chief of the Bureau of Construction and Repair had observed that in wartime a third torpedo mounting could be substituted for No 5 gun. In effect the *Mahans* achieved this improvement with no sacrifice of gun armament: they substituted a quadruple torpedo tube for the No 3 gun of their predecessors, moving the latter to a shelter deck extended forward, and moving the two waist torpedo tubes from the centreline to either beam to provide the necessary centreline space. Thus the torpedo broadside remained unchanged but there were four reload weapons. Another major armament innovation was the provision of gun crew shelters for the superimposed guns fore and aft, one before the bridge and one atop the shelter deck aft. Each served as the base for two single .5in machine guns. The forward crew shelter was not repeated in later ships in view of the adoption of fully enclosed base-ring mountings; the one aft survived through to the *Bensons*, the last of the pre-war classes. With regard to armament, the significance of the crew shelters lay in their size: it was unnecessary, in ships so fitted, to provide special structures to bring light AA guns and later even twin Bofors clear of the 5in weapons.

In some ways the *Mahans* were the most satisfactory of the 48 US '1500-ton destroyers' completed in 1934-39. Their 5-gun main battery admitted reductions to provide adequate automatic weapons, but the Navy in the Pacific was extremely reluctant to reduce torpedo batteries for this purpose. On the other hand, even so modified, they were far superior to the relatively frail *Farraguts;* in 1945 emergency AA modifications were designed for the *Mahans*, but not for the flimsier *Farraguts* and *Gridleys*.

Right: The *Benson-Livermores* were the ultimate development of the series of US 1500-ton destroyers. Here *Madison* (DD425) is shown off Boston, 6 November 1940. As yet she is unmodified: she has no depth charge projectors, and no Oerlikons or Bofors guns. Her .5in machine guns are barely visible: one, wrapped in a tarpaulin, is just forward of her second funnel, and two more can be seen before her bridge.
By courtesy of A D Baker III

Below: *Anderson* (DD411), second ship of the *Sims* class, on trial. She is complete except for her Mk 37 director. Note her waist torpedo tubes (one of which would later be remounted on the centreline) and uncovered Nos 3 and 4 guns aft.

The basic *Mahan* design was repeated in two more ships, *Dunlap* (DD384) and *Fanning* (DD385), which differed in that they had fully enclosed guns forward and consequently no forward gun crew shelter. At first, the ships up to DD393 had been scheduled as repeat *Mahans*, but in fact while the former class was under construction advocates of the torpedo, who previously had failed to secure adoption of SP guns to provide more weight for torpedoes, became more vocal; it turned out that one of the five DP guns could be exchanged, in effect, for an additional quadruple tube. Developments in torpedo design suggested that in action a destroyer could fire all of her wing tubes at once, using 'curved ahead fire', ie gyros to correct the courses of the torpedoes once they had been fired. In effect, then, a destroyer with four quadruple tubes mounted two on each beam could fire all of them as a single massive salvo.

An additional consideration at this time (March 1935) was the fear that torpedoes fired from centre-line positions, especially elevated ones such as had been adopted in the *Mahans*, might fail to clear a ship's side on launching. Thus came about the series of 22 sixteen-tube destroyers of the *Gridley, Bagley,* and *Benham* classes, interspersed with other types. The four *Gridleys*, built on both coasts by Bethlehem Steel (DD380, 382, 400 and 401) introduced a single-funnel arrangement with immense trunked intakes. They appear to have suffered somewhat from light construction, perhaps adopted in order to

achieve very high speed. The *Bagleys* (DD 386–393), built by Navy Yards, were very similar but apparently more satisfactory. These ships were interspersed with the *Somers* class 'Leaders' (DD 381, 383, and 394–396) in which the two funnels of the *Porters* were trunked into one and the reloads of the earlier ships were replaced by a third quadruple tube. The *Benhams* (DD 397–399 and 402–408) were modified *Bagleys* with less prominent uptakes, reflecting a reduction from four to three boilers. They also had all four guns in base-ring mountings, whereas the earlier ships had had only Nos 1 and 2 so mounted. It is worth noting that all these ships had been designed with very little operational experience of modern destroyers. The *Farraguts* first entered service in 1934-35, and the *Craven* design was essentially approved by the middle of 1935. The former had been built very carefully to conserve weight under treaty limits and the fleet considered them rather flimsy, and at the end of 1935 the Chief of Naval Operations began a general review of destroyer policy, looking towards greater ruggedness, perhaps at the expense of characteristics such as high trial speed which might be more valuable in theory than in practice.

THE POST-1936 CLASSES
While this review was under way a new naval treaty (the 1936 London Treaty) was signed eliminating the former destroyer and 'Leader' sub-categories and substituting a limit of 3000 tons; however, the

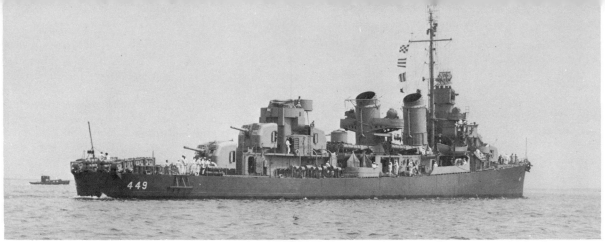

limit on *total* tonnage in this category remained, so that the need for large numbers of destroyers would keep unit displacement in the same 1500-ton range. The same need, incidentally, would cause the Navy to prefer the modification of existing designs to new types which might well require extensive redesign.

The general review reaffirmed the value of five DP guns, especially as the likely opposition would be Japanese destroyers armed with six such weapons. It is interesting in retrospect to note that US experts felt that the Japanese ships would be able to put out only a reduced volume of fire, as their twin mountings would not have twice the rate of fire of single mountings.

The 1935-36 review led to the last cycle of pre-war US destroyer designs, the *Sims* (DD409) and *Benson* (DD421) classes. In the *Sims* class the displacement

limit was raised to 1570 tons and No 5 gun was restored and one torpedo tube mount eliminated in a return to the *Mahan* arrangement (which had only just entered service and so had not yet been tested). No 5 gun, that furthest aft, was shielded for the first time, and another improvement was an actual provision for depth charge racks. Although the torpedo battery appeared to be sharply reduced, the design provided for four reloads which, in the context of US destroyer design and operational doctrine, meant almost no reduction in the effective torpedo battery.

Further weight was expended on general strengthening and on some limited protection against bomb fragments. In consequence the twelve *Sims* class destroyers (DD409–420) turned out decidedly overweight and topheavy – at light displacement the first ships were nearly 120 tons over. The Bureau of Construction and Repair proposed a series of revisions including the elimination of one of the two waist torpedo tube mountings and the relocation of the other to the centreline atop a new deckhouse. Thus the broadside was unchanged; in fact the after tubes could be used in more severe weather. The Secretary of the Navy approved this proposal on 25 September 1939, in time for many of the *Sims* class to be completed to the new standard. Tubes made surplus were installed aboard the new *Atlanta* class light cruisers.

Above: The *Fletchers* were designed to mount a quadruple 1.1in machine gun but only a few were completed with this battery, including USS *Nicholas* (DD449), shown off Boston 15 August 1942. She also had six Oerlikons, two forward and four abeam the after superstructure. Note the early-type depth charge stowage (for side projectors) abaft the latter guns, and the 8-charge depth charge tracks on the 'fantail'.
By courtesy of A D Baker III

Left: There were many variations on the *Fletcher* secondary battery. Here USS *Guest* (DD472) is shown off Boston Navy Yard on 5 February 1943, with two twin Bofors amidships in what was soon to become a standard arrangement, but none in the raised superstructure aft. She carries an SC-2 air-search radar without the integral IFF panel that was later standard, and on her yardarm she carries an early model ('stovepipe') IFF and the TBS tactical voice radio. She also has the standard US SG surface-search centrimetric radar.
By courtesy of A D Baker III

This did not end the problems of the *Sims* class. Their design was not well suited to the North Atlantic, which in 1940 was increasingly the ocean of greatest concern to the US Navy. The last ship in the class, USS *Buck*, ran her trials in December 1940 and experienced severe icing on Nos 3 and 4 guns. This inspired BuOrd to design a half-gunhouse for the 5in/38, the top of which could be closed with canvas so that it resembled the more usual fully enclosed type. Such mountings provided shelter without the topweight penalty of the gunhouse; they appeared in the raised after positions of the *Sims* and succeeding *Benson-Livermore* types. During wartime some of the earlier *Benhams* had half their tubes removed and their two after guns enclosed, No 3 in a half-shield and No 4 in a full gunhouse.

As the *Sims* class was being built, the next class

was well in hand. It began as an enlarged *Sims:* new boilers had made it possible for Construction and Repair to adopt a unit machinery arrangement, reflected visually by a switch from one to two widely separated funnels. Four boilers replaced the previous three; the less compact machinery required a longer hull, and additional weight could also be provided for greater strength. Late in 1938 the new class was envisaged as a 1620-tonner with three quadruple torpedo tubes, as in the *Sims;* in fact the main improvement to the battery would be a pair of bulwarks to shield the waist tubes. The latter became characteristic of US destroyers built or modified during World War II; but the 1620-ton class did not repeat the *Sims* tube arrangement. One important reason why was the accumulating Fleet experience of corrosion and sea damage to waist

tubes; sentiment began to favour the high tube location which had been so severely criticised in the *Mahans*. The General Board was willing to return to an 8-tube centreline arrangement in view of the existence of 22 units with sixteen tubes each. In fact even this sacrifice proved unnecessary: BuOrd developed a new quintuple mount, which increased broadside fire by a quarter. It is interesting that the new 10-tube destroyers were still required to carry four rather than five reloads.

The resulting *Benson-Livermore* or 1620-ton type was the ultimate development of the pre-war destroyer design cycle. It had the five guns specified in 1936, as well as ten tubes and depth charge racks; it had even been possible to increase the light AA battery to six .5in machine guns. DD421–444 were ordered under the 1937–39 programmes, after which production was to have ceased in favour of the much more powerful *Fletcher* class; thus the last units were to have been DD453–464, ordered in mid-1940. However, production continued, largely as a means of keeping up destroyer deliveries: DD483–497, 598–628, 632–641, and 645–648 were all ordered during Fiscal Year 1941 (1 July 1940 – 30 June 1941); and it was nearly decided to keep building 1620-ton destroyers even during Fiscal Year 1942 as specialised 'sea control' types.

Top: *Charles Ausburn* (DD570) refitted at Mare Island, 27 September 1944. Alterations are circled: two twin Bofors forward, with Mk 51 directors atop the pilot house to control them, and an ECM mast aft surmounted by an SPR-2 radar intercept receiver.

Above: Three *Fletchers* were completed with catapults to carry aircraft. Here *Halford* (DD480) is shown off Point Jefferson, Washington, on 24 April 1943. Note that she has one Oerlikon atop her pilot house and another before it, on the centreline. This was a very common installation in *Fletchers* with closed bridges.

Left: Most *Fletchers* ended the war with two twin Bofors before their bridges, for a total of five such mountings. Here *Harrison* (DD573) passes mail, 5 March 1935. Note the pair of Mk 51 directors added on the pilot house roof to control these two mountings. In addition, *Harrison* shows ECM gear on a stub mainmast aft, including the dipoles of the SPR-2 intercept receiver. Her Mk 37 DP director carries the Mk 12 fire-control radar and, alongside it, the 'orange peel' of the Mk 22 used against low-flying aircraft. This was a standard modification towards the end of the war, but could not be accommodated on Mk 33 directors, nor on some Mk 37s.

By courtesy of Norman Polmar

There were actually two series: *Benson* (DD421–428, 459, 460, 491, 492 and 598–617) built to Bethlehem Steel plans and characterised by flat-sided funnels; and *Livermore* (DD429-444, 453-458, 461-464, 483-497, 618-641 and 645-648) designed by Gibbs & Cox, with round funnels and officially ten tons heavier. In fact the prototype *Livermores*, DD423 and 424, were always listed as *Bensons*. Two unofficial distinctions were far more important. From USS *Bristol* (DD453) onwards, all were designed for five rather than ten torpedo tubes and four 5in guns; the weight thus saved went into depth charges. Thus DD453 (or 453 and 459) were the lead ships of a significant sub-class. In addition, during 1941, the Navy ordered the elimination of unnecessary curves in superstructures as a time-saver in production: all ten ships built at Seattle-Tacoma (DD493–497 and 624–628), and the last ten (DD618–623 and 645–648) built by Federal at Kearny thus had square-faced bridges with directors atop their pilot houses rather than atop pedestals. DD645–648 had their 40mm tubs staggered and no 20mm mounted at the fore end of their pilot houses.

The first series of *Benson-Livermores* was completed with the original battery of five guns and ten tubes, but repeat ships were affected by the AA improvement programme. As in other classes, it was deemed preferable to eliminate one out of five guns rather than one out of two banks of tubes; two multiple machine guns could be fitted in its stead. Elimination of the six .5s and of four reload torpedoes would permit the installation of two twin Bofors with directors and four Oerlikons. This was at the end of 1941; AS improvements decided upon in August eliminated the after bank of tubes in favour of one Y-gun (with ten 300lb charges) and depth charge track extensions to take a total of twenty-four 600lb charges (with stowage for seventeen more), as well as improved splinter protection, degaussing and radar. This decision prompted the General Board to suggest that it would be wise to distinguish between fleet destroyers and destroyers for sea control, ie to fight submarines, aircraft and surface raiders. The *Bensons* could be reserved for the latter rôle, with a depth charge battery of thirty 600lb charges and thirty-two 300lb in eight (later reduced to six) K-guns. In fact the removal of No 4 gun would permit a *Benson* to carry eighty 300lb charges. This option, which at one time was intended to be applied to nearly all DD453s, was dropped only in January 1943. The twin Bofors, as it happened, was not available until late in 1942, and actual batteries are described in Chapter 3.

If the *Bensons* were to be relegated to sea control, the fleet would be screened by a new class: the big

Fletcher. In layout the latter followed its predecessor, with three 5in guns aft, the two high mountings without shields but with a crew shelter between them. However, the two .5s carried aft atop the crew shelter in a *Benson* were replaced by a 1.1in machine gun. Early in 1941, following the *Buck* trials, the after superfiring 5in guns were enclosed (weight prohibited more than a half-shield in a *Benson*, although these ships did get full gunhouses upon surrendering one of their two high weapons). The earliest units were completed with the 1.1in gun, but quite soon the approved battery was one twin Bofors there and four Oerlikons in place of the .5s. Most early-completion *Fletchers* which did receive Bofors also had a twin mounting at the extreme stern.

New Characteristics of May 1942 added another Bofors on the 'fantail'; weight compensation was to include the removal of the four reload torpedoes and the lowering of the 5in director 'where possible'. In fact the latter change was coupled with the provision of a new open bridge more suitable to air action. Meanwhile more Oerlikons were mounted, particularly in the forward sector: many closed-bridge ships had one atop the pilot house and one raised in front of it, together with the two mounted either side of the shelter deck. The waist guns were doubled in number.

Early in 1943 the approved ultimate *Fletcher* battery included three twin Bofors: two abreast the second funnel and one aft. Three Oerlikons would be mounted on the 'fantail' – not many ships had been completed with a second Bofors there. Ships

with the closed bridge would now mount eleven Oerlikons and ships with an open one ten (the pilot house top could not be used owing to blast). Even this was not enough. In April the assigned battery was briefly set at four twin Bofors, the 'fantail' position having been restored, but in June it was revised once more, the 'fantail' position finally eliminated, and two twin Bofors replacing all of the forward Oerlikons, for a total of five (and seven Oerlikons), a battery which remained until 1945. This modification was coupled with the installation of a CIC. Many later *Fletchers* were completed to the 5-Bofors standard.

This expansion in AA battery could not be carried out without cost. In November 1941 the *Fletchers* were intended to carry two 5-charge depth charge tracks as well as four projectors, with ten 600lb and eight 300lb charges. In December two more projectors were added. Not long afterwards the standard was set at two 7-charge tracks and four projectors (five 300lb charges each), with an additional eight 600lb and sixteen 300lb charges in the torpedo warhead locker. Unfortunately, the warhead locker was needed for automatic weapons ammunition; the *Fletchers* could not have any depth charge stowage below decks. However, in that case they could lay only four patterns (less one 600lb charge), whereas the standard requirement was for five. The ultimate solution was special stowage racks on the 'fantail'.

Out of over 200 destroyers ordered in the second half of 1942, 119 were *Fletchers*: DD445–451, 465–481, 498–502, 507–597 (of which 523–525, 542, 543 and 548–549 were cancelled on 16 December

1940), 629–631 and 642–644. The gaps are repeat *Bensons* and abortive experimental types (DD452, 482 and 503–506). The squared-off open bridge was introduced in some late-production ships, probably DD518–522, 526–541, 544–547, 554–568, 581–591, 594–597 and 629–644. It was also incorporated in 56 repeat *Fletchers* ordered under the Fiscal Year 1942 programme: DD649–691 and 792–804.

Six units (DD476 481) were to be modified to carry a catapult in place of No 3 gun and No 2 bank of torpedo tubes; three, DD477, 479 and 480, were actually so fitted. They mounted one twin Bofors on the 'fantail' and a complete outfit of Oerlikons – eight guns, four of them forward. Operational experience with the catapult was disappointing: the equipment was landed in October 1943 and the remaining three conversions were cancelled. For a time the three converted ships had only two Oerlikons on the shelter deck between Nos 3 and 4 guns, a modification adopted in order to reduce the workload on West Coast shipyards.

Even the *Fletchers* were not entirely satisfactory. In the autumn of 1941 BuShips began work on a new destroyer to take advantage of the twin enclosed 5in/38 DP mounting already in production for capital ships and cruisers. One important advantage of the twin mounting was that it freed deck space for light AA weapons – structures such as torpedo tubes could be spread out along the deck for greater survivability. This *Sumner* class design, adopted in April 1942, had one other important armament feature: the after twin 5in mounting could fire quite close to the bow, so that on most bearings ahead fire was six rather than four guns. Seventy were built. Out of the series DD692–808 ordered on 7 August 1942, DD692–709, 722–741, 744–762 and 770–781 were completed as *Sumners*. Most of the others were modified during construction and emerged as *Gearings* (see below); in addition DD857 (USS *Bristol*) was completed as a *Sumner*.

The *Sumners* emerged with extremely heavy AA batteries, the result of a long evolution in the design stage. They began with two twin Bofors between their torpedo tubes, as well as four Oerlikons forward, but in March 1943 two twins were added on raised positions abreast the forefunnel. Two Oerlikons were added on a raised platform around the second funnel, three on the 'fantail' and two more on the shelter deck abreast the after twin Bofors. In April DesPac asked urgently for six rather than four twin Bofors; instead in May the amidships twin mountings were replaced by quadruples, for a total of twelve 40mm and eleven Oerlikons. The March revisions also included the provision of a pair of 5-charge (600lb) storage racks on the 'fantail', between the main depth charge tracks. The only other major development in this class was in the bridge, which had begun as a British type with an enclosed pilot house forward of the open bridge. A sonar hut built out from the pilot house restricted athwartships movement on the bridge and was severely criticised when the ships began to enter service. All were modified to the more familiar configuration, based on the *Fletcher* open bridge, but not before Destroyer Division 119 had served in the Normandy invasion.

The new destroyers were overweight and their speed and endurance were somewhat disappointing, but any fundamental change in design would have been impossible. The quick solution was the insertion of 14ft of extra length (for speed and fuel tankage) amidships, to produce the 'long hull' *Sumner* or *Gearing*, the ultimate US wartime destroyer. Of 152 ordered, including 36 planned for 1945 (DD891–926), 93 were completed: DD710 (*Gearing*)–718, 742, 743, 763–769, 782–790, 805–808, 817–823, 826, 828–853 and 858–890. In addition DD719, 824, 825 and 827 were completed after the war as the prototypes of a new generation of AS ships; five others were retained unfinished for over a decade after the war and their completion was frequently considered. DD828, *Timmerman*, though nominally a *Gearing*, was actually a test ship for new propulsion machinery.

DESTROYER EMPLOYMENT 1941–45

The realities of US destroyer operations in World War II did not quite match pre-war expectations. In the brief notes which follow, the reader should keep in mind the existence of a substantial force of 'flush deckers' left over from the First World War build-

All *Sumners* were refitted with an open bridge based on that of the later *Fletchers*. Here is *Laffey* (DD724), as refitted after she returned from service off Normandy. She has both banks of quintuple torpedo tubes, as well as pairs of single Oerlikons forward and amidships (including one abreast her after quadruple Bofors).

ing programme and used largely as AS escorts; they do not figure in the present account.

Throughout the war US destroyers were generally organised in 9-ship Squadrons ('Desrons') consisting of a 'Leader' and two 4-ship Divisions ('Desdivs'); the 'Leader' or flagship was considered one of a 5-ship Desdiv. In 1939 all modern destroyers were concentrated with the US Fleet, the main fleet in the Pacific. At this time there were not enough modern destroyers to absorb all of the 1850-ton 'Leaders'; seven of them formed Desron Nine, with *Moffett* as flagship. Subsequent US practice appears not to have been to build specialised 'Leaders', and it is not clear whether particular destroyers were used consistently as Squadron and Division Flagships. On the other hand, an examination of Atlantic and Pacific Fleet organisation tables suggests that Desdiv membership was fairly stable through the war.

With the outbreak of war in Europe, the US government declared a wide Neutral Zone in the Western Atlantic, and began to move warships into the area to enforce it. At the same time interest in AS and cold-weather operations increased, and Atlantic destroyers were specially modified. New destroyers were assigned to the Atlantic Fleet. Thus in January 1941 the Atlantic Fleet included 5 Divisions of modern destroyers: DD362 and 394 as 'Leaders', plus DD402–404, 409, 410, 414–416, and the whole of the new *Benson-Livermore* class. By June all of the *Sims* and all but two (DD397 and 398) of the *Benham*s had joined; and there were eight 'Leaders' (DD358, 359, 362, 363, 381, 383, 395 and 396) formed into two Desdivs. All of the 1500- and 1620-ton Atlantic destroyers were scheduled for AS modifications, including the installation of Y-guns; but the battle fleet ships were scheduled only for the installation of a pair of 5-charge DC racks aft.

Matters began to change after Pearl Harbor. None of the older modern destroyers was transferred out of the Pacific, and many of the *Sims* and *Benham* class ships went back, leaving only DD402–405 and 418–420 in the Atlantic. However, new *Benson*s, even those from Pacific yards, con-

tinued to be assigned to the Atlantic Fleet; no more than nineteen (DD459, 460, 483–488, 598, 599, 602, 605–608 and 628–631) served only in the Pacific. One Desdiv – DD609–612, built by Bethlehem – went to the Atlantic after shakedown but was released to the Pacific in the autumn of 1943 as new DEs joined the Atlantic Fleet. Two Atlantic Desdivs, DD418, 441–443 and 645–647 went to the Pacific in January 1944. Remaining *Benson*s went to the Pacific in 1945 either as fast minesweepers or as destroyers; in July 1945 there remained only *Nields* (DD616) on detached duty and one Desdiv (DD613–615). Of the 'Leaders', five spent the entire war in the Atlantic: DD359, 362, 381, 395 and 396. In fact DD358 was the last to be detached to the Pacific, in September 1942. Nearly all of the newer destroyers served only in the Pacific. There were two exceptions: Desdiv 119 (DD722–726) fought at Normandy, and *Capps* (DD550) was temporarily attached to Desdiv 20 for a raid with the British Home Fleet (and USS *Ranger* and *Tuscaloosa*) in Norwegian waters in October 1943.

The 13 pre-war 'Leaders' were a special case, as their lack of a DP armament made them less than ideal screening units for the air-sea war of the fast task forces. Pacific 'Leaders' fought at Midway and then at Guadalcanal (where *Porter* was sunk), but by 1943 four (DD 361, 358, 383 and 394) had been assigned to Balboa in the Canal Zone as convoy escorts, seeing action only when they brought convoys into combat areas. However, even though they retained their SP batteries, three (DD357, 360 and 363) fought with the main fleet at Attu and the Marianas. Plans had been drawn up for extensive AA refits as early as 1942, but only six ships were ever modified: DD357 and 360 at Charleston just

before joining the Atlantic Fleet in the autumn of 1944, DD358 and 359 in 1945; and of the *Somers* class only two Atlantic units, DD395 and 396, were ever done. The other units at Balboa had been scheduled for conversion, but their transfer to the Atlantic took precedence: they were required to replace the large *Bibb* class Coast Guard cutters as convoy flagships; the cutters themselves were required for conversion to amphibious flagships. Thus by the end of 1944 all 11 surviving 'Leaders' were serving with the Atlantic Fleet.

There was one other interesting case. The 4 *Gridleys* (DD380, 383, 400 and 401) appear to have been too unstable to accommodate even one twin Bofors gun. In the spring of 1945, then, as the fleet as a whole received AA rearmament for employment near Japan, they were detached as a Desdiv for the Atlantic Fleet, and in fact two banks of torpedo tubes were removed. Of all other Pacific types, only the *Farraguts* had no approved rearmament plan, but it is not certain that this was a matter of their inadequacy. They were being considered for subsidiary duties at the end of the war.

Gearing was the name ship for the 'long-hull' destroyers, although she was not the first ship completed. Here she is shown on 21 May 1945, with her second bank of torpedo tubes removed, but no quadruple Bofors as yet mounted in its place. Note also that her single Oerlikons have not been replaced by twin mountings.
By courtesy of Norman Polmar

10. Weapons & Sensors

One remarkable feature of US destroyer armament of the Second World War was the degree of standarisation achieved. The 5in/38 served throughout the war, and all three major variations – the pedestal mount, the base-ring, and the DP twin – were in production before the outbreak of war in Europe. Of the light weapons, the two major pre-war types, the 1.1in and the .5in machine guns, were superseded by only two wartime types, the twin Bofors and the single Oerlikon. Even the principal variation on the Bofors, the quadruple mount, was little more than two twins joined together. This situation stands in great contrast to the British experience. The reasons for the success of the US probably include a greater willingness to enforce standardisation in the interest of a high rate of production and the success of the pre-war US concept of future naval warfare already described – in particular there was no urgent need for powerful AA weapons, as the original main batteries of the ships sufficed. Finally, in selecting the Bofors and the Oerlikon, the US Navy had the advantages both of British experience and of an additional period of peacetime in which to try to achieve some degree of sophistication.

ARMAMENT

The need for three distinct AA weapons, the 5in gun and a heavy and a light AA automatic weapon, can best be explained in terms of evolving air threat. In the 1930s the air threat was understood to have four components: level bombers (probably operating in formation at relatively high altitudes), dive bombers, strafers and low level torpedo planes. The level bombers required careful aim, and their approach could be upset if the sky near them were filled with shell bursts. This task could best be accomplished a long range weapon firing time-fuzed shells, and US DP fire control systems were designed with such targets in mind. Gun mountings (in base-ring installations and with ammunition hoists) were designed with fuze-setters.

The primary US destroyer gun of World War II was the 5in/38, here shown in a half-shielded mounting aboard the destroyer *Kearny* (DD432) at Reykjavik, Iceland, October 1941. To the right is visible the .5in machine gun, which vanished from US service with the widespread introduction of Oerlikons early in 1942.

Dive bombers were a far more difficult problem as a rapidly diving aircraft might be impossible for a gun to follow, or, for that matter, for a fire control computer to adjust to. Indeed, the US Navy adopted dive bombing as its principal anti-ship weapon in the 1930s on exactly this theory. At the time the best counter appeared to be a heavy automatic gun which could hose down the approach path of the bomber; its contact-fuzed shells would probably score a few hits, and if they were made far enough from the ship they would disable the bomber in time. However, if the bomber were hit too close to the ship, it would continue downwards and complete its mission, albeit, perhaps, with a dead pilot. This consideration was of particular consequence during Kamikaze attacks: although a dive bomber pilot might well pull up if he experienced too dense a barrage, a Kamikaze would continue to dive until his aircraft broke up.

Strafers were best engaged at short range: a weapon with a range roughly equivalent to that of the strafer's guns would suffice. Since strafing was understood to be a menace to warships long before dive bombing was well known, work on anti-strafing guns began earlier and these weapons appeared as early as the mid-1930s as .5in water-cooled machine guns.

Finally, the torpedo bomber had to approach fairly close at very low altitude. From the gun's point of view such a bomber was not so very different from a destroyer approaching to fire torpedoes; clearly it could be attacked by anti-ship weapons. The favoured tactic before World War II was to fire into the water to create shell splashes which might disable an approaching bomber. Clearly this required no more than the low-angle use of any standard destroyer gun.

Of the weapons evolved to meet these perceived threats, the 5in/38 has been described in considerable detail elsewhere (see *Warship 7* pp 171-177). The major wartime changes were increases in the ammunition supply aboard ship and the provision, from 1942 onwards, of proximity (VT) fuzes. The latter contained miniature radar sets,which could detonate a shell when it approached to within a lethal distance of its target. Such shells required no fuze time-setting (hence the variable time, or VT, designator) and so could tolerate fairly inaccurate fire control situations. Moreover, they could often kill targets which more conventional shells would merely dissuade. By the end of the war, with the Kamikazes the main air menace, the major problem of VT fuzes was that they became active too far from a ship and so could not kill aircraft very close by.

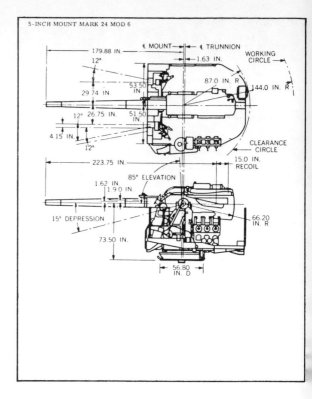

5-INCH MOUNT MARK 24 MOD 6

AMMUNITION

Prior to World War II, the standard ammunition capacity for modern destroyers was 300 rounds per gun of AA Common (Common in 'Leaders' with single-purpose guns) plus 200 rounds per ship of illuminating ammunition; 100 rounds of AA Common per gun and 100 rounds of illuminating ammunition were to be carried in peacetime. Mobilisation supplies were to be carried aboard tenders. Unfortunately the tenders had very limited capacities, and in April 1937 the CNO increased the allowance to 150 rounds of AA Common per gun. As ammunition figured in the standard displacement regulated by treaty, it was necessary for the CNO and the Secretary of the Navy to use fairly tortuous logic to add these rounds without exceeding stated displacements. In the end Admiral Leahy, as Acting Secretary, observed that the additional rounds were merely intended to reduce the load on destroyer tenders, and so were not for carriage in peacetime; they could not therefore affect the standard displacement.

Right: No 4 5in mounting of *Rhind* (DD404), New York Navy Yard, 3 March 1944. Note her SC-1 air-search radar. The stovepipe-shaped object on one yardarm is an early form of the US IFF antenna; TBS is on the other.

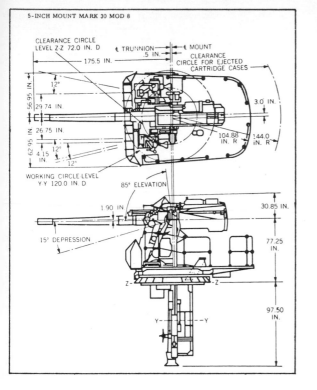

5-INCH MOUNT MARK 30 MOD 8

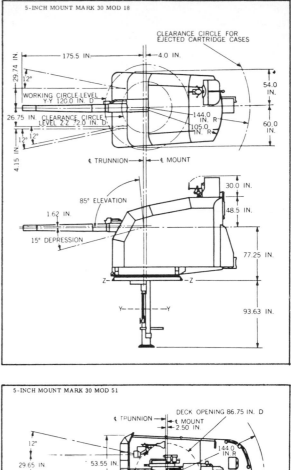

5-INCH MOUNT MARK 30 MOD 18

5-INCH MOUNT MARK 30 MOD 51

Ammunition capacities rose beyond the pre-war requirements in ships built just before and during the war. Thus the *Benson-Livermores* could carry 1800 rounds and the *Fletchers* and *Summers* were designed for 2100. In fact one reason the *Fletchers* could not make their originally required speed of 38kts on trial was that before they were completed the standard for trial speed changed from one with standard displacement ammunition aboard to one with full mobilisation supply on board.

Ammunition capacities increased still more in wartime. Thus a typical late *Fletcher, Van Valkenburgh,* inclined in July 1944, had 2775 (525 per gun) rounds in magazines, plus 250 in ready-service stowage. The minelayer *Fraser,* typical of *Sumner-Gearings,* had 300 rounds of ready-service and 48 of ready-service illuminating shell, plus 2110 of 5in Common and 292 of 5in illuminating shell in her magazines. Such increases in ammunition borne in wartime were a major factor in the sea-going behaviour of US destroyers, but they are generally ignored.

Pre-war destroyers could accommodate no such increases. For example in 1944 *Aylwin* (DD355) had about 1000 rounds in magazines for her four guns, plus 50 rounds per gun in ready-service stowage. *Craven* (DD382) could accommodate only 40 rounds per gun of ready-service ammunition, but she had magazine stowage for 1225 rounds and 230 of illuminating shell. The relatively tender ex-'Leader' *Selfridge,* rebuilt at Mare Island, ended up with only 214 rounds of ready-service and 1312 of magazine 5in, as well a 22 rounds of ready-service and 85 of magazine illuminating shell.

The ration of 50 ready-service rounds per 5in gun was fairly general, and it was carried in boxes near pedestal-mounted guns or in the upper handling rooms of base-ring mounts.

5IN FIRE CONTROL SYSTEMS

Essential to the success of the DP-armed destroyer was a DP fire control system. The first American efforts in this direction produced the Mk 19 and then the turret-like Mk 28; the latter appeared aboard some cruisers, as well as in the reconstructed *New Mexico* class battleships. It employed a manual drive, and contained its own stereo rangefinder, range keeper (computer), and stable element; the operators fed target data into the computer by keeping the rangefinder on target. The Mk 33 was developed specifically for the new destroyers, and incorporated a power drive to permit it to track targets despite the liveliness of its platform. Late models raised its target speed limit from 275 to 320kts, and incorporated a 'dive attack' feature to control fire against a target diving at up to 400kts.

Prewar Mk 33s were open on top, but wartime modifications included provision for a complete weather shield and radar. However, the Mk 33 was never completely satisfactory. It was difficult to add weight without unbalancing its rotating structure, and its computer was too slow, both in initial solution and in accommodating a manoeuvering target.

The Mk 33 could accommodate the early US Mk 4 DP fire control radar, but it could not carry the increased weight of the Mk 12 (and certainly not that of the Mk 22 which generally accompanied the Mk 12): by the end of the war almost all Mk 4s had, therefore, been replaced instead by the dish of the Mk 28. The Mk 35 was a specialised SP director for the 1850-ton 'Leaders'. Units modernised with DP guns surrendered their MK 35s for Mk 37s and the surplus directors were converted to 8in ballistics and

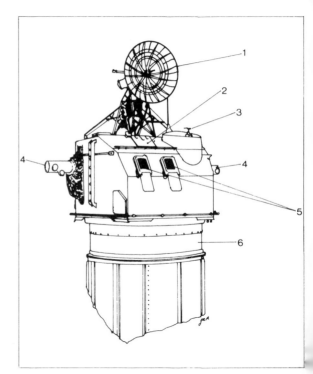

MK 37 DIRECTOR (EXTERNAL VIEW)

1 Radar aerial (post-war radar Mk 25)
2 Observation hatch (closed)
3 Slewing sight
4 15ft stereo rangefinder
5 Telescope ports
6 Barbette

installed in heavy cruisers. The Mk 37 was the culmination of pre-war fire control design. Work began in 1936, and the first unit was ready for testing in 1939. For the first time the stable element and computer were moved below decks, connected by wiring to a compact turret-like mounting which carried optical equipment and operators. For the first time the computing mechanism was designated a computer rather than a range-keeper; it could accommodate 400kts horizontal or 250kts vertical speed, which sufficed until the advent of the Baka bomb late in the war. The computer Mk 1 incorporated a fully automatic rate control. Wartime improvements in the aloft director included a slewing sight, by means of which the Director Officer could slew very rapidly to his selected target, tracking it after getting on, until the pointer and trainer could take over.

The Mk 37 design incorporated provision for radar, reflected in its clear flat top and its tall barbette, to bring an antenna well clear of the deck. Beginning in 1941, Mk 37s were fitted with the Mk 4 DP fire control radar; later Mk 12/22 was fitted in many ships. Some installations could not take the weight of this system and were fitted with the single dish of Mk 28 instead; in other cases Mk 28 was fitted to save weight for emergency armament installations in 1945. The Mk 37 made unusual demands of below-decks space for its plotting room (stable element plus computer) and required a somewhat larger hull than the original 1500-tonner; it was introduced in the enlarged Sims class. Of the earlier ships, only the rebuilt 'Leaders' and the rebuilt *Cassin* and *Downes* received it.

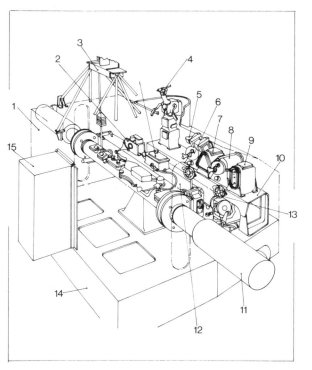

MK 37 DIRECTOR (INTERNAL VIEW)

1   Shield
2   Range spot transmitter
3   Radar antenna mounting
4   Slewing sight
5   Radar elevation indicator
6   Telescope
7   Elevation indicator
8   Telescope
9   Train indicator
10 Optical box shelf
11 Rangefinder
12 Rangefinder beam
13 Port closure handwheel
14 Carriage weldment
15 Blister for amplifier power assembly

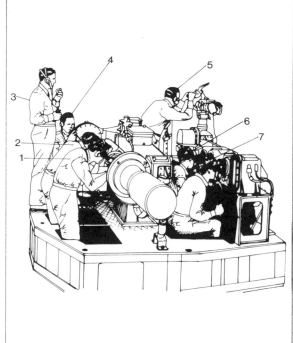

CREW POSITIONS IN A MK 37 DIRECTOR

1   Range talker
2   Rangefinder operator
3   Illumination control officer
4   Talker
5   Control officer
6   Pointer
7   Trainer

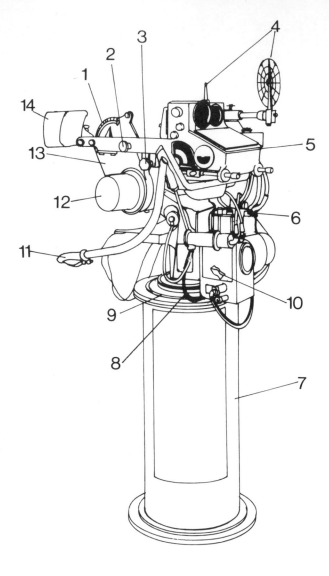

MK 51 DIRECTOR

1 Elevation scale
2 Elevation lock pin
3 Range setting knob
4 Peep and ring sight
5 Mk 14 gun sight
6 Power unit
7 Pedestal
8 Ships supply cable to power unit
9 Train scale
10 On-Off switch
11 Right handle with firing key
12 Transmitter
13 Gear case
14 Counter weight

Of wartime director designs, the Mk 51 designed at first for 40mm control was also used for close-in control of 5in guns; for example the after Mk 51 of *Sumner/Gearings* with after quadruple Bofors guns

could also control their after twin 5in mount, and some ships which did not receive the FRAM modernisation did retain this director even after their Bofors were removed. During the war a new Mk 56 director was developed for 3in fire control; it was first tested aboard the experimental destroyer *Winslow* just after the war, and was very widely used post-war for 3in control in modernised destroyers. It was the main fire control of the converted DDE825 and 827, whose main battery was 3in guns, and it was retained when these two ships were rearmed with 5in guns under the FRAM programme.

AUTOMATIC WEAPONS

Of the four main US wartime automatic AA weapons, the .5in machine gun dated from soon after World War I. It was intended as an anti-strafer weapon and by the late 1920s was already considered somewhat inadequate. By the summer of 1940 it was no longer acceptable even where the 1.1in could not be mounted, and the Navy began to move towards the classic Oerlikon.

However, the .5in had been ripe for replacement long before that. The Bureau of Ordnance convened a special Board to plan for a machine gun of 1in or greater calibre in October 1928, and the result was the unfortunate quadruple 1.1. Design began in March 1929 and tests were run on initial models from March to May 1931. By 1933 a rate of fire of 140 rounds per minute had been attained, and the gun was turned over to the Naval Gun Factory for production. A quadruple mounting was adopted in order to match the rate of fire of the .5 – 550 to 600 rounds per minute – and the mounting incorporated a third axis of rotation as there was a strong feeling that a technique of vertical dive bombing would be developed and mountings with only two axes would not be able to cope. The first mounting appeared in April 1935. It was extremely elaborate, being power-operated in view of the weights of its parts. Despite incomplete testing, it was rushed into production – and its complexity caused numerous problems. For example, the complicated traverse was often locked out.

In service the 1.1in gun received mixed reviews. At first it earned a bad reputation for unreliability, but by the end of the war it was well enough liked as a gun. However, its shell was far too small to stop attacking aircraft. A DE commander wrote in 1945 that in spite of its high rate of fire it had neither the range nor the stopping power of the Bofors. Moreover its power 'has been erratic and at times dangerous, necessitating an inordinate amount of overhaul by ship's force to be kept in even fair operating condition'.

Thus in 1940 both standard US automatic

weapons were considered unsatisfactory. Several foreign weapons were available: both the 20mm Oerlikon and the 40mm Bofors had established a considerable reputation in the Spanish Civil War, and hence both were obvious candidates as replacements. Ironically, both guns had benefited from the efforts of the Axis powers. The Navy rejected a Model 1934 Oerlikon in 1935 in view of its low muzzle velocity and low rate of fire (265 rounds per minute); but the Japanese Navy adopted it, and so saved the Oerlikon Company from bankruptcy, while permitting it to make the improvements which made the gun so effective in British and American hands a few years later. The great selling point of the Oerlikon was that it required no external power supply, and so could be bolted down in any available deck space; the Royal Navy adopted it as armament for merchant ships, suitable for use by non-specialists. The US decision was affected by excellent reports, in the autumn of 1940, from the Royal Navy, and its installation aboard US warships began late the next year.

At first the Fleet's reaction was extremely enthusiastic, and an analysis of Pacific Fleet kills between Pearl Harbor and September 1944 showed the Oerlikon to be responsible for 32% of all identifiable ones. However, after that date ranges increased, the Japanese shifted to night attacks, and heavier Bofors batteries and improved VT-fuzed 5in guns began to increase their share of kills. Thus, whereas in the second half of 1942 the Oerlikons had accounted for 48.3% of aircraft shot down, in 1944 they were down to 25% and the Fleet was asking for more Bofors guns and fewer Oerlikons.

Above and overleaf: The two primary US 5in fire control systems were the Mk 37 and the Mk 33. Here a Mk 37 is shown aboard *C K Bronson* (DD668) on 17 June 1945; it carries on its roof the large Mk 12 DP fire control radar, flanked by the 'orange peel' of Mk 22, which was effective against low flying aircraft by virtue of its narrow beam. The object on the front of the director is the slewing sight; many Mk 37s were built with bulges on their forward faces to accommodate it. The open-topped Mk 33, shown overleaf on USS *Mahan* (DD364) on her refit to mount Bofors guns (24 June 1944, at Mare Island), carries the dish of Mk 28 radar. Note the rangefinder at the fore end of the director; most of the rest of it is taken up by the mechanical computer ('range keeper') and the stable element. As in open-topped British directors, there was a weather cover, indicated here in the framework surrounding the director.

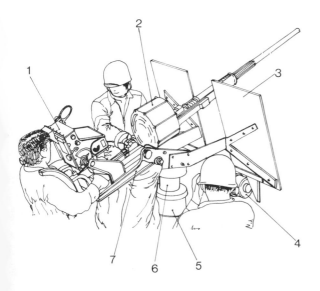

20MM OERLIKON

1   Mk 14 gun sight
2   Magazine
3   Shield
4   Power unit
5   Pedestal
6   Raising column
7   Cradle

The Bureau of Ordnance continued to favour the Oerlikon, citing its high rate of fire (450 rounds per minute) and its value as a free-swinging weapon which could be brought into action at very short notice and independently of shipboard power systems. Even though the Oerlikon had a short range it could still destroy enemy aircraft flying over a ship after they had dropped their weapons, and so keep them from fighting another day. The Fleet disagreed. In May 1945 the Commanding Officer of USS *O'Brien* (DD725) 'after experience with suicide attacks at Leyte, Ormoc, Mindoro, Lingayen and Okinawa advocated heavy continuous fire as the ship's best defence and recommended replacing 20mm with 40mm guns. He reported that the 20mm had a negative psychological value, the saying the crew being, "When the 20mm opens fire, it's time to hit the deck".' The SCB report containing this anecdote continued that 'a recent DD action report reported that 20mm fire was a signal to the engine room to shut down the blowers to keep the flash of the explosion from the suicide hit being drawn down into the machinery spaces. This worked successfully'.

As the Bureau of Ordnance wanted to retain at least some free-swinging unpowered automatic weapons in the face of the Fleet's desire for more Bofors guns, it began the development of a twin Oerlikon early in 1944, the first mounting being completed and tested by the September. Most late war rearmament plans therefore called for the replacement of single by twin Oerlikons, and twin mountings remained with the Fleet well after the war.

The other major wartime automatic AA gun was the 40mm Bofors, which had begun life as a Krupp design shortly after 1918. In 1940 the Navy Department AA Board was worried that the 1.1in gun was too light to bridge the gap between itself and the 5in, yet too heavy to function as a last-ditch free mounting. The Board considered the lack of a close range AA gun 'the most serious weakness in the readiness of the Navy for war' and recommended immediate increases in 1.1in production as well as an effort to procure another more effective weapon. That was the twin Bofors. The Bureau of Ordnance bought one, which arrived in New York at the end of August 1940.

The standard Navy twin Bofors was a water-cooled power-driven weapon requiring a director and rather elaborate wiring; its installation was a shipyard job. The first example was mounted aboard the destroyer *Coghlan* (DD606) on 1 July 1942. As noted elsewhere, installations aboard destroyers in service proved relatively slow, and the Bofors rearmament programme was not completed until the summer of 1944.

The Army also adopted the Bofors, but in an air-cooled version, which weighed about a third as much as a twin mounting, even with power drive. It was, therefore, very suitable for temporary armament improvement – as in the case of three Destroyer Divisions in 1944 prepared for the invasion of Europe. However, since these weapons were generally not director-controlled, they had no automatic cut-offs to prevent them from firing into the ship and so required pipe guards.

By 1945 even the twin Bofors was not considered powerful enough to destroy an incoming Kamikaze. The Bureau of Ordnance undertook a crash programme to develop a more powerful replacement, a 3in/50, two of which could replace the four 40mm of a quadruple Bofors. Single automatic 3in/50s were intended to replace the twin Bofors. Despite the urgency with which the programme was pursued, these weapons were not ready until 1947, but they eventually armed most of the post-war destroyer force. BuOrd also tried to develop a new free-swinging machine gun to replace the Oerlikon and at times after the war to favour a 35mm weapon, but this never appeared.

ANTI-AIRCRAFT FIRE CONTROL SYSTEMS

US wartime AA fire control systems were generally descended from the Mk 14 Sight, which was developed for the Oerlikon at MIT. It incorporated rate gyros which measured the rate at which the sight (and hence the gun) tracked a moving target, and then computed that target's future position. Most Oerlikons were so equipped; the same sight, mounted on a 'dummy gun', was used as a director to control Bofors guns. It was very simple and could follow very rapidly moving targets; not surprisingly, it could not incorporate much in the way of ballistics, and it required range estimation by eye. Towards the end of the war many ships were using Mk 51s interconnected to their 5in batteries, for local control against short range targets.

The great defect of the Mk 51 was its inability to operate at night. Late in the war a variety of 'blind-fire' systems was developed, one of which, Mk 63, was applied to many Bofors guns and, after the war, to many 3in/50s. It incorporated a Mk 35 radar dish carried on the gun mounting itself, with the radar receiver below decks.

The Mk 56 director for 3in control has already been mentioned.

RADAR

A variety of gunnery control radars has already been mentioned. The US Navy introduced its first radar in 1937, and by 1941 it had two destroyer sets, SC and SA, in production. Both were metric-wave air-search types; a sea-search set, SG, using centimetric waves (and thus comparable to the British 271/272/273 series) soon appeared as well, and the standard US destroyer suit was SC-2 (a modified SC with a rectangular antenna) at the masthead and SG below. All of these sets are more fully described elsewhere.

The Atlantic Fleet destroyers *O'Brien* (DD415) and *Walke* (DD416), refitting at Norfolk on 16 December 1941, show early AS modifications. On her 'fantail' *O'Brien* carries a Y-gun, served by two davits and two stowage racks of 300lb depth charges. She carries her Y-gun arbors in a rack on her starboard side, just abaft No 4 gun; *Walke* appears to have a K-gun installed aft, and her Y-gun may be in the process of being removed. She already has Oerlikons aboard, whereas *O'Brien* is just receiving foundations for them. Although not visible in these views there are torpedo directors forward of the main (Mk 37) directors but as yet no fire control radar for the 5in guns.

One other electronic search device deserves mention here: HF/DF, or 'huff-duff'. One essential feature of German submarine tactics was the extensive use of radio, as 'wolfpack' attacks were controlled from U-boat headquarters in France. One reason why the Germans were willing to break radio silence was that they assumed, very incorrectly, that it was impossible to fit a high frequency radio direction finder aboard a small ship. However, HF/DF became a valuable Allied weapon; many destroyer escorts and some US destroyers received it at their mastheads in place of air-search radars. By 1944 it was more typical for the HF/DF 'birdcage' to be mounted atop a short mainmast. Even so, it was common for Atlantic destroyers, which would normally encounter little air opposition, to retain their original SC-1 antennae long after their Pacific sisters had been fitted with the much more effective SC-2: the radar which mattered in the North Atlantic was the surface-search set which could detect a submarine or which could assist a ship attempting to keep station on a convoy at night.

In 1944 SC-2 and its immediate successors began to be replaced by the similar SR, which could be distinguished by its lack of a secondary IFF array above the antenna and by its rounded edges. Meanwhile development work proceeded on a new generation of shorter wavelength air-search radars: for given dimensions, the shorter the wavelength the sharper the radar beam and hence the greater the accuracy of its indications. SC and SR operated at about 1.5m, but the new SR-6 was to operate at about 23cm. It was fitted to several ships just after the war, but its antenna proved unsuccessful and was replaced by the familiar parabola of SP-6. (The latter was probably the most characteristic US destroyer radar of the 1950s.) SR and its cousins, however, did not disappear. It was not only that the longer wavelengths proved to have properties uniquely valuable; in addition, it soon became clear that there was much to be said for having a spread of radar frequencies in the Fleet, simply as an insurance against enemy action.

The only other major US destroyer search radar of World War II was SP, a dish which produced a narrow beam for height-finding by radar pickets. Given a range and bearing by an air-search set such as SC-2, SP could be scanned in elevation until it found the target. The resulting altitude data was necessary for fighter control. In the absence of SP, a fighter control ship would have to operate by means of a 'fade chart'. The metric radars experienced fading due to the interference between reflections off the sea surface and waves transmitted directly to a target and reflected directly from it. Fading would occur at particular angles, and the ranges at which an aircraft passed through a fade zone would indicate its altitude. The trickiness of this procedure shows in the preference for a specialised height-finding radar, even at some considerable cost in ship modification. SPS-8 was a post-war replacement for SP.

Many destroyers also carried electronic warfare equipment in the shape of radar search receivers to pick up enemy emissions and direction finders to locate them more precisely, and by the end of the war many, including all the radar pickets, had the TDY jammer as well. All of this equipment is noted in the photographs. After the war the TDY jammer gradually disappeared and few destroyers were fitted with its far more powerful successors, although the warning and direction finding devices remained.

Presumably among their virtues was the ability to detect a submarine's surface-search radar emissions.

Finally there were communications devices. These included TBS, a short-range, very high frequency voice radio, important in that it greatly facilitated tactical communication. From a tactical point of view, its very short range, which made interception by an enemy difficult, was as important as its voice character. Late in the war a higher-frequency system, RDZ/TDZ, appeared – this could carry many more channels, and it had an even shorter range, its shorter wavelength showing in its smaller dimensions. Another wartime communication device was 'Nancy', an infra-red beacon carried at the masthead.

Two other devices can also be categorised as communications systems. IFF was a radar recognition device, carried both as an interrogator for shipboard radars and as a transponder to reply to ship and aircraft sets. In destroyers the interrogator was an integral part of the SC-2 and later radars; in SC-2 there was actually provision for two alternative IFF systems, reflected in sets of aerials both on the main antenna and on an auxiliary antenna above it. In the post-war SPS-6 series the IFF function was not visible as it was incorporated in the big waveguide feed to the main antenna. IFF transponders were carried on the yardarm.

The other communication device was an aircraft homing beacon, YE, which was carried only by radar pickets; it was necessary if the picket were to control its section of fighters. YE was also adopted by the Royal Navy, and appeared aboard many British ships after the war.

TORPEDOES

The classical destroyer weapon was the torpedo, and US torpedo mounting doctrine has already been discussed in some detail. Each ship was fitted with a torpedo warhead locker for peacetime stowage of warheads; part of the mobilisation procedure was to fit the warheads to the torpedoes, leaving the locker free to accept the mobilisation allowance of depth charges. In fact this applied to most classes, but in the *Fletchers* the warhead locker was instead allocated to 40mm ammunition and all depth charges had to be stowed on deck.

Each bank of tubes carried a local sight, although torpedoes were generally fired by means of a centralised torpedo director in the bridgework. From the *Mahan* class on, tubes exposed to blast – in general those aft – were provided with special cylindrical blast shields. In many cases these shields were removed in wartime for weight reduction.

One characteristic of all US destroyer torpedo installations from the *Mahans* on was a T-shaped torpedo handling crane. Generally, torpedo main-tenance, in which each torpedo was hauled from its tube, was a standard feature of destroyer operation in port; this required considerable clearance, and was a determining factor in limiting the depth charge projector battery of Pacific Fleet 1500-ton destroyers (see below).

The standard US destroyer torpedo of World War II was the Mk 15, a 21in diameter weapon 288in long. It had three speed settings: 26.5kts for a range of 15 000yds; 33kts for 10 000 yds; and 45kts for 6000yds. In its Mod 3 version of 1945 it could carry 800lb of TNT. An experimental Mk 17 was powered by Navol (hydrogen peroxide plus fuel) and was expected to exceed 18 000yds at 46kts, carrying 950lb of Torpex, which was at least 1.5 times as powerful as TNT. However, with the end of the war, interest in surface-launched torpedoes waned, and ultimately the destroyers retained their tubes mainly as space and weight reservation for AS torpedo launchers. Even so, it is noteworthy that the US Navy, unlike the Royal Navy, was willing to retain full torpedo batteries nearly to the end of World War II.

ANTI-SUBMARINE WEAPONS

The primary AS weapon of modern US destroyers of World War II was the depth charge, rolled off a stern track or projected from a side launcher (depth charge projector or K-gun). Installation of ahead-thrown weapons was restricted to 'Hedgehogs' in some flush-deckers (and in all destroyer escorts and frigates) and 'Mousetrap' in a few *Bensons* (see below); this was in distinct contrast both to wartime RN policy and to the US policy of the 1950s.

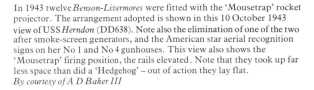

In 1943 twelve *Benson-Livermores* were fitted with the 'Mousetrap' rocket projector. The arrangement adopted is shown in this 10 October 1943 view of USS *Herndon* (DD638). Note also the elimination of one of the two after smoke-screen generators, and the American star aerial recognition signs on her No 1 and No 4 gunhouses. This view also shows the 'Mousetrap' firing position, the rails elevated. Note that they took up far less space than did a 'Hedgehog' – out of action they lay flat.
By courtesy of A D Baker III

SONAR

The chief AS sensor was sonar which the US had developed independently of the Royal Navy after both (and the French) had collaborated at its beginning in 1917-18. The first US set, designated QA, was tested at sea in 1927. It operated at high frequency (20 to 40kc) and hence at short range, and it was useless above about 4kts. An improved QC began to appear in service in 1934, and this was the primary US destroyer sonar of World War II. It was a searchlight device, sending out a 'ping' in one direction. The operator would wait for an echo, then try another bearing. The beam was about 14° wide. Because sound does not travel very fast in water, the search rate of such a sonar was low and in fact a sonar mounted aboard a moving ship would leave large areas uncovered. Thus the searchlight sonar was less a search device that a means of maintaining contact with a submarine which had already betrayed its position, eg by firing a torpedo. In fact a serious defect of the searchlight system was that a manoeuvring submarine could evade attack by moving out of the relatively narrow beam which, moreover, was so wide vertically that it could give only range and bearing, and not the depth data essential for a depth charge attack. In addition, the sonar beam sloped downward in such a way as to leave a wide dead space near the ship, so that a destroyer approaching a submarine would lose contact before she passed over to drop depth charges.

Pre-war US sonars were encased in rubber domes which limited effective sonar speed to 15kts. However, the US Navy adopted a Royal Navy steel dome in the autumn of 1941 which was said to permit a destroyer to hold a contact made at 15-20kts and to search at 20-24kts; these figures, however, proved to be somewhat over-optimistic.

In 1941 standard installation policy was to fit two sonars to each modern destroyer, presumably to improve the search pattern. However, the standard fit was reduced to one in order to provide sufficient sonars for destroyer escorts (1942). In addition, in 1942, many destroyers had the Ship Magnetic Submarine Detector (SMSD), which appears from sparse contemporary references to have been a magnetometer to detect submarines lying on the sea bed. It cannot have geen particularly successful, and vanished in 1943.

Wartime sonar development addressed the defects of the system, which had been apparent even before the war. Thus the Bearing Deviation Indicator (BDI) assisted a sonar operator in maintaining contact with a manoeuvring target. A new QGB sonar, introduced in the *Sumner*, tilted to maintain contact with a submarine as the ship approached. Finally there was scanning sonar, QHB, the ances-

tor of all post-war US destroyer sonars. In this system an omni-directional 'ping' was sent out, and the receiver scanned in direction, to achieve a much better search rate and far more solid detection. The significance of QHB was that submarines in prospect at the end of the war might well fail to show themselves, and their torpedoes might well be wakeless pattern-runners, so that it was essential for AS ships to improve their chances of initial detection.

The US Navy did not deploy a depth-determining sonar such as the British Type 147, used with 'Squid'. Depth estimates were generally made using the slope of the sonar beam, the rule of thumb being that target depth was about one third of the range at loss of sonar contact. However, a series of depth-determining sonars, essentially QHBs turned on their sides, were under development in 1945, and some of them were used after the war in conjunction with 'Weapon Alfa'.

DEPTH CHARGES

The standard depth charges throughout most of the war were a 600lb Mk 7 rolled from stern tracks and a 300lb Mk 6 fired from projectors, either a K-gun or a Y-gun. These weights referred to the weight of explosive; the charge itself was heavier, being 720 and 420lb respectively. Mks 6 and 7 had been developed from the much older Mks 3 and 4 to improve sink rates from 6fs to 8 and 9fs; during the war a lightweight teardrop-shaped Mk 9 (340lb, of which 200lb was TNT) was developed to sink at 14.2fs. As an interim measure, 155lb was added to the Mk 6 to produce the 11-13fs Mk 8. Faster sinking was important in view of increases in the crush depth of war-construction U-boats. Thus the standard maximum setting of 300ft had to be doubled by 1942; note that even at 10fs it would require a full minute for a depth charge to reach 600ft, during which time a submarine escaping at 6 kts might travel about 600ft. The US Navy appears not to have considered any ultra-deep heavy depth charge comparable to the British Mk X.

The pre-war standard depth charge track carried five 600lb charges and could be extended by standardised fixtures. In typical installations two were fixed to the 'fantail', toed inwards at the stern to clear the two smoke screen generators there. This installation was approved for all destroyers of the Battle Force in January 1941, and had appeared in the *Sims* and later classes as completed. Additional depth charge stowage was to be provided in the locker used in peacetime to hold torpedo warheads. In fact Atlantic destroyers received far more. Thus by January 1942 many *Benson-Livermores* had a pair of 12-charge stern racks (plus stowage for sixteen 600lb charges) and a Y-gun with ten 300lb charges.

In October the CNO had ordered the installation of 8 K-guns in each of the repeat (DD453/459 class) *Bensons*, with an allowance of not fewer than thirty-two 300lb and thirty 600lb charges. In fact this was not practical: some ships actually carried 8 throwers, but the standard was changed to 6 in December 1941, which became the standard for Atlantic destroyers. Nor did the unwieldy 12-charge tracks remain for long.

Y-guns were fitted to some Atlantic destroyers, but they presented difficulties in that they required clear athwartships space. As early as 1936 the Bureau of Ordnance had devised a side projector (AS Projector Mk 6, the K-gun) which could be mounted in clear space alongside the superstructure, and production began in 1941. An important adjunct was a roller rack alongside the projector to hold three or four 300lb charges. The rack did require some athwartships space, however, and the *Farraguts* had an alternative stowage spread out along the deck.

So at the end of 1941 the Atlantic Fleet standard was 6 K-guns, to form an adequate pattern. However, ships of the Battle Force generally did not have enough clear deck space to accommodate 3 K-guns

on one side without fouling their torpedo tubes, at least when those tubes were emptied for port maintenance: the CNO agreed early in 1942 to limit them to 4 projectors each. However, the larger *Fletchers* and *Sumner-Gearings* all had 6 projectors each. The capacity of depth charge modification of 1941 was an increase from 5 to 7 charges. Later there were 8- and even 12-charge racks. Unfortunately, attempts to gain depth charge capacity by lengthening depth charge tracks also greatly reduced space on the 'fantail'. This problem was particularly critical in the *Fletchers* and *Sumners*, which carried automatic weapons aft but which also had no magazine stowage for depth charges and so had to carry all of their charges topside. The solution was a pair of 8-charge rails, toed outwards, with a pair of 5-charge stowage racks inside them, for a total of 26 charges aft. With 5 charges in each K-gun/roller rack combination, a *Fletcher* could lay 5 patterns. The stern reserve racks were unique to the large fleet

Detail view of depth charge projectors and roller racks aboard *Mugford* (DD389) as refitted at Mare Island, 2 May 1944. The objects in the rack above are parts of a floater net, a standard US fitting by this time.

destroyers – all others had magazine stowage.

By March 1944 allowances had stabilised. Of the 1500-ton ships, the *Farraguts* alone carried five 300lb charges per projector; they had the standard 5-charge stern tracks and magazine capacity for eighteen 600lb charges. Later Pacific 1500-tonners had a similar allowance of 600lb charges, but only four 300lb for each of their 4 K-guns. The *Benson-Livermores* carried twenty charges in throwers and another twenty-two 300lb charges in a magazine.

Atlantic destroyers were better endowed. All had the 7-charge stern rack, with another eight 600lb charges in reserve; this reserve capacity was also characteristic of Atlantic and Pacific *Benson-Livermores*. Of all these ships, only the Pacific ships of the original *Benson* class had the 10-charge stern tracks. All Atlantic destroyers had 6 K-guns, each with 2 charges in DD402-404, 5 in DD419 (the only remaining Atlantic *Sims*), 3 in early *Benson-Livermores* and 4 each in later ones, from DD453 onwards. There was also magazine stowage: 24 charges in DD402-404, 16 in DD419 and 22 in *Benson-Livermores* (including those in the Pacific). As for the 'Leaders', the interim *Porter* battery was a 5-charge stern track with stowage for 18 charges, plus twenty 300lb charges in 4 throwers and their stowage racks. The *Somers* class had 7-charge stern racks with 9 charges in reserve, as well as 24 charges in 6 throwers, plus 15 more in reserve. The ultimate batteries envisaged for both classes included 5-charge stern racks (with the magazine capacities above) and, in each case, 4 projectors with a total of 16 charges (plus, in the *Somers* class only, the 15 in reserve).

The fast-sinking depth charge promised far more capacity with no increase in total weight. Thus the standard 5-charge track could accommodate 7 Mk 9s, the 7-charge track 10, and the 26-charge capacity of a new destroyer would translate to 36. Even projector capacity would increase in some cases: in a *Bristol*, the throwers would now hold 30 charges, and the magazine another 26. The effect of a switch to the lead-weighted Mk 8 was similar but less dramatic.

A view of the Mk 33 director, here as mounted on the carrier *Ranger* (CV4), from the rear, with the calculating portion of the director clearly visible, and the rangefinder projecting from both sides in front. The photograph is dated August 1942.

AHEAD-THROWING INSTALLATIONS

All of these stern- and side-dropped charges were of limited value, in that they could be fired only well after a destroyer had lost contact with a submarine. By 1943 it was understood that the most effective AS weapons would be ahead-fired ones, similar to the British 'Hedgehog'. 'Hedgehog' was a spigot mortar firing 24 contact-fuzed charges; its main defects were its weight and the deck reaction felt by the ship firing it, which in British practice required that one main battery gun be surrendered in exchange. The US National Defense Research Committee developed a rocket projector, 'Mousetrap', which in its Mk 22 version could fire eight 'Hedgehog'

charges to 300yds (compared to 200yds for 'Hedgehog'). Early in April 1943 the commander of the Atlantic Fleet ASW Unit at Boston recommended a variety of AS improvements for Atlantic fleet destroyers, including an ahead-throwing weapon, which he considered valuable enough to be worth the surrender of a boat or even of depth charges – especially as it was rare to find any destroyer which had exhausted its supply of depth charges.

The Commander of Atlantic Destroyers agreed, and considered ahead-throwing weapons particularly valuable because a submarine could not turn inside a destroyer before the attack was made. He preferred 'Mousetrap' to 'Hedgehog' in view of its simplicity (one might be fitted to each side of the forecastle) and its greater range; its charge matched that of 'Hedgehog'. On the other hand, 'Hedgehog' was designed to compensate for roll. DesLant was particularly impressed by recent 'Mousetrap' tests at sea in small escort vessels. CinC Atlantic Fleet agreed, although he was worried that a projector which could not be corrected for train or tilt might not be worthwhile. He approved experimental installations in not more than four 1500-ton or larger destroyers, with temporary weight compensation to be effected by a reduction in the number of depth charges carried and/or in 5in ammunition.

The CNO also agreed, but felt that at least 12 ships would have to be fitted to allow for a quick evaluation. He also suggested that three 'Mousetraps' be fitted in each ship, one on the centreline with perhaps a blast shield to protect No 1 gun. Priority of installation was to be higher than for any other class. Atlantic Fleet now nominated 12 late *Livermores*: DD493, 620, 622, 623, 635, 637-9 and 645-8. In November, 1943 DD645 was removed from this list and *Gillespie*, DD609, substituted.

DesLant's enthusuasm did not stop at the *Bensons*. He proposed the removal of one bank of torpedo tubes in *Sims* and 10-tube *Bensons*, as one of the two boats had already been removed from these ships as compensation. No compensation was available in the *Benhams*, so they were eliminated from

consideration. The 'Mousetrap' installation included stowage for 144 rounds (7 attacks), including 48 of ready-service (in the former Captain's bath abaft No 1 gun).

Admiral King was right: 12 installations did make for a quick evaluation – but not for a positive one. He approved their removal on 9 March 1944 in view of unsatisfactory service experience, which was not cited in detail. The only installation which survived for very long was that aboard *Gillespie:* she transferred to the Pacific, and still had her 'Mousetraps' in April 1945. She never received the 1945 AA modifications, but no longer had this weapon by the end of the war. Ahead-firing AS projectors did not reappear aboard US fleet destroyers until after 1950.

11. AA Improvements

The US Navy was extremely fortunate in its close ties with the Royal Navy. From 1940 onwards, British war experience was made freely available to the United States, and the two navies even went so far as to exchange observers. Thus the US Navy appreciated the importance of aircraft in Norway and in the Mediterranean quite early, and determined to mend its ways in regard to close range anti-aircraft protection. Then Rear Admiral E J King was asked to make special studies of AA batteries for the fleet in the spring of 1940, and in August a Navy Department AA Board was created by the Chief of Naval Operations, primarily to implement King's suggestions. By mid-1941 the General Board, acting on the King Board guidelines, had worked out the AA batteries which US destroyers, other than the new *Fletchers*, would carry up to 1945. This level of foresight seems remarkable in view of the continuous changes evident in British practice; but it is well to keep in mind that the US Navy had equipped its newer destroyers from the first with powerful DP guns and, just as importantly, with DP fire control systems.

Initial war modifications to the *Farraguts* were limited to the installation of 20mm guns and the removal of No 3 5in gun, as seen here on *Aylwin* (DD355), at Mare Island, 30 March 1942.

The King Board was loath to sacrifice existing capabilities to AA armament, especially as the 5in gun was expected to be valuable in breaking up high-level bombing formations as well as torpedo attacks. Nor did it want to sacrifice torpedo tubes for automatic weapons: one gun out of five might be a 20% reduction in battery, but one bank of torpedo tubes would be half or a third of a destroyer's complement. Matters would be different in a 16-tube boat, but in that case the removal of one mounting would require extensive rearrangement – which might in fact be impossible in any case in view of insufficient centreline space. In that case a pair of tubes would have to go, and that was not acceptable in destroyers whose mission was still with the Battle Fleet.

In either case it seemed to the Board that, given the best existing weapons, the .5in and the quadruple 1.1in machine guns, the best that could be done for existing destroyers was to double their machine gun battery to eight .5s, so arranged that four could fire in the ahead sector and four simultaneously on some other sector. Nothing more could be done without landing major weights. However, by that time (December 1940) it was clear to many that a heavy machine gun would be required to fight off dive bombers. On 14 February 1941 the General Board suggested that the interim *emergency* battery for all 5-gun 1500- to 1600-ton destroyers envisage the replacement of one 5in weapon by a quadruple 1.1in machine gun. The Board had already observed that, in view of the inadequacy of both the .5 and the 1.1, destroyers should be armed instead with the 20mm and 40mm weapons already on order. These weapons would not, however, be available for some time.

Top left: Later two twin Bofors guns replaced the Oerlikons mounted abaft the second funnel; this photograph shows *Dewey* (DD349) as refitted at Mare Island, 1 December 1942. She had early radar sets: SC-1 at the foretop, with the SG surface-search set below it, and a Mk 4 fire control set on her Mk 33 director. Note that she has no roller-loaders for her depth charge projectors aft.

Top right and right: Initial modifications to the *Mahan* class included the removal of No 3 gun and the addition of Oerlikons. Note that the detail view, of *Mahan* (DD364) at Mare Island, 28 April 1942, shows the after gun crew shelter in use to support these weapons, whereas it has been removed in the photograph of *Cushing* (DD376), out of the same yard, 15 July 1942.
Second photo: by courtesy of A D Baker III

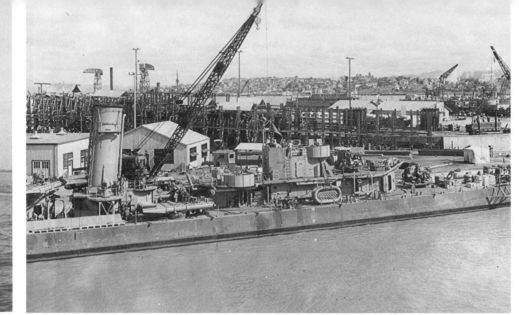

A feature of war modifications that did not concern armament was the considerable reduction in overhead structure in destroyer bridges, to allow Captains a better view during air actions. The modifications were not radical: for example, there was no provision for any walkway around the bridge front, although in a few ships windshields were fixed on the pilot house roof for a conning officer. However, in the modified *Fletchers* and their successors, the pilot house was reduced in size and moved back from the fore part of the bridge, leaving a broad open space surrounding it.

Given these directives, the Bureau of Ships (successor to Construction and Repair) in co-operation with the General Board proposed class-by-class rearmament plans; to some extent these were modified in practice for the Atlantic Fleet by the exigencies of Atlantic warfare. In the detailed notes which follow, it is important to distinguish between 'temporary approved' and 'ultimate' batteries, both of which were given for each ship. The temporary approved battery consisted of weapons immediately available, and often included some structural provision for the battery ultimately desired (which might not be fitted for some years, given the shortage of the twin 40mm Bofors guns which were among its principal constituents). Temporary approved batteries were also altered for special missions, such as invasion duty in 1944 in the Atlantic and anti-Kamikaze warfare in 1945, although ships so altered might not be converted back to their 'ultimate' configurations.

Finally, it should be borne in mind that it was always far easier to bolt down Oerlikon guns or even to remove a 5in gun than to install power-operated Bofors with their directors: fitting the latter was a major shipyard job which had to await either repair after action damage or else a major overhaul. Pacific Fleet destroyers were worked so hard that it was some time before they could be spared for return to West Coast yards. As late as the beginning of 1944 it was considered a great improvement for ships to be assigned for overhaul after 100 000 miles or 18 months of operation.

Actual rearmament plans must be treated on a class-by-class basis. Emergency AA modifications will be discussed separately.

1500-TON 5-GUN TYPES

Farragut class The major feature of wartime armament modifications was the elemination of No 3 5in gun in favour of a pair of twin Bofors; each twin Bofors was roughly equivalent in weight to a quadruple 1.1, but by mid-1941 it was clear that the weight saved by the removal of a 5in gun would buy two heavy automatic weapons rather than the one which had initially been assumed. As an interim modification, No 3 gun could be replaced by four single Oerlikons; others could replace the four original machine guns. The temporary approved battery also included four K-guns. *Farragut* and *Dewey* were among the first to be refitted to this standard (May 1942).

One defect of this battery was insufficient ahead fire. When the *Farraguts* were refitted with two twin Bofors amidships in place of the former quartet of Oerlikons, an Oerlikon was mounted on the centreline forward, raised above the two shelter deck guns

before the bridge – the prototype conversion was probably *Dewey* (December 1942) and the last appears to have been *Monaghan* (April 1943). *Monaghan*, and possibly others, had seven 20mms, with two single guns mounted in the future twin Bofors positions. No further increases were planned in 1945, as by then the *Farraguts* were considered obsolescent.

Mahan class In 1941 these were probably the best units of the Battle Force. Their ultimate battery was, therefore, a matter of some discussion, and some unorthodox schemes were suggested. Commander Destroyers Battle Force wanted to retain all the guns and torpedoes originally mounted; he would also add two twin Bofors and six Oerlikons, not to mention 24 depth charges and their projectors. Recognising that he could not have all of this, he suggested in September 1941 that if necessary either No 2 or No 3 gun could be sacrificed; No 2 'is generally considered to be the poorest gun in the

ship for AA fire because it interferes with the director and fire control. Its removal, however, would seriously reduce surface fire ahead, which is considered essential in destroyer torpedo attacks'. No 3 would have to go instead. Twin Bofors might replace the paired .5s atop the gun crew shelters fore and aft, flanked by Oerlikons at the shelter deck level; another pair of Oerlikons could flank the second funnel. No torpedo tubes would be landed; weight compensation would include the replacement of the tripod foremast by a pole, the removal of the navigational rangefinders, and the removal of the blast shields from the wing torpedo tubes.

Although this scheme would have given excellent ahead AA fire, it was rejected; *Mahans* were ultimately rearmed with two twin Bofors on the forward end of the after shelter deck, replacing both No 3 gun and the gun crew shelter there. Also mounted were five Oerlikons, three before the bridge and two flanking the second funnel. The temporary approved battery was eight Oerlikons, one replacing each of the former .5s, as well as two abreast the second funnel and two replacing No 3 gun. Prior to their rearmament with Bofors guns, some ships, such as *Cushing*, mounted single Oerlikons in the future Bofors tubs, and another (for a total of seven) in the future Bofors director position.

Actual rearmament with the Bofors guns was very slow, reflecting the high rate of use of these ships. Probably the first to rearm was *Flusser* (DD368, January 1943). That spring four more rearmed (DD364, 369, 371 and 378), but ships were still being rearmed the next spring and in fact the last of the group, *Lamson* (DD367), was not complete until July 1944.

Three *Mahans* deserve special mention. *Shaw* (DD373) was severely damaged at Pearl Harbor, her bow blown off. She was repaired and refitted, and was probably unique in mounting one quadruple 1.1in machine gun and four Oerlikons as an interim AA battery. In the course of reconstruction she gained about 60 tons, which was to prove unfortunate when she underwent an emergency AA refit in 1945.

Left and overleaf: Most of the *Mahans* were not rearmed until 1944. The detail views show *Mahan* at Mare Island, 24 June 1944. Her refit included a new Mk 28 fire control radar (circled), whilst on her yardarm can be discerned two IFF aerials at the ends, as well as the characteristic crossed whips of TBS. Note also her new roller-loaders in the aft view. The overall view shows *Lamson* (DD367), out of Mare Island 24 May 1944. Little more was done to these ships during the war. *Third photo: by courtesy of A D Baker III*

145

Cassin (DD372) and *Downes* (DD375) were almost completely destroyed at Pearl Harbor, but their machinery and main batteries were placed aboard new hulls and the names were retained. They were unique among *Mahans* in having the new Mk 37 director, and also in having two banks of torpedo tubes raised on their centrelines, like later destroyers; AA armament was two twin Bofors and six Oerlikons, two abreast the second funnel, two in the bridge wings, and two abreast the British-style bridge rather than before it as in other US destroyers. Apart from machinery and guns, they were essentially new construction destroyers, and they did not enter service before 1943/4.

Sims class The *Sims* class marked a return to the 5-gun pattern of the first US Treaty destroyers;

however, unlike the two earlier classes, it was first modified for the Atlantic Fleet. In June 1941 the Bureau of Ships ordered for this class the removal of No 3 gun, as well as the gun crew shelter aft, the 2.5m navigational rangefinder on the bridge, the smoke generator, one torpedo director, and both 24in searchlights. The two .5s atop the gun crew shelter would be relocated to the shelter deck itself, two more would be added at the fore end of that deck in place of No 3 gun and two would be added on the main deck forward of that, to make up the King Board total of eight. A Y-gun with ten 300lb depth charges would be mounted on the 'fantail' and the depth charge tracks extended to take fourteen 600lb charges. Splinter protection would be provided and the foremast modified to take radar equipment. The

main deck bulwark, so characteristic of later US destroyers, was to be extended aft to provide protection for the main deck machine guns. Finally, AA ammunition lockers would be increased to a capacity of 40 000 rounds of .5in. These (and similar alterations for the Atlantic Fleet *Benham*s) were all carried out during the summer of 1941.

This battery did not remain in force for very long; in particular, ships were soon refitted with Oerlikons (either four, in place of the original four .5s or, later, six, with an additional two on the centreline, one forward of the bridge and another abaft and above the after pair). The proposed ultimate battery was two twin Bofors (in place of the shelter deck Oerlikons aft, leaving the superimposed one in place) and four Oerlikons (three before the bridge, one aft). Four depth charge projectors abreast the after deckhouse would replace the cumbersome single Y-gun. K-gun production was far swifter than that of Bofors guns – as early as April 1942 six ships had the new projectors. On the other hand, ultimate armament refits began about January 1943 (DD411) and continued at least until that October (eg DD413). As refitted, Pacific units had the half-shield on No 3 gun removed, as did the Atlantic units which later went West. Of the five war losses, only *Buck* (DD420) lasted long enough to be refitted.

9958-43
PLAN VIEW, AFT.
MARE ISLAND, CAL. 30 NOVEMBER 1943
(DD375)

In March 1944, four Atlantic Destroyer Divisions were modified, apparently for the invasion of Europe: Desdivs 13 (DD421-4 and 431), 14 (DD425-8, of which 426 was sunk in April 1944), 21 (DD429, 430, 432 and 440), and 25 (DD419, 'Leader', and 437-9). In each case the second bank torpedo tubes was replaced by Army-type single Bofors, three for *Wainwright* (DD419) and two for the *Benson-Livermores*. Following the major invasions, the CNO ordered these guns to be removed from returning *Benson-Livermores* (November 1944), but he authorised the retention of the increased battery in *Wainwright*. It was not removed until the spring of 1945, when the after torpedo tube was restored.

Benson-Livermore class The original planned battery, to which few vessels were completed, has already been discussed. 5-gun ships were modified to take six Oerlikons in place of their original .5s, the after torpedo tubes being surrendered. As in the *Sims* class the gun crew shelter was eliminated, the two superfiring 5in guns aft being half-shielded. The searchlight was moved forward to the position vacated by the after tubes, and six K-guns replaced the Y-gun installed in 1941. In April 1942 it was expected that ultimately No 3 5in gun and the two aftermost Oerlikons would be replaced by a pair of twin Bofors, the four other Oerlikons being retained (two before the bridge and two abreast the second funnel). Later, however, the ultimate armament was amended to two banks of torpedo tubes. Nine ships (DD421-8 and 431) had an alternate ultimate battery of one bank of tubes and four extra Oerlikons on a 'portable' platform in its place; some

operated in this configuration, but by 1944 all surviving ships of the DD421-444 series had ten tubes and four guns.

For repeat *Bensons* (DD453 onwards) the temporary approved battery was one quadruple 1.1in machine gun to starboard with an Oerlikon opposite it aft, and the four Oerlikons of earlier units amidships and forward. Some were completed with the twin Bofors aft – *Coghlan* (DD606) was the first US warship to mount twin Bofors (1 July 1942). However, not all had these weapons until mid-1944. Meanwhile, in November 1942, the ultimate AA battery of repeat *Bensons* was increased by three Oerlikons: one on a raised platform before the bridge and two more on the bridge wings (a position almost unique in US practice).

Two *Mahans* were so badly damaged at Pearl Harbor that new hulls were built to accommodate their machinery and weapons. Here *Downes* (DD375) is shown completing at Mare Island, 30 November 1943. She was unique in having the modern Mk 37 fire control system, and both of her tubes were raised on the centreline, as in later destroyers. In the detail view of her bridge, the torpedo director can be distinguished just forward of the Mk 37 barbette. Note the Admiralty-style bridge and the Oerlikon mounted in its wings.

The four divisions of 10-tube ships refitted for special European service surrendered their after banks of tubes in return for two Army-pattern single Bofors and four more Oerlikons. Because, unlike Navy weapons, the Army Bofors were not director-controlled, they required pipe guards to prevent them from firing inboard. All of these weapons were removed, and the after tubes restored, during refits carried out when the ships returned to the United States in November 1944.

1500-TON 4-TUBE TYPES

Gridley class The *Gridley* and the very similar *Bagley* classes remained with the Pacific Fleet before the outbreak of war, and consequently were little modified. By April 1942 the temporary approved AA battery was eight Oerlikons, with an ultimate battery of two twin Bofors and two Oerlikons. Presumably it was felt that the principal armament weights were so low in these ships that neither 5in guns nor torpedo tubes would have to be surrendered to achieve this; of course that could not be the case. In fact most ships replaced their four .5s with Oerlikons and added another pair, on raised platforms abeam the single large funnel. This was the temporary approved battery as of August 1942. The question of an ultimate Bofors battery was still under study; at the end of November the Bureau of Ships ruled that the four *Gridleys*, apparently deficient in stability, were to have no Bofors but ultimately eight Oerlikons. The AS battery was set at four depth charge projectors.

The 6-Oerlikon battery remained until mid-1943, when a seventh was added, in a third position on the platform surrounding the funnel. The eighth gun, added a few months later (in all but *Maury*, DD401), was mounted on a centreline platform forward of the bridge. This progression suggests that the *Gridleys* were deficient in stability, and in the spring of 1945 the two after tubes were removed from all four.

The *Bagleys* were rather more heavily modified. When ultimate batteries were fixed at the end of November 1942, they were scheduled for one twin Bofors, which would be mounted atop the gun crew shelter aft, and six Oerlikons, one to either side of the funnel, one to either side of the shelter deck forward of the bridge, and two more on the centreline, one forward of the bridge above the other two, and one abaft the funnel. There would be four depth charge projectors abreast the after deckhouse.

Above: The two *Fannings*, very like the *Mahans*, were similarly rearmed. Here *Fanning* (DD385) is shown after rearmament at Mare Island, 22 November 1943. The foundations for a set of smoke generators can be distinguished outboard of one depth charge track. Her foremast shows SC-2 air-search and SG surface-search radars, and on the yardarm, left to right, are IFF, TBS, and another IFF antenna.

Above right: USS *Hughes* (DD410) (top) after early war modifications (Mare Island, 1 August 1942) and USS *Anderson* (DD411) (centre) of the *Sims* class later in the war, after rearmament. For an earlier view of this class, see Chapter 10. Note the half-shield aft in *Hughes*. *Anderson* shows several standard wartime weight-saving measures incidental to rearmament: blanking off the port hawsepipe, eliminating No 3 half-shield, and (not visible) elimination of one of the two 26-ft motor whaleboats normally carried. This photograph must have been taken late in the war, as she shows a Mk 22 'orange-peel' radar alongside her standard 5in fire control antenna. Note also that this Pacific Fleet destroyer did not have the HF/DF antenna common in the Atlantic. *By courtesy of A D Baker III and Norman Polmar*

Bottom right: *Wainwright* (DD419), one of the few Atlantic *Sims* class ships, was modified for the invasion of Europe: her after torpedo tubes were replaced by three Army pattern single Bofors guns. Note her HF/DF mast aft and her shielded superfiring after 5in gun, both characteristic of Atlantic destroyers. She was returned to her earlier configuration in 1945, and is shown here at Pearl Harbor on 24 March 1946.

This battery was not of course realised at first. For example, as initially refitted *Ralph Talbot* (DD390) had no centreline Oerlikons; these had, however, been added by December 1942 (after gun) and early 1943 (bridge gun, filling an empty gun tub installed in December). Some ships carried a seventh Oerlikon in the gun tub aft intended for the twin Bofors. As in the case of other Pacific Fleet destroyers, armament refits extended well into 1944, the last to be completed probably being *Helm* (DD388) in May.

Although an emergency AA rearmament plan was drawn up in 1945, none of the *Bagleys* was refitted.

Right, top and bottom: *Benson* (DD421) in two very different configurations. In the first photograph, 10 May 1943, she is shown with five 5in guns, two of them in half-shields, and five torpedo tubes. She has as yet neither Bofors guns nor the 1.1in weapons installed in many cases as an interim battery, and her radar (not very clear in this photograph) is the early SC-1 search set. On 30 April 1945 (second photograph) she shows ten tubes, Bofors guns, and four 5in, one of which is half-shielded. Her mainmast carries HF/DF gear.
Second photo: by courtesy of Norman Polmar

Below: *Livermore* (DD429) shows the ultimate battery of the original *Benson-Livermores*, before the 1945 emergency rearmament. Although there is good evidence that the European invasion rearmament was carried out, no photographs of rearmed *Benson-Livermores* have been found, nor is it clear where the two additional single Bofors guns would have been accommodated.

Benham class Almost all the *Benhams* served with the Atlantic Fleet before the outbreak of war; they were subjected to modifications roughly analogous to those carried out in the *Sims* class. The two after banks of torpedo tubes were removed, as well as the gun crew shelter aft and various structures (for example one window on each side of the bridge was removed as part of the reduction of covered area). Depth charge track extensions and a Y-gun (in place of the torpedo tubes) were added, as well as two .5in machine guns (on the deckhouse aft); the refit also added foundations for three more .5s around the base of the single funnel. With these filled, the battery on the outbreak of war was generally seven .5s, and the temporary approved battery was six Oerlikons – a one-for-one replacement, except for the omission of the centreline gun amidships. The ultimate battery, as of April 1942, was a pair of twin Bofors (on the after deckhouse) and four Oerlikons.

At that time only the two ships which had remained in the Pacific (*Benham*, DD397, and *Ellet*, DD398) retained all four tubes. Their battery throughout most of 1942 was to be four Oerlikons and four tubes. *Benham* was sunk probably in this configuration, but *Ellet* was refitted in the autumn of 1943.

The completion of the ultimate armament refit was relatively quick: *Stack* (DD406) had twin Bofors as early as August 1942. At that time she had open mountings aft, but ships still in the Atlantic Fleet had a full shield on No 4 gun and a half-shield on No 3. These were removed upon armament conversion in the Pacific.

The *Benhams* retained their original ultimate batteries until early 1945 although they were subject to the emergency AA improvement programme described later.

Far right, top: The later *Benson-Livermores* were designed for five tubes and four guns from the start. Although, like *Emmons* (DD457, shown here on 1 November 1943 off Hampton Roads), they were designed to mount a pair of twin Bofors aft, many were completed with one quadruple 1.1in machine gun and one Oerlikon aft instead.
By courtesy of A D Baker III

Far right, second from top: *Turner* (DD648) photographed 23 August 1943, is an Atlantic Fleet variation on the same theme as *Frazier*. Note her staggered Bofors guns, characteristic of the DD645-648 group. She has HF/DF in place of her air-search radar, a modification extended to several Atlantic destroyers and to many destroyer escorts; and she has the triple 'Mousetrap' forward of No 1 gun mounting.
By courtesy of A D Baker III

Far right, bottom two photographs: The four *Gridleys* were little altered during the war. *McCall* (DD400, Mare Island, 1 December 1943) shows mid-war modifications amounting to additional Oerlikons, better radar, and more modern depth charge projectors. All were transferred from the Pacific to the Atlantic in 1945; *Craven* (DD382) shows their final 8-tube configuration in a 26 March 1946 photograph. By this time she had a Mk 28 fire control radar in place of the Mk 4 earlier mounted on her Mk 33 director.
By courtesy of A D Baker III and Norman Polmar

Right: The very similar *Bagleys* received a twin Bofors aft. This detail view shows *Mugford* (DD389) at Mare Island on 2 May 1944 for this refit; at Mare Island in February 1945 she received additional, relatively minor alterations such as the substitution of a Mk 28 dish for her former Mk 4 fire control radar.

Below: *Frazier* (DD607), shown here on 20 September 1944 after a refit at Mare Island, illustrates the appearance of the later *Benson-Livermores* just prior to the big armament refits of 1945. Note that as a Pacific Fleet destroyer she needs no HF/DF mast aft.
Fahey Collection by courtesy of Norman Polmar

Right: Some of the 1850-ton 'Leaders' retained their original eight 5in/38 SP guns until quite late in the war. *Moffett* (DD362) is seen here off Charleston, 1 March 1944. Note that the 5in fire control radar was not the Mk 4 of the other destroyer classes, but rather the Mk 3 of some battleships and cruisers. The HF/DF is sited on a stub mainmast. The next stage, prior to reconstruction (see Chapters 5 and 6 for photographs), was the removal of No 3 twin 5in mounting.

Above: *Rhind* (DD404) served in the Atlantic fleet; this view shows her off New York, 16 January 1944; note her two twin Bofors mounted aft and the half-shielded 5-in gun characteristic of Atlantic destroyers.
By courtesy of A D Baker III

Left: *Moffett* again, off Hampton Roads on 13 July 1944 with a new quadruple Bofors aft and still retaining her early SC-1 air-search radar on her foremast. Note the catwalk connecting her forecastle to her after deckhouse.
By courtesy of A D Baker III

1850-TON 'LEADERS'

Porter class The 1850-ton 'Leaders' were unique among modern US pre-war destroyers in mounting SP main batteries; to some extent they made up for this by mounting two quadruple 1.1in machine guns, fore and aft. However, even this was clearly insufficient, and studies of DP main batteries for these ships began in May 1940. It turned out that the increase of 30 000lb *per mounting* was impossible to absorb: not merely would the mountings have to be replaced but an entirely new fire control system would be required, and fuze-setters (for the time-fuzed AA shells) would have to be inserted into the ammunition hoists, which would require additional modifications to accommodate the longer AA rounds.

The suggested solution was to adopt a battery of two twin mountings with a single enclosed 5in DP gun superfiring over each. The General Board approved this 'ultimate' battery in August 1940 with the proviso that any procurement be deferred in view of the fact that the ships already had 1.1in guns and that all other destroyers had DP main batteries, so that Fleet air defence would suffer little from the temporary retention of a few SP guns. Meanwhile the General Board raised informally the question of a third 1.1; on 29 August 1940 the Bureau of Ships replied that it would cost the after 5in director and the mainmast. These proposals were held in abeyance, although all the 'Leaders' had their after directors removed in consequence.

The question was reopened in the summer of 1941 as part of the general review of destroyer air defence. It was expected that three twin Bofors could be substituted for the 1.1s and six Oerlikons for the original pair of .5s: BuShips suggested mounting one twin Bofors on the shelter deck before the bridge and the other two on a cleared shelter deck aft, with two Oerlikons just forward of No 3 gun-house there, another two on the searchlight platform around the second funnel, and the third on deck just forward of the base of the after bank of torpedo tubes. Weight compensation would include the torpedo stowage lockers amidships and the tripod foremast, and the superstructure above the shelter deck level aft would be eliminated as well. The CNO approved these alterations on 19 September and they were carried out in *Porter*, at Mare Island, and in *Clark*, at Pearl Harbor. The other ships of the class were scheduled to be refitted after 7 December 1941, but they were considerably delayed.

Neither Bofors guns nor Oerlikons were available at first, so the interim battery was to be two quadruple 1.1s (the after one offset on the new starboard sponson) and .5s. Stability problems made it impossible to add the third 1.1 (January 1942), and waves washed over the main deck Oerlikon positions, which had to be abandoned. In July 1942, *Porter* had two twin Bofors and five Oerlikons, and Commander Destroyers Pacific (who considered these ships inadequate in any waters where 'encounters with enemy aircraft are probable' until they were given their ultimate battery of five 5in DP guns) wanted the after twin mounting relocated to the centreline, raised to allow for low-angle fire and surrounded by a triangle of Oerlikons at shelter deck level.

Above and below left: The single-stack 'Leaders' were similarly modified: *Davis* (DD395) (above) at Charleston, 23 July 1943, shows a light battery of Oerlikons, whilst *Jouett* (DD396), off Charleston on 20 April 1944, shows the standard 6-gun configuration. Modifications at this time included the installation of the stub mainmast for HF/DF, three twin Bofors aft, one twin Bofors forward, SG surface-search and SA air-search radars, and a ram bow – the latter was being installed in many destroyers at this time.
By courtesy of A D Baker III

Right: *Mayo* (DD422) refitting at Boston Navy Yard, 14 August 1944. She shows two Mk 51 directors atop her pilot house, and a torpedo director relocated there from her navigating bridge.

Other 'Leaders' were brought up to this standard throughout 1942; for example *Moffett* (DD362) was completed at Charleston in October with two twin Bofors and six Oerlikons. Meanwhile the Bureau of Ships reviewed the situation, and in December revised the temporary approved battery to six 5in SP guns: No 3 gunhouse would be replaced by a quadruple Bofors, and there would also be three twins and six Oerlikons, as well as four depth charge projectors. Ships varied. For example, when *McDougal* was refitted she received two 1.1s aft and her forward mounting was eliminated in favour of a pair of Oerlikons at shelter deck level. *Moffett* was similar. At least in *Phelps* (DD360), when No 3 gunhouse was removed in December 1942 it was replaced by a quadruple 1.1; similar guns were mounted on either side of the shelter deck aft and in the raised position forward, and there were two Oerlikons on the shelter deck forward and another four around the searchlight platform. A seventh was later mounted on the 'fantail' just forward of the depth charge tracks, though there were as yet no depth charge projectors.

By 1944 only *Selfridge* (DD357) retained all four gunhouses. That May all 1850-tonners in the Pacific, except for *Clark* and *McDougal* which had been assigned to the Canal Zone force, were transferred to the Atlantic. *Selfridge* was refitted in her 'ultimate' configuration, which by now meant two twin 5in and one single superfiring aft, plus a quadruple Bofors in No 2 position. The single 5in aft replaced the after quadruple Bofors; Oerlikons were retained on the searchlight platform (4) and in the bridge wings (2); the low bridge resembled that in the rebuilt *Cassin* and *Downes*. *Phelps* and the *Somers* class *Davis* (DD395) and *Jouett* (DD396) soon followed at Charleston, while material was assembled at Balboa for the two ships retained in the South East Pacific force. However, they were reas-signed to the Atlantic at the end of July – their material would be shipped to Charleston. *McDougal* was converted in 1945, along with *Winslow*, which had been in the Atlantic from the first; *Clark* was never done, and *Moffett* ended the war half-converted at Charleston. No conversion of *Balch* appears to have been contemplated.

Somers class The problems of the *Somers* class roughly paralleled those of the *Porters*, except that the former had even less reserve of stability. Initial modifications, therefore, were to include the removal of the amidships bank of torpedo tubes as well as No 3 gunhouse – at the beginning of the war the planned ultimate armament was six 5in/38 DP (singles superfiring over twins), three twin Bofors, six Oerlikons and eight torpedo tubes. Interim modifications roughly matched those of the *Porters:* one twin Bofors replaced the forward 1.1, another was set to starboard on the deckhouse aft and a third was mounted on the port side of the searchlight platform surrounding the single funnel. The forward Bofors was flanked by two Oerlikons, the amidships one counterbalanced by one to starboard and the aft one by one to port, and two more were mounted in the former position of No 3 gunhouse, giving a total of six. Prior to the removal of No 3 gunhouse, the aftermost heavy AA position was filled by an Oerlikon, with another opposite: *Somers* had her No 3 gunhouse removed only in the autumn of 1944, and *Jouett* only that spring. The others were refitted during 1943. Only *Davis* (DD395) and *Jouett* were rebuilt; their lesser stability shows in the fact that they had only a twin Bofors in No 2 position.

A detail view of *Wainwright*'s (DD419) additional armament, taken at New York Navy Yard. Note the pipe guards to prevent her three extra Bofors from firing into the ship.

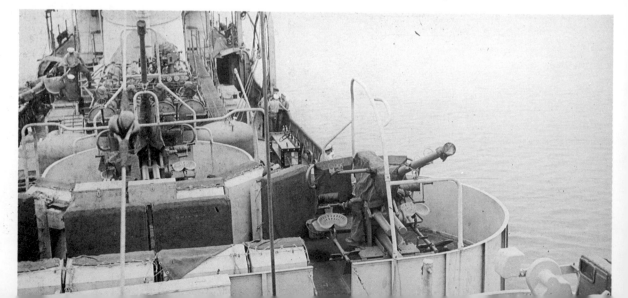

12. Special Versions

During World War II the US Navy produced four major series of destroyer conversions: minelayers, minesweepers, radar pickets, and fast troop transports. All of the original fast transports were former flush-deck destroyers of World War I origin and so fall outside the scope of this work, as do their successors, converted destroyer escorts. The minesweepers to be discussed here were successors to a series begun in 1940 with flush-deck conversions; but the minelayers were the continuation of a class begun as early as 1920. Only the radar pickets were true products of World War II technology and new tactics: they presaged the general shift in surface combatant rôles towards the support of aircraft through their operation as sensor platforms.

MINELAYERS

Fourteen of the World War I mass-production flush-deck destroyers were converted to fast minelayers in 1920-21; their torpedo tubes were replaced by tracks for up to 80 mines and their designators were changed from DD to DM. This programme appears to have been inspired by the wartime British use of fast offensive minelayers. Six were scrapped in 1930, and another four converted in their place. Four more were converted in 1937, when the remaining eight original DMs were discarded. The force of eight elderly destroyers was somewhat inadequate, and from 1940 until 1944 a variety of schemes to produce new destroyer minelayers was mooted; all but the last were rejected in view of the desperate need for destroyers in the Pacific. Finally, with mass production in high gear, twelve new *Sumners* were released for conversion.

Probably the first expression of interest in converting modern destroyers is to be found in a letter to the General Board from the Commander of Battle Force Minecraft at Pearl Harbor. In March 1940 he

Right and overleaf: Twelve new *Sumners* were converted to destroyer minelayers in 1944. The aerial view of *Shannon* shows her mine rails, and also the way four depth charge projectors could be set up to straddle them when they were not in use. Note the absence of Oerlikons on her 'fantail'. The side view of *T E Fraser* (DM24) shows the typical post-war refit configuration, with a tripod foremast and a semi-enclosed bridge. Note that although she has the new Mk 25 fire control radar on her 5in director she retains her old SC-2 air-search and SG surface-search radars. However, she does have post-war ECM gear: note the radomes on her second funnel, and the search antennae on her first.
By courtesy of Norman Polmar

asked for more flush-decker conversions, and suggested that the *Farraguts* would be even better. Looking mainly at deck space, he felt that the removal of No 5 gun and the torpedo tubes would permit the installation of tracks for 120 mines, and quite possibly a second series of tracks inboard for 80 or more – over twice the load of an old destroyer. Such ships might be useful in a fleet engagement, in which they could lay drifting mines. Moreover, the fleet would lose only eight torpedo tubes per ship, which would be far less serious than the loss entailed in any conversion of a more recent ship. Unfortunately this proposal, like several later ones, fell foul of topweight considerations: mines were heavy, and tightly-designed Treaty destroyers were unable to take large additions of weight at the main deck level (in 1944 new destroyer-minelayers were carrying 120 Mk 16 mines – 109.3 tons).

The Bureau of Construction and Repair stated that stability precluded the conversion of any ships from DD348 to DD420. The weight compensation suggested would suffice only for 40 mines; the removal of No 3 gun and the addition of about 20 tons of fixed ballast would be required to take another 45 mines; alternatively 20 more tons of ballast might be added. The matter was then dropped, only to be revived early in 1943 when Commander Service Squadron Six, responsible for Pacific Fleet minelayers, asked for the conversion of four more destroyers. Admiral King rejected this request, citing the shortage of destroyers – perhaps aircraft could substitute. However, the CNO did authorise the Bureau of Ships to design kits for quick temporary conversions, for specific mining operations. The formal request to the Bureau, in mid-April, suggested the use of prefabricated mine rails, interchangeable among ships of the same class. The maximum number of destroyer guns was to be retained.

Until this time the destroyer minelayers had been engaged almost entirely in AS and escort operations, but those in the South Pacific were now beginning to lay mines offensively. Ideally they would operate in units of three or four, but in the spring of 1943 two were operating as AS escorts in Hawaiian waters and three more in Alaska in support of the Aleutians landings. All suffered from low speed (25kts) and age (hence requiring frequent and lengthy repair). Admiral Nimitz, commanding the Pacific Fleet, saw the distribution of the minelayers as evidence that not even the eight existing units were required. His scepticism would affect later proposals as well.

The Bureau of Ships studied the conversion of both *Bristol* (DD453) and *Fletcher* class destroyers. Results for the 1620-ton class were disappointing: even with all the depth charges, smoke generators and the after 5in gun removed, only 54 of the old Mk6 or 38 of the new Mk16 or 18 mines could be carried. The *Fletcher* was far more encouraging. In the scheme ultimately adopted, all main deck machine guns (seven Oerlikons or one twin Bofors and four Oerlikons), the depth charge throwers (but not two stern racks without extensions), No 5 gun, No 2 bank of torpedo tubes and the smoke generators would have to be landed and 5in ammunition limited to 2100 rounds. Either 90 old pattern or 84 new type mines (the latter could not be carried by a converted flush-decker) could be carried; and if cross tracks were used the capacity would rise to 100 Mk 6, although no more Mk 16/18 could be carried due to topweight. This conversion could be undertaken in a week by a suitable destroyer tender – five had the crane capacity to remove a 5in gun and

mounting. In September 1943 Admiral King ordered Mare Island Navy Yard to fabricate four conversion kits, and these were ready in December 1943.

They were never used. That same month, Commander Destroyers Pacific asked that 1850-ton destroyers be substituted for the *Fletchers*, which he considered too valuable for such a secondary assignment. In fact he thought in terms of the removal of No 2 twin 5in SP mount; this, together with a reduction in 5in ammunition, would perhaps compensate for as many as 90 Mk 6 mines. Late in January 1944 the CNO asked BuShips for plans for both temporary and permanent conversion of the 1850-tonners. Three of the Pacific units, *Sampson*, *Warrington* and *Phelps*, were then scheduled for overhaul (including the installation of 5in DP guns) by May. On 5 April Admiral King proposed the permanent conversion of these ships, although Nimitz protested that he considered 'the number of light minelayers in this area now adequate. Subject vessels more valuable as destroyers than as minelayers'. In any case all of the Pacific 'Leaders' were ordered to the Atlantic on 29 May.

This did not end BuShip's interest in conversions. A conversion plan of 14 June for the *Somers* class was based on the DP gun version, the torpedo tubes and No 2 (single) gun being omitted. The full automatic AA battery of three twin Bofors and six Oerlikons would be retained; mine capacity would be 97 Mk 16 or 99 Mk 6. The *Fletcher* class conversion kits would be used, but the upward sheer of the 1850-ton hull would require recesses cut in the stern. A parallel plan for the *Porters* showed their quadruple Bofors in the superimposed position forward.

By this time Admiral Nimitz was more convinced of the value of fast light minelayers, and on 24 June he recommended the conversion of twelve *Sumners* while they were being completed. Admiral King suggested as an alternative the conversion of four new ships and eight existing *Fletchers;* but Nimitz preferred all new ships, perhaps to avoid breaking up experienced crews. He wanted all to be ready for combat by 1 February 1945; training time would require the selection of ships scheduled to be so completed by 1 November 1944. Three yards were selected: Bath (DD735-740 became DM23-28), Bethlehem Staten Island (DD749-751 became DM29-31), and Bethlehem San Pedro (DD771-773 became DM32-34). The prototype, *R H Smith* (DM23), was commissioned as a minelayer on 4 August 1944. The whole programme was carried out very quickly. King only directed that the conversion be carried out on 17 July, and it proved necessary to transfer two ships for conversion, DD735 from Bath to Boston Navy Yard, and DD771 from Staten Island to New York Navy Yard. In each case the delay was small – ships completed by their original builders were delayed only a few days by the installation of mine gear. This of course jibed with the original intention of designing a conversion which could be carried out by a destroyer tender within a week.

The Bureau was finally willing to accept decreased stability in view of the urgent requirement for minelayers, and it argued that in any case they would rarely operate with all 120 mines (then estimated at 90 tons) aboard. About 1-1.5kts would be lost by a fully loaded DM; weight compensation was limited to both torpedo tubes, three Oerlikons at the stern, and two of the six depth charge projectors. One of the great wartime problems of BuShips was the constant pressure to relax stability standards in order to fit more light AA and more ammunition aboard destroyers; in its letter to the CNO describing the DM conversion the Bureau was careful to point out that the relaxed standard it had accepted for the DM was not to be a precedent for any other destroyers.

It appears in retrospect that much of Nimitz's scepticism regarding the fast minelayers was warranted. However, by 1945, Pacific destroyers required neither torpedo tubes nor much AS armament: fast minelayers joined the picket line off Okinawa, where *Aaron Ward*, *Lindsey*, and *J W Ditter* were severely damaged by Kamikazes and *Shea* by a piloted Baka bomb. Most of the minelayers were laid up after the war; in 1950 only four, all in the Atlantic, remained active, and even after the great Korean War call-up there were only two, *Gwin* and *Shea*, one on each coast. At this time interest was expressed in a *minesweeping* capability, and *Gwin* was converted at a cost of nearly 20 tons of topweight. The Mine Force protested that this was a very expensive way to gain a secondary capability, and the issue was mooted when the *Benson-Livermore* class minesweepers reverted to destroyer status in July 1955. Both minelayers outlived their minesweeper counterparts, remaining in service until April 1958.

A measure of the topweight associated with the mines is the fact that post-war modification plans incorporated four rather than the usual *Sumner* battery of six 3in/50s. However, they did include a substantial AS battery: dual 'Hedgehog', SQS-4, and depth charge tracks aft. In fact none of the DMs was ever rearmed.

DESTROYER MINESWEEPERS

The US Navy had no equivalent of the British practice of fitting destroyer flotillas for high-speed minesweeping, but in 1940-41 it converted 18 flush-deckers into specialised fast minesweepers. As in the case of the minelayers, the question of converting more modern ships was raised. In December 1939 the then Bureau of Construction and Repair observed that DD364-408 would be unsuitable as they would hogg under the strain of towing sweep gear. A later study showed that no 1500-ton destroyer would do; as for the new *Benson-Livermores*, all torpedoes and tubes would have to be removed from the 4-gun ships, and No 3 gun from in the 5-gun units. At this time sweeping appears to have meant classical wire sweeping using trailing wires aft. However, war experience must already have shown the importance of more sophisticated mines, particularly magnetic ones.

As in the case of the minelayers, it was clearly desirable for more modern ships to be converted; the Bureau of Ships produced a sketch design for a conversion of *Bristol* (DD453) class destroyers in August 1944. This called for the removal of No 4 5in gun and the single bank of torpedo tubes, as well as the reduction of the stern depth charge racks to a capacity of seven 300lb charges each. By this time the fast minesweeper (DMS) was expected to cope not only with moored mines but also with magnetic and acoustic types; considerable extra gear was required, as well as a new 540kw turbo-generator. After the CNO ordered 24 ships to be converted (7 October), the Bureau undertook more detailed studies, which showed that the four depth charge projectors and two 24in searchlights would have to be landed, whilst below deck depth charge stowage would have to be reduced from sixteen 300lb and eight 600lb to fourteen 300lb. That would reduce the depth charge battery to two projectors, each with 5 charges (one in the thrower) and the two stern tracks; light AA would not be affected, which shows that the conversions were ordered with the Pacific Theatre in mind. In view of the critical weight situation, the winches fitted would not be suitable for target towing. One invisible modification was degaussing to DMS standards.

Although the CNO had ordered a total of 24 conversions, only 12 Atlantic Fleet destroyers were converted during 1944: DD454-458, 461, 462, 464, 621, 625, 636 and 637 became DMS19-30. In 1945 12 more were converted, their designs being modified to reflect the AA modifications developed that spring: DD489, 490, 493-496, 618, 627 and 632-635 became DMS31-42.

The DMS task was well understood after the end of World War II: in 1950 12 were maintained in commission, in three Mine Divisions, two in the Atlantic; 8 more were in reserve, 4 having been disabled off Okinawa. One, *Hobson*, was lost by collision in 1952, and the others were reduced to reserve in 1954-5. The DMSs all reverted to destroyer status at this time. The sole exception was *Fitch* (DMS26), which remained in service with the Operational Development Force until February 1956.

Below: The radar picket conversion was probably the most extensive of the three wartime series. Here USS *Leary* (DDR879) is shown in New York harbour, probably just after the end of the war for the Navy Day celebrations of October, 1945. She has undergone both DDR (shown by her tripod mast) and emergency AA (shown by the absence of her after tubes) conversions; note the practice of painting up the ship's name amidships, which appears to have lasted only until ships were repainted in peacetime light grey with large bow or funnel numbers.

Right: The prototype picket *Frank Knox* (DD/DDR742) under refit in 1946, when the remaining bank of torpedo tubes was removed.

RADAR PICKETS

The specialised radar picket destroyers were, above all else, symbolic of the shift in the character of naval warfare experienced by the Pacific Fleet. They were essentially platforms for fighter-control radars; their main batteries, then, were sections of carrier combat air patrols. On-board armament was of course secondary. The other major picket task was the early warning of enemy air attack.

Destroyers were first used as pickets in 1943, USS *Trathen* (DD530) being the first ship so used, in the invasion of the Baker and Howland Islands. VHF radio transmitters taken from fighters on board the carrier *Princeton* were installed in her CIC, where a specialist fighter direction officer was stationed. During the approach she was stationed in the van, 30-65 miles ahead of the carrier, and no Japanese aircraft penetrated to within sight range. For the approach to the Gilberts in November 1943, the picket and fighter direction tasks were combined in *Kimberley* (DD521); others were used in the Marianas operation, where they performed useful early warning functions. By 1945 most Destroyer Divisions included one specialist Fighter Director ship. However, the radar systems of these ships were not particularly suited to such a rôle, for example there were no height-finding sets aboard them.

On 31 December 1944 representatives of the Third and Fifth Fleets, Air Forces Pacific, Destroyers Pacific and Service Squadron Pacific staffs jointly recommended the conversion of twelve 2200-ton destroyers (long hull) for picket duty. Alterations would include the provision of an SP height-finding radar on a tripod mast, which would replace the forward bank of torpedo tubes. Admiral King approved this suggestion in January, designating DD742, 743, 805-808, 829 and 873-877. Alterations would have to be post-shakedown on all but the incomplete DD806-808 and 829, all of which would be converted at Boston (with 742 and 743). The others would be done at Norfolk. Conversion required 6-9 weeks, and the programme had high priority. In May 1945 the CNO designated 12 more *Gearings* for conversion: DD830-835 and 878-883. By this time the emergency AA conversion orders had been promulgated, and new radar picket destroyers were to have their after banks of tubes, as well as their forward banks, removed. It is not clear how many of the original batch of pickets ever retained their after tubes following conversion.

Although the pickets saw little action at the end of the war their value was perceived at once, and they spent the next decade and a half in carrier screens. Twelve more (DD711-714, 784, 817, 838, 842, 863, 870, 888 and 889) were converted under the Fiscal Year 1952 programme. They differed from the earlier ships in that they were designed from the first to carry the heavy SPS-8 height finder, which had to be mounted at superstructure deck level. They also had improved electronics, including a new type of CIC, and the new 3in/50 secondary battery was installed as well. All 36 were to have been rebuilt under the FRAM programme; their SPS-8 radars were to have been replaced by the new and extremely powerful SPS-30. However, by the end of the 1950s there were already in existence, or else in prospect, numerous guided missile destroyers and frigates, all of which had fighter-control radars; most of the radar picket destroyers were rebuilt as pure AS craft.

Left: *Chevalier* (DD805), like *Knox*, shows the radar mainmast topped by a YE aircraft homing beacon, and the SP pencil-beam radar tops the tripod. The yardarm carries radar warning receivers. On the platform below is a TDY jamming transmitter and the associated DBM radar direction finder. This photo was also taken in 1946.

13. Emergency AA Armament 1945

When the Pacific Fleet reached the Philippines late in 1944, it encountered a new level of Japanese air opposition, culminating in the Kamikaze. The destroyer staff of the Fleet proposed that ships be rearmed, sacrificing torpedoes for additional automatic weapons. It should be noted that, in contrast to the Royal Navy, the US Navy had retained its heavy pre-war torpedo batteries, often mounting automatic weapons at the expense of 5in guns.

The first class to be affected was the *Mahans*: apart from the 4-tube ships, which had very light AA batteries, they had the most powerful torpedo armament in the fleet. In January, the elimination of the two waist tubes was approved; with this weight compensation, the two twin Bofors could be replaced by quadruple mountings, and their Mk 51 directors replaced by Mk 63 blind-fire directors. Only *Lamson* (DD367) had been refitted to this standard (at Puget Sound, completed in April 1945) when far more radical alterations were approved. These originated with an April 1945 order by the CNO: as ships were refitted or repaired after battle damage (the work being undertaken at the utmost speed) they would be rearmed: *Sumners* and *Gearings* would exchange their after bank of tubes (the only tubes in radar pickets) for a quadruple Bofors. In *Fletchers*, one bank of tubes would be replaced either by two twin or one quadruple Bofors. Earlier destroyers would lose all or half their torpedo tubes as necessary. At the same time blind-fire directors would be installed to control the Bofors guns and single Oerlikons would be replaced by twins.

The Bureau of Ships began at once to produce detailed plans, the highest priority being reserved for the newest ships. The notes which follow are on a class-by-class basis.

Most *Sumner-Gearings* were refitted in 1945: USS *Beatty* (DD756) is shown here post-war. She had lost her after tubes in 1945 but remained essentially in wartime configurations with, unusually, twin Oerlikons still in place on the 01 level forward and no dual 'Hedgehog' as yet installed. However, she had the new SPS-6C air-search radar on a tripod mast. Thus although the photograph is dated December, 1959, it was probably taken about 1950, as the 'Hedgehog'-fitting programme was just getting under way.
By courtesy of Norman Polmar

SUMNER/GEARING CLASSES

Plans dated 24 and 25 April 1945 called for the addition of one quadruple Bofors mounting and the replacement of the former 11 single Oerlikons by 10 twins, in both fleet destroyers and radar pickets. The radar pickets, then, would lose all of their torpedo tubes. *Sumner* class destroyers converted to minelayers had already had all their tubes removed. On 16 June the CNO approved the replacement of their 8 single Oerlikons by 5 twins. In August he approved a Pacific Fleet suggestion that an additional third quadruple Bofors be mounted atop the aft deck house in place of the depth charge projectors; the latter would be in portable mountings which could be laid over the mine rails when mines were not being carried. About 25 Mk 16 mines would have to be landed, leaving 94.

Of the 58 *Sumners* not converted into light minelayers 4 were lost, and in November 1945 30 remained unconverted: DD692-3, 696-9, 701-3, 705-6, 722-3, 727-31, 745-6, 748, 752, 754-5, 757, 770, 775-6, 778 and 781. However, all but two *Gearings* had been refitted, the converted radar pickets DD742 and 743 each retaining one bank of tubes. Of the light minelayers, only *Tolman* (DM28) and *Wiley* (DM29) appear to have been refitted; all surviving units except *Wiley* were listed with three quadruple Bofors by 1960, which suggests that the November 1945 listing for *Wiley* was a clerical error. All had twin Oerlikons except for DM23, 27, 28 and 32.

Benson-Livermore refits required considerable weight compensation, including replacement of the usual Mk 4/22 5in fire control radar by the small dish of Mk 28 – a radar so small that it can hardly be seen in these photographs. Note also the emplacement at the aft end of the main deck bulwark for single Oerlikons pending availability of the Mk 63 blind-fire director, an alteration particularly visible in the photograph of USS *Parker* (DD604) (top left), 27 June 1945. USS *Frankford* (DD497) (right) shows the modification effected on square-bridge ships, whilst USS *Swanson* (DD443) (top right) shows that carried out on the original *Benson-Livermores* – she is shown at Puget Sound on 24 June 1945. *First two: Fahey Collection by courtesy of Norman Polmar*

FLETCHER CLASS

Plans adopted on 27 April 1945 called for the replacement of the forward bank of torpedo tubes; the two amidships twin Bofors would be replaced by two quadruple mountings and two Mk 63 blind-fire directors retained to control them. Structures for ready-service ammunition would be added on the shelter deck. The standard battery of 7 Oerlikons would be replaced by 6 twin mountings.

The *Fletcher* refit programme was not so extensive as that applied to the 6-gun destroyers, many of which were completed to the altered configuration. In November 1945, 53 had been modified (ships denoted thus * were under refit at the end of the war): DD445-448, 473, 478, 481*, 499, 502, 520, 521, 528, 530, 531, 534-539, 541, 550, 554, 556, 563, 577, 578, 580, 583, 586*, 589, 590, 592, 643, 657, 661, 665, 668-676, 681, 682, 685, 686, 800, 802 and 804.

BENSON-LIVERMORE CLASS

A plan of 26 April called for the refit of Destroyer Division 32 (DD600-601, 616 and 617): the bank of 5 tubes would be removed, and quadruple Bofors would replace the former twin mountings, although the single Oerlikons would remain. On 11 May a plan for all ships of the DD421 and later groups called for the retention of the twin Bofors and the installation *in addition* of two quadruple mountings. The Oerlikon battery would be reduced ultimately to two twins forward of the bridge, but until blind-fire directors could be fitted, the two single mount-

ings amidships would be retained as emergency cover for the after quadrants, on the theory that in some circumstances there would not be enough time to bring Bofors guns into operation. As weight compensation these ships would carry only one motor whaleboat, four depth charge projectors, one anchor and cable, one 24in searchlight (no 36in), 300 rounds (ready-service) per Bofors gun, and 960 per Oerlikon. The radio direction-finder would be removed, and although all four 5in guns would be enclosed, this would be weather shielding only. As further weight compensation, the combination of Mk 4 and Mk 22 5in fire control radars would be replaced by a single lighter Mk 28 dish.

Even so, the ships would be weight-critical. For example, Commander Destroyers Pacific really wanted one twin Oerlikon per quadrant. To get that, further weights would have to be removed; this could be achieved by installing lighter furniture for the Captain's emergency cabin, removing the top of No 3 gunhouse, the ram bow (originally fitted for AS duties) and the hawsepipe, and eliminating ECM electronics and some safes in the coding room – among other rather desperate expedients.

Plans for modifications to the light minesweepers converted from *Benson-Livermores* were similar to those initially planned for Destroyer Division 32. Once again more heroic measures of weight reduction were required: the remaining pair of depth charge throwers was eliminated, as well as the boat winch, one of the two anchors and the entire secondary conn, and ready-service ammunition was reduced to the level of the refitted destroyers (see above). All of this bought only two quadruple Bofors, plus two twin Oerlikons forward (and two singles aft pending the fitting of blind-fire directors).

Of the 19 surviving 10-tube ships, 12 were refitted: DD423, 424, 429-432, 435, 437-440 and 443. Of the later ships originally completed with five tubes, 16 out of 37 were refitted: DD497, 600, 601, 603, 604, 608, 610, 612-617, 623, 624 and 628. Of these, *McLanahan* (DD615) had four twin Bofors pending availability of two more quadruple mountings.

There were two groups of light minesweepers. DMS19-30, converted in 1944, were not refitted, the sole exception being *Hobson* (DMS26), which was refitting, and in fact had no Bofors at all, at the end of the war at Norfolk following battle damage. However, all 12 units (DMS31-42) converted in 1945 were completed to the new armament standard.

The *Benson-Livermores* went into reserve after the war, but many were refitted for foreign navies. USS *Macomb* (DD458) received a reduced version of the 1945 refit for transfer to Japan – here she is shown, just prior to transfer, on 13 October 1954. She has the two quadruple Bofors aft but no twins and only two single Oerlikons forward. Torpedo tubes and depth charge projectors have been removed, but she has no 'Hedgehogs'. Note the elimination of the IFF array normally associated with her SC-2 series air-search radar.
By courtesy of A D Baker III

Above: USS *Shaw* (DD373) was the only *Mahan* subjected to the full 1945 armament change; she was not stable enough, and No 3 gun had to be landed. Here she is shown off Mare Island Navy Yard, 5 August 1945.
By courtesy of A D Baker III

Far left: Newly-converted destroyer minesweepers were also given enhanced AA batteries: here USS *Thompson* (DMS38, formerly DD627) emerges from Charleston Navy Yard on 4 July 1945. Note that she has an SA air-search set in place of the more common SC-2; note also the position on her second funnel for the future installation of ECM gear.
By courtesy of Norman Polmar

Left: The pre-war 'Leaders' were refitted in 1945. Here *Phelps* (DD360), 8 August 1945, is shown off New York with three quadruple and two twin Bofors. Note the long catwalk between her forecastle and the twin Bofors amidships, and also the absence of AS equipment: both depth charge projectors and the usual HF/DF mast are missing. Radar dishes on her after quadruple mountings are characteristic of the Mk 63 blind-fire director.
By courtesy of A D Baker III

173

SIMS CLASS

The planned refit called for the removal of both banks of torpedo tubes and their replacement by a pair of twin Bofors; in addition the four single Oerlikons would be replaced by four twins. In fact this alteration was never completed; the three ships refitted, *Mustin* (DD413), *Morris* (DD417) and *Russell* (DD414), all retained single Oerlikons (two twin and two single in the case of *Russell*). The refit included the substitution of a Mk 28 fire control radar for the Mk 4 these ships had carried.

BENHAM CLASS

The armament modifications here consisted of the removal of the two remaining banks of torpedo tubes and their replacement by twin Bofors, to make four twin mountings in all; the four single Oerlikons would be replaced by twin mountings, two of these being on the main deck just abaft the two new twin Bofors. Only *Lang* (DD399), *Sterett* (DD407), and *Wilson* (DD408) were refitted.

BAGLEY CLASS

All four quadruple torpedo tubes were to be removed; the structure on the after deckhouse which had carried a twin Bofors would be replaced by a pair of quadruple Bofors, and a pair of twin Bofors would be mounted on a deckhouse extension forward of them. The amidships Oerlikons would be removed and the 20mm battery reduced to two twin mountings on the deckhouse between the bridge and No 2 gunhouse. Ammunition limits as in the *Benson-Livermores* would be imposed.

Although this scheme was promulgated on 8 June 1945 no ships were refitted. Studies of *Gridley* class refits were made, but they were held at low priority in view of the assignment of these four ships the Atlantic (which presumably reflected their unsatisfactory character).

Kidd (DD661) was no sooner refitted with five twin Bofors than she had to return to Hunters Point Naval Shipyard for an emergency AA refit, following Kamikaze damage sustained on the picket line off Okinawa, 11 April 1945. She is shown (bottom) at Mare Island, newly refitted, on 8 February and (below) at Hunters Point in July. The detail view shows her as refitted in July 1945. She received ECM gear as well as two quadruple Bofors and new Mk 63 directors to control them. The object circled before her navigation bridge and that on her forefunnel are both ECM search antennae; others, operating at shorter wavelengths, were located on her second funnel. She also had two twin Oerlikons on her main deck aft of the former single Oerlikon position, and a new ECM mast aft which carried radar direction-finders and a TDY jammer to exploit their data.

MAHAN CLASS

In June the CNO approved the removal of the one remaining authorised torpedo tube, on the centreline, and the addition of a pair of twin Bofors between the funnels to give a total battery of twelve 40mm. Only the two twin Oerlikons between the bridge and No 2 gun would be retained, although two more were to be installed on the main deck forward of the twin Bofors pending the availability of blind-fire directors. Weight compensation would include the replacement of the 36in searchlight by a 24in type, and ready-service ammunition would be limited as in the *Benson-Livermores*.

Only one ship, USS *Shaw* (DD373), was refitted. When she was inclined at Mare Island after the removal of a second (unauthorised) motor whaleboat and the completion of this refit she was found to be grossly overweight; it was believed that much of the 64-ton rise in light displacement since her completion could be traced to battle damage repairs, presumably those carried out after Pearl Harbor. About 30 tons at the main deck level had to be landed as her seaworthiness in heavy weather was considered unacceptable. Ultimately No 3 5in gun was removed, largely negating the gains in battery, and at the insistence of Commander Destroyers Pacific she was reassigned to the Atlantic Fleet and her place taken by *Drayton* (DD366).

It does not appear that rearmament plans were drawn up for *Cassin* and *Downes*; nor were any promulgated for the *Farraguts*, which by 1945 were being relegated to less hazardous duties.

PORTER CLASS

Rearmament plans applied only to those ships already modernised with DP main batteries. They were to surrender all their torpedo tubes, the two twin Bofors aft would be replaced by quadruple mountings and two twins would be mounted just abaft the second funnel. The Oerlikon battery would be reduced to two twin mountings forward, and weight compensation would include the elimination of the two forward depth charge projectors and one of the two depth charge tracks. This plan was approved on 12 June and *Selfridge* (DD357), *Winslow* (DD359) and *Phelps* (DD360) were all refitted. *McDougal* (DD358) had the DP battery but had not been refitted at the end of the war.

SOMERS CLASS

The plan for this class, which applied to refitted ships only, generally followed that for the *Porters* except that the Bofors in No 2 position was a twin rather than a quadruple mounting, so that the ultimate battery was 14 rather than 16 40mm. Both modernised ships, *Davis* (DD395) and *Jouett* (DD396), were refitted to this standard.

The *Benham* and *Sims* classes were subject to very similar emergency AA modifications. Here *Lang* (DD399) is shown off Mare Island on 17 August 1945.
By courtesy of A D Baker III

14. Postwar

The United States ended World War II with the largest destroyer fleet in the world, much of it newly built. Unfortunately, all of these ships had been built for a war which was unlikely to recur – there was no probable enemy on the horizon who might be expected to build a new battle fleet. On the other hand, the Russians, the probable enemy, had captured the German submarine technology which in 1945 had promised to reverse the Allied victory in the Atlantic. At the same time, with the advent of nuclear weapons, the US Navy became more and more interested in fast carrier strike operations, with destroyers forming an AS and radar picket screen for the carriers as they approached launching positions off the borders of the Soviet Union.

The new submarines were so fast that it appeared that war-built destroyer escorts would not be able to cope with them. On the other hand the war-built fleet was so large and so new that there could be no hope of a new large-scale building programme. The only solution was the reconstruction of many new hulls: in the late 1940s several ships were entirely rebuilt, and in the early 1950s a somewhat more austere programme modified several hundred others. Air defence requirements produced a large rearmanent programme using the war-developed 3in/50 as well as a new series of radar picket conversions.

USS *Winslow* (DD359) was the last active survivor of the pre-war destroyers. She operated as an experimental radar picket destroyer with the Operational Development Force until 1950. Here she is shown leaving Boston Navy Yard after conversion in 1946. Her tripod mainmast carries a height-finding SP radar, and abaft it is the prototype Mk 56 fire control system.

Three stages in the evolution of postwar *Sumners*. USS *Maddox* (DD731) (above left), photographed in December 1959, had two twin 3in/50s aft with a Mk 56 fire control system between them, as well as two singles just abaft her bridge; she retained her five torpedo tubes as well as two stern depth charge tracks (but no stowage racks) and six depth charge projectors, but added two 'Hedgehogs' on the 01 level forward of the bridge. Note the tripod mast carrying SPS-6C and an SU-2 surface-search radar, a hallmark of post-war US destroyers. Note also that the Mk 12/22 combination atop wartime destroyer DP directors has been replaced by the dish of Mk 25. USS *J R Pierce* (DD753) (left), photographed in Hampton Roads in July 1964, shows further modification in lieu of the more complete FRAM overhaul. Her wartime bank of tubes has been replaced by a pair of triple Mk 32s for small AS homing torpedoes, and her depth charge projectors and one track aft have been discarded, the other track being retained as a quick-reaction weapon against submarines suddenly detected at short range. By this time SU-2 had been retired in favour of the SPS-10 surface-search set. Finally, USS *H R Dickson* (DD708) (above), May 1964, shows the AS torpedo tubes uncovered and additional spaces built out from her bridge; note also her new SPS-29 air-search radar and the prominent ECM radomes which both she and *J R Pierce* had sprouted from their second funnels by this time.
By courtesy of Norman Polmar

Even with these major changes, it was not until the end of the 1950s that destroyer rôles and technological developments demanded really radical changes to the surviving US destroyers, resulting in the FRAM reconstructions and in the discarding of the surviving ships of the *Benson* and *Fletcher* classes deemed unsuitable for FRAM. Thus the beginning of the FRAM programme seems a suitable end to the story of American destroyers of the Second World War.

The post-war active destroyer force consisted entirely of *Fletchers* and *Sumner-Gearings*; all of the *Benson-Livermores* were laid up in 1946-7 (the sole exception being *Woodworth*, DD460, assigned to Naval Reserve Training). All earlier destroyers were disposed of although one, *Winslow*, was retained as an experimental radar picket. In the summer of 1946 five *Fletchers* (DD540, 596, 658, 684 and 687) were assigned to Naval Reserve Training but all the others were laid up, five badly damaged ones, DD476, 481, 514, 552 and 555, being scrapped. On the other hand, all the *Gearings* were kept in commission, and the economy cuts of the post-war period threw only 17 *Sumners* (DD699, 700, 722-725, 744, 752, 754, 757, 760-762, 775, 776, 779 and 780) into reserve; DD774 was scrapped on account of Kamikaze damage. By January 1950 so much money had been cut from Navy operating funds that it was necessary to place newly converted *Fletcher* class AS ships into reserve; but the outbreak of the Korean War in June changed matters, and for the rest of the 1950s most of the *Fletchers* and all the *Sumner-Gearings* were active.

ANTI-AIRCRAFT REFITS

From 1947 onwards BuOrd advocated the replacement of all Active Fleet Bofors guns with the new 3in/50. Not merely was the new gun far more destructive, but its shell was large enough to take a VT fuse, which the Bofors shell was not. However, although the twin 3in/50 was designed to replace a quadruple Bofors on a one-for-one basis, it suffered the usual weight growth during design and ultimately could replace the earlier weapons only on a two-for-three basis. The standard *Sumner-Gearing* battery was six such weapons, two twin mountings aft on the 01 level on the centreline, controlled by a single Mk 56 director abaft the second funnel, and two single mountings abaft the bridge where twin Bofors had been carried.

USS *G K Mackenzie* (DD836), photographed about 1958, shows the reinforcement of No 1 gunhouse adopted in view of damage experienced in heavy weather: the *Sumner-Gearings* were notoriously wet, presumably in view of their overloading as compared to their original design. Note that her open bridge has been enclosed, a common modification after the war.
By courtesy of Norman Polmar

The conversion of a *Fletcher* was more complex: No 5 gun was removed, and a twin 3in/50 replaced the former after twin Bofors, with a Mk 56 director forward of it. Two more twin 3in/50s were mounted between the funnels, and a pair of 'Hedgehogs' replaced the two twin Bofors formerly mounted before the bridge.

The FY51 (10 ships) and FY52 (109 ships) programmes financed the conversion of 41 *Fletchers* (of which 39 were carried out), 40 *Sumners* and 38 *Gearings* (of which 33 were carried out). Another 75 would have completed the programme: 13 *Sumners*, 11 *Gearings*, 11 *Lloyd Thomas* DDEs and 40 *Fletchers*. However, destroyer rearmament had insufficient priority, and this programme was deleted from the FY53 and later budgets. Existing radar pickets (24 ships) were rearmed under the FY52 programme, which also paid for 12 new conversions, all with 3in/50 guns.

Thus 13 *Sumners* (DD699-701, 730, 734, 747, 756, 759, 760, 761, 778, 781 and 857) and 13 *Gearings* (DD710, 712, 782, 783, 785, 787, 836, 837, 848, 851, 864, 869 and 886) retained their Bofors guns throughout the 1950s. *Gyatt* (DD712) was rearmed in 1956 during her conversion to a missile destroyer; *Kraus* (DD849) was reclassified as an experimental ship (AG151) and was not rearmed; and *Timmermann*, completed as an experimental engineering ship, was commissioned with Bofors guns.

All 17 'mothballed' *Sumners* and 76 *Fletchers* were

activated for Korean War service. Only 39 *Fletchers*
(DD519, 520, 527, 528, 530, 532, 535, 537, 544,
547, 556, 561, 564, 566, 629, 630, 642, 644, 650-
652, 655, 659, 666, 669, 670, 674, 677, 678, 679,
681, 685, 687, 689, 793-796, 799 and 804) were
converted. Others were to have interim modifications: quadruple Bofors in place of the forward torpedo tubes and 'Hedgehogs' in place of the pair of
twin Bofors formerly mounted before the bridge.

Above: *Fletcher* reconstruction was quite elaborate, as this view of USS
Braine (DD630) shows (15 August 1955). Note that she retained her full
wartime AS battery: six throwers, two depth charge tracks, plus two
stowage racks aft. Her stub mainmast carries the standard US ECM
warning antenna, which looks like a segment of a wagon wheel, but as
yet there are no radomes for radar threat direction-finding. Her twin
3in/50s amidships are controlled by Mk 63: the radar is on the gun, the
director perched nearby. The after 3in/50, by contrast, has its radar in
the Mk 56 director.
By courtesy of Norman Polmar

Left: Eleven *Gearings* underwent an austere DDE conversion. USS
Norris (DDE859), off Guantanamo, Cuba, in June 1956, shows its main
features: a trainable Mk 15 'Hedgehog' in place of No 2 gun, the wartime
quintuple torpedo tube, and the DAU HF/DF aft. Note that she retains
her wartime depth charge battery (although without reserve racks), but
that she appears to have been refitted with 3in/50s. She has lost the usual
dual 'Hedgehog' installation forward.

Most also had tripod foremasts to support new SPS-6 radars: DD521, 531, 534, 536, 538, 539, 540, 541, 545, 546, 558, 562, 565, 567, 568, 596, 631, 643, 653, 654, 656, 657, 658, 661, 667, 668, 671, 672, 673, 675, 676, 680, 682, 683, 684, 686, 688, 793, 794, 797, 798, 800 and 802. Those ships remaining active as late as 1960 were modified further: their Bofors guns and remaining torpedo tubes were removed, and a pair of triple Mk 32 tubes for homing torpedoes were fitted. Note that at least a few ships, such as *Brown* (DD546), were initially recommissioned with 'Hedgehogs' forward and 10 tubes (3 twin Bofors). *Sumners* not refitted with 3in/50 guns nevertheless lost their after torpedo tubes.

ANTI-SUBMARINE CONVERSIONS

After World War II US efforts at countering the expected flood of Russian copies of German Type 21 and 26 submarines included a series of prototype AS destroyers converted from *Gearings* and a series of conversions of *Fletchers* to mobilisation prototypes of a new generation of fast convoy escorts. So many of the latter would be required in wartime that it was planned to convert all surviving *Fletchers*. Because they would be used in the event of war, the plan was to convert *Fletchers* and then place most of them in reserve, as personnel were scarce. The *Gearings*, on the other hand, were maintained in commission to develop tactics against fast submarines.

In each case the AS battery was an ahead-throwing weapon, either a trainable Mk 14 or 15 'Hedgehog' or the new 'Weapon Alfa'. The latter was a rapid-firing rocket-launcher capable of sending a stream of fast-sinking 250lb depth-fuzed rockets to a range of about 800yds. Like the contemporary British 'Limbo', it required a depth-finding sonar (SQG-1). In addition, the AS destroyer was to be armed with homing torpedoes.

Fletcher DDE conversions were intended as mobilisation prototypes. Although they were intended to mount 'Weapon Alfa' forward in No 2 position, most, like USS *Waller* (DDE466), shown here on 20 July 1950, had to make do with a trainable Mk 15 'Hedgehog'. Note the installation of an open bridge around the front of *Waller*'s original closed one: she was a round-bridge/high-director ship. Note also the provision of four twin Oerlikons, two on the 01 level forward and two on the 'fantail', and the deletion of her forward bank of torpedo tubes. The built-up superstructure amidships was to enclose four fixed AS tubes plus their reloads. USS *Fletcher* (DDE445) in October 1966, shows the 'Weapon Alfa' installation, together with the usual dual fixed 'Hedgehogs' on the 01 level. By this time the HF/DF had given way to other ECM gear, and Mk 32 tubes had been fitted between the funnels, but otherwise she was little changed. Note, however, that the bridge had once more been enclosed.
By courtesy of A D Baker III

Four *Gearings* suspended at the end of the war were completed as specialised types: two AS destroyers (sub-killers, DDK825 and 827) and two prototype escorts (DDE719 and 824). The 'killers' were to have 3 'Weapon Alfas', 4 torpedo tubes and 1 depth charge rack, but in fact DDK825 was completed with 4 K-guns, 2 'Weapon Alfas' and a Mk 15 trainable 'Hedgehog' perched on the 01 level just

forward of one of the 'Weapon Alfas' and intended ultimately to be replaced by it. There were four fixed torpedo tubes. The escort conversion was more conventional. The DDKs had 3in/50s (ultimately to be replaced by the ill-fated 3in/70) in place of Nos 1 and 3 5in guns (controlled by Mk 56), whilst the DDEs retained both twin 5in/38s. One 'Weapon Alfa' replaced No 2 gun, and 2 Mk 11

'Hedgehogs' were mounted on the 01 level forward. In addition, two depth charge tracks and four fixed torpedo tubes were fitted.

There were also more austere conversions. In 1946 an AS Conference recommended that two Task Groups be set up to work out tactics. Five *Gearing* class destroyers of Desdiv 81 (DD818, 819, 820, 847 and 871) had their No 2 gunhouses replaced by a large trainable 'Hedgehog'. A second group was converted under the FY50 programme, this comprising DD764, 765 and 858-861. In both cases the Bofors guns and the quintuple torpedo tubes were retained. The first series of conversions was designated DDE on 4 March 1950, and at the same time the DDK and DDE categories merged as DDE.

Two more *Gearings*, *Witek* and *Sarsfield*, were 4-gun ships used for experimental purposes, and classified as DDEs from time to time. *Sarsfield* was the prototype for the FY50 conversions.

No other *Gearings* were converted – they were too valuable as general-purpose destroyers in view of their heavy AA batteries and good endurance. Moreover, by the late 1950s the specialised weapons and sensors of the DDEs were no longer much better than those which all destroyers would soon have, and they merged back into the destroyer category when they were refitted under FRAM.

The *Fletcher* conversions were similar in spirit: No 2 gun was replaced by a 'Weapon Alfa' or a Mk 15 trainable 'Hedgehog', and two fixed 'Hedgehogs' (except in Mk 15 ships, which had two twin Oerlikon there, and two more on the 'fantail') were mounted on the 01 level forward. Nos 2 and 4 5in guns were also removed, and the secondary battery was replaced by two twin 3in/50 aft with a Mk 56 between them. There were also to be four fixed torpedoes in the after superstructure, but many units retained their forward bank of torpedo tubes as weight and movement reservation against the availability of the new tubes. The original battery of depth charge tracks and projectors was retained against the ultimate availability of 'Weapon Alfa', production of which could not meet demand.

Eighteen *Fletchers* (DDE445-7, 449, 450, 465, 466, 468, 470, 471, 498, 499, 507, 508, 510, 517, 576 and 577) were converted. Twelve were complete at the beginning of the Korean War, of which four had been returned to reserve; eleven more had been authorised. Of these, the President approved the commencement of seven, but one was cancelled in favour of the fast underwater target *Albacore*.

In the 1950s the US destroyer force was by far the largest in the world. Here is part of it, waiting at the piers to begin the naval parade of the International Naval Review at Hampton Roads, June 1957.
By courtesy of Norman Polmar

At this time 'Weapon Alfa' had not yet been proven in trials. Only units converted from reserve after the outbreak of war (DDE446 and 465) had it; the rest had short-range 'Hedgehogs'. In 1950 a review of the AS programme suggested that far less impressive measures might well be effective against a Russian underwater fleet still overwhelmingly composed of wartime and pre-war submarines. The *Fletcher* programme was curtailed and in its place all general purpose destroyers and all the radar pickets were fitted with a pair of 'Hedgehogs' at the 01 level forward of the bridge; in addition all destroyers received scanning sonars. The large amount saved went instead into the development of advanced weapons, against the day when the Soviet submarine fleet would indeed be the menace forecast just after the war.

As a footnote to this AS story, plans were cast for conversions of *Benson-Livermores;* but although prototype conversions figured in several programmes of the mid-1950s they were always edged out by more urgent projects.

Index

Page numbers in *italics* refer to illustrations

INDEX TO PART I

INDEX TO PART II